POLITICAL
WARFARE

POLITICAL WARFARE

Strategies for Combating China's Plan to "Win without Fighting"

KERRY K. GERSHANECK

MCUP
MARINE CORPS UNIVERSITY PRESS
Quantico, Virginia
2020

LIBRARY OF CONGRESS CATALOGING-IN-PUBLICATION DATA
Names: Gershaneck, Kerry K., 1953- author.
Title: Political warfare : strategies for combating China's plan to "win without fighting" / Kerry K. Gershaneck.
Description: Quantico, Virginia : Marine Corps University Press, 2020. | Includes bibliographical references and index. | Summary: "Political Warfare provides a well-researched and wide-ranging overview of the nature of the People's Republic of China (PRC) threat and the political warfare strategies, doctrines, and operational practices used by the Chinese Communist Party (CCP). The author offers detailed and illuminating case studies of PRC political warfare operations designed to undermine Thailand, a U.S. treaty ally, and Taiwan, a close friend"—Provided by publisher.
Identifiers: LCCN 2020032647 | ISBN 9781732003125 (paperback)
Subjects: LCSH: Information warfare—China. | Propaganda, Chinese. | Political persecution—China. | China—Foreign relations—Thailand. | China—Foreign relations—Taiwan.
Classification: LCC DS740.4 .G47 2020 | DDC 327.1/40951—dc23
LC record available at https://lccn.loc.gov/2020032647

The production of this book and other MCUP products is graciously supported by the Marine Corps University Foundation.

Published by
Marine Corps University Press
2044 Broadway Drive
Quantico, VA 22134
www.usmcu.edu/mcupress

First edition, 2020
ISBN: 978-1-7320031-2-5

CONTENTS

FOREWORD

Professor Kerry K. Gershaneck's study on the People's Republic of China's (PRC) political warfare stands as a major contribution to the body of knowledge regarding this existential threat to the United States, its freedoms, and its values. He provides a well-researched and wide-ranging overview of the nature of the PRC threat and the political warfare strategies, doctrines, and operational practices used by the Chinese Communist Party (CCP). Further, Professor Gershaneck offers detailed and illuminating case studies of PRC political warfare operations designed to undermine Thailand, a U.S. treaty ally, and Taiwan, a close friend.

This book is not merely an academic study. It is also based in great part on Gershaneck's extensive experience working in the fields of national intelligence, counterintelligence, international relations, strategic communications, and academia during the course of more than 35 years, at times literally on the front lines combatting PRC political warfare. He witnessed firsthand the United States at its zenith in the political warfare fight as well as its subsequent abandonment of high-level political warfare organization, education, and operations at the end of the Cold War.

As commander of U.S. Marine Corps Force Pacific in the early 2000s, I observed a disturbing trend, based in large part on the United States' dismantlement of its own political warfare apparatus. It was becoming increasingly apparent that American government, business, academics, culture, and other elites were losing the ability to identify and confront PRC political warfare. By the time I assumed duties as U.S. assistant secretary of defense for Asian and Pacific security affairs in 2009, America's unwillingness and inability to recognize and challenge Beijing's malign persuasion, intimidation, coercion, infiltration, and subversion was even more evident. Even within the highest levels of the U.S. Department of Defense, with senior leadership focused more on combat operations in Southwest Asia than the rapidly emerging threat from China, it was very difficult to shift focus and resources to addressing the PRC.

As this book goes to print, the United States is engulfed in the Coronavirus disease 2019 (COVID-19) pandemic and a massive PRC political warfare campaign to rewrite history regarding its role in the epidemic. The circumstances of this pandemic may be unusual, but this is a typical PRC political warfare campaign of cover-up, deception, misinformation, coercion, repression, and intimidation. Consequently, there is a rapid awakening in the United States about the nature of the threat from the PRC. This makes the publication of this book all the more pertinent and timely.

During the more than 25 years that I have known Professor Gershaneck, he has demonstrated superior abilities as a strategic planner, researcher, analyst, and operator in the field. He superbly masters both the realm of academic research and theory and the world of street-smart operational practice, and he brings his unique perspective and capabilities to this important project.

This book is a call to arms as well as a valuable study of the history and nature of the PRC political warfare threat. While the United States has recently begun to more seriously engage on the political warfare battlefield, much more work and investment of national resources lie ahead. Professor Gershaneck provides useful strategic-, operational-, and tactical-level recommendations to deter, confront, and defeat PRC political warfare operations, all of which are crucial to development of a coherent, successful national response.

Lieutenant General Wallace C. Gregson Jr., USMC (Ret)
U.S. Assistant Secretary of Defense for Asian and Pacific Security Affairs, 2009–11

PREFACE

Political warfare is not a new phenomenon. Its practice spans thousands of years, and it is not unique to the People's Republic of China (PRC). Still, the Chinese Communist Party (CCP) is devilishly good at conducting its own particularly virulent form of it.

The PRC version of political warfare poses more than a unique challenge—it presents an existential threat to the United States and its friends and allies. The CCP no longer hides its disdain for concepts such as democracy, rule of law, freedom of speech, and human rights, nor does it conceal its intent to create a new world order based on its totalitarian model. Political warfare is a primary tool that the CCP employs to defeat the United States. It is the PRC's magical path to victory, to win not so much without struggle but without having to resort to open kinetic conflict.

The PRC's intent is not a theoretical conjecture. Beijing demonstrates on a daily basis its eagerness and ability to subvert and defeat—or, to use CCP parlance, to "divide and disintegrate"—the United States and other foreign nations. This intent and capability is explored in considerable detail in this book, which includes case studies of PRC campaigns to co-opt Thailand, a treaty ally of the United States, and take possession of Taiwan, with which the United States shares a special relationship.

The PRC's complex and remarkably successful political warfare campaign against Thailand will surprise many readers, as will the extent and viciousness of its relentless efforts to capture Taiwan. What will be the result of PRC victory in these campaigns? Thailand risks assuming tributary-state status to Beijing, while Taiwan faces extinction as a sovereign entity, loss of its hard-fought freedom, and brutal repression of its people.

Of particular concern is that in the PRC's war to divide and disintegrate us, we are not winning. Victory is not a given—nor, at this point, even in sight.

This is the main reason this book was written. We in the United States must reverse what appears to be inevitable defeat, which requires us to relearn the means to deter, counter, and defeat the PRC's daunting political warfare threat. But first, we as a nation must be willing and able to recognize that threat. This statement might seem like a blinding flash of the obvious, but the task is significantly harder than it appears.

While it took roughly 12 months to research and write this book, it is fair to say that this work is the culmination of more than 35 years of experience and study. As a young Marine Corps counterintelligence officer, I was initiated in PRC malign influence operations during a particularly dismal era of the Cold War, just after the fall of South Vietnam, Cambodia, and Laos to PRC-backed Communist forces. At that time, I studied political warfare as practiced by the PRC and the Soviet Union, learning their approaches to espionage, sabotage, and subversion. I then had a golden opportunity to help combat their political warfare and espionage activities in Asia and elsewhere, albeit in a minor supporting role.

It is important to note that combatting political warfare was easier in that era, as most senior U.S. government security and diplomatic officials, as well as American business, industry, and news media leaders, had at least some rudimentary understanding of that hostile threat. We are not so fortunate today.

This formative experience, combined with subsequent broader involvement in the fields of intelligence and counterintelligence, strategic communications, international relations, and academia, provided a strong foundation on which to write on this topic. As important was serving with the U.S. Information Agency as the Office of the Secretary of Defense liaison and experience acquired during assignments at U.S. Information Service offices abroad.

While the path to this book was filled with many inspiring experiences, it sometimes revealed deeply disappointing realities as well. Following is a brief overview of some of the disturbing insights I gained that convinced me that a book on this subject would be of great value.

First, the CCP is quite good at employing political warfare. By contrast, the United States is not. Yes, we mastered it pretty well during the Cold War, but we then declared victory over the Soviet Union—the "end of history," in fact! We were living in a unipolar, nonthreatening world, we were told. Consequently, we shut down our cornerstone political warfare institutions and capabilities and dropped our guard for nearly three decades, during which our offensive and defensive political warfare skills atrophied. Despite some effort devoted to combating radical Islam and a nod to Russia, we paid little focus to the greatest threat: the PRC.

Second, during the course of these three decades, we lost sight of how to prepare our elected officials and policy makers, military and foreign service officers, and business, industry, entertainment, commerce, news media, and academic leaders for the never-ending struggle that is the nature of hostile political warfare. Since the end of the Cold War, many American elites rose to lofty positions in these important fields with nothing to inform them of the dangers posed by political warfare or how to combat it.

After 1992, political warfare-related courses disappeared from the curriculum of the universities that traditionally produced America's diplomats, elected officials, and military leaders. Consequently, there exists no systematic way to educate emerging national leaders about the political warfare threat and help inoculate them to its strategies and tactics. As evidence, I routinely talk with recent graduates of reputable master's degree programs and U.S. military command and staff colleges. Invariably, the graduates tell me that at these esteemed institutions, they were generally taught that the PRC is our "partner" and not a threat. They learned a little about soft and hard power, but they were taught nothing about political warfare.

One consequence I have observed firsthand is that many U.S. government officials and bureaucrats cannot recognize political warfare at all. For many who at least acknowledge it exits, it is "too complex" or at most a mere "niche issue," as I was told by a senior U.S. official at a major American mission in Asia who was assigned to assist my research in 2018.

Moreover, in stereotypical bureaucratic style, many in government and the private sector see political warfare waged by hostile countries against the United States as "important, but not my job." In his superb book *Stealth War: How China Took Over while America's Elite Slept*, former senior U.S. National Security Council (NSC) official Robert S. Spalding III details his painful experience dealing with the "not my job" syndrome as he tried to enlist the private sector and government officials to counter the PRC's malign influence.[1]

At the governmental and institutional levels, the United States has lost its ability to recognize the political warfare threat, educate its elites and officials about it, prioritize resources to engage it, and plan and conduct operations to deter, counter, and defeat it. In other

[1] BGen Robert Spalding, USAF (Ret), *Stealth War: How China Took Over while America's Elite Slept* (New York: Portfolio/Penguin, 2019), 1–4, 72.

words, we have created the perfect prescription for defeat on the information battlefield.

Third, sometimes our failure to recognize and confront PRC political warfare is through simple ignorance and ineptitude—but often it is willful, resulting from co-option, coercion, bribery, indoctrination, intimidation, or psychological manipulation. Grant Newsham, a noted security analyst with extensive political warfare expertise, explains how the CCP sets the conditions for conscious decisions to aid, enable, apologize, and/or cover for its totalitarian regime. Newsham observes that the Chinese understand "their target's vulnerabilities" and capitalize "on American avarice, ignorance, naiveté, vanity, and hubris." Beijing, he says, attacks "on a broad front . . . successfully manipulating American business and Wall Street, government officials and the political class, academia, and even U.S. military leaders."[2]

Fourth, the CCP does not simply direct the behavior of the willing—it conditions behavior. Americans at the highest levels of government, business, and academia have proven surprisingly susceptible to PRC psychological manipulation. My experience with the U.S. government, particularly the Departments of State and Defense, provides useful examples of this important slice of American social structure. The following anecdotes highlight some of the challenges the United States faces to turn its "ship of state" in the right direction to face the PRC political warfare challenge. Cumulatively, they helped propel me to write this book.

In August 2017, *Foreign Policy* magazine ran what it must have considered to be a shocking exposé, with part of the headline declaring that "Foggy Bottom has shown inexplicable deference to Beijing." The author urgently asserted that the U.S. Department of State had begun "tilting dangerously toward China"—but only since January 2017.[3] While the allegation of the department's tilt toward China is valid, the timeline provided offers a false narrative. For many years, key State Department officials seemed quite deferential to the PRC and, to put it charitably, inattentive to malign activities such as political warfare. How else can one explain why the acting U.S. assistant secretary of state for East Asian and Pacific affairs, Susan A. Thornton, a career foreign service officer, asserted in late 2018 that she had never "seen any evidence" of PRC covert influence operations in the United States?[4]

---

[2] Grant Newsham, "Chinese Psyops against America: One Hell of a Success," *And Magazine*, 1 December 2019.

[3] Ely Ratner, "The State Department Is Tilting Dangerously toward China," *Foreign Policy*, 24 August 2017.

[4] Koji Sonoda, "Ex-diplomat: U.S. Must 'Figure out a Way to Work with China'," *Asahi Shimubn* (Osaka, Japan), 6 November 2018.

Oddly enough, by the time that stunning statement was made, there was a flood of evidence available from the Federal Bureau of Investigation (FBI) and Central Intelligence Agency (CIA) regarding the massive PRC campaign to influence U.S. public opinion.[5] It is not clear how Thornton, who was responsible for Washington's China policy, could have been inattentive to such compelling evidence, nor is it clear why she would repeatedly "improperly block [U.S.] law enforcement agencies in their efforts to deal with China's repeated violations of U.S. sovereignty and law," as was alleged by a senior NSC official and is detailed in this book.[6]

Moreover, in December 2016, the American chargé d'affairs at the U.S. embassy in Bangkok related during a 75-minute discussion that "Russian election interference" posed the greatest threat to the United States, while "China's political warfare is not a threat" and that "we [Americans] can handle it."[7] His skewed threat assessment alone is deeply worrisome, but the story of why I was in his office in the first place is of equal concern.

Two months earlier, in October 2016, I was invited to the U.S. embassy in Bangkok by a U.S. House of Representatives staff delegation to brief its members on PRC political warfare against Thailand. I was a professor at Thammasat University and the Royal Thai Military Academy at the time, and I had gained unique insights regarding PRC political warfare campaigns in the region during the previous three years. For two hours, I provided the staff delegation key elements of what is written in chapters 5 and 6 of this book.

Ten minutes into my presentation, the U.S. embassy foreign service officers escorting the staff delegation looked agitated. Twenty-five minutes into the discussion, they neared hysteria and, in one case, became teary-eyed. They frantically tried to cut me off and convince the delegation to leave. The delegation leader calmly shut down their protests, and we completed a very fruitful two-hour discussion. But why the hysteria and tears? A confidant in the embassy later told me that these young foreign service officers felt I was being "too hard on China." When I learned the astonishing reason for their inappropriate conduct, I asked to see the chargé d'affairs, hoping their view would be more enlightened than those of the young staffers. After our 75-minute discussion, it was very clear they were not.

---

[5] Natalie Johnson, "CIA Warns of Extensive Chinese Operation to Infiltrate American Institutions," *Washington Free Beacon*, 7 March 2018.
[6] Bill Gertz, "Controversial State Department Nominee in Trouble," *Washington Free Beacon*, 15 May 2018.
[7] Kerry K. Gershaneck, interview with a senior U.S. Department of State official, Bangkok, Thailand, 30 December 2016.

In another instance, as a guest lecturer at the Foreign Service Institute in Arlington, Virginia, several years ago, I asked instructors teaching courses on public affairs about the curriculum they used to educate State Department public affairs officers about PRC political warfare. I may as well have asked them to explain how they taught quantum mechanics or matter-antimatter asymmetry, for they had no idea what I was talking about. These instructors were responsible for shaping the State Department's strategic communicators, to help them compete and succeed on the perilous information battlefield, and yet they did not understand what the term *political warfare* meant.

At numerous meetings and conferences I attended with senior U.S. diplomats since 1995, I heard many sneeringly deride the "Cold War mentality" of those who expressed concern about the PRC's totalitarian governance, expansionist nature, or global political warfare. Though the PRC openly acknowledges that it is at "war" with the United States, there appears to be no more damning a personal denunciation in the foreign service community than to accuse someone of exhibiting "a Cold War mentality" toward China. Savvy young foreign service officers take their cues from senior diplomats on how to succeed in the State Department's corporate culture. Those who learn quickly to withhold concerns about the PRC are generally promoted to more senior positions.

The State Department has recently begun reversing decades of ignorance, apathy, and appeasement toward the PRC, but there is still much to repair. Unfortunately, the situation has not been any better on the side of the U.S. Department of Defense, at least until rather recently.

At defense education institutions such as National Defense University, command and staff colleges, and the Defense Information School, systematic education about the PRC's extensive global political warfare simply disappeared. In an experience similar to my visit to the Foreign Service Institute, I gave a guest lecture at the Defense Information School at Fort Meade, Maryland, and visited with the school commandant in their office. I proposed that the school begin a program of instruction to prepare the Defense Department's strategic communicators to combat PRC propaganda, media warfare, and other forms of political warfare. The commandant smiled politely, but was clearly unfamiliar with political warfare as a topic. After asking me to better explain it, they informed me that they could not initiate such a program without being directed by higher authority.

Implied in their words and tone was that they were not going to ask for any such direction.

Within the Department of Defense, like the State Department, for many years it was a likely career death sentence to speak the truth about the nature of the PRC threat, whether it be political warfare, expansion into the South or East China Seas, or the increasingly threatening People's Liberation Army (PLA). Senior officials set the tone: as the chief of staff of the U.S. Army, General Raymond T. Odierno, cheerily applauded U.S. Army-PLA camaraderie while visiting Beijing, he confidently proclaimed to America's astounded allies that he saw no evidence of a PLA threat to neighboring Japan.[8] Similar to Thornton's perplexing declaration that she had seen no evidence of covert PRC influence operations in the United States despite ample public evidence to the contrary, there was then a flood of evidence of PLA threats and preparations for military operations against Japan's southwest islands.[9] Perhaps the U.S. Army's massive G-2 intelligence staff could not find this evidence, but Google could.

Comparably, the commander of U.S. Army Pacific, Lieutenant General Francis Wiercinski, declared in 2013 that "the Chinese army no longer poses a threat" to the U.S. military, while a former vice chairman of the Joint Chiefs of Staff, Admiral William A. Owen, who had business interests in China, lobbied Congress and the Pentagon on behalf of Beijing in 2012 to end U.S. arms sales to Taiwan.[10]

Meanwhile, highly respected U.S. senior intelligence officers who spoke up about the PRC threat were silenced. In one case, the U.S. Navy's most respected China expert, Captain James E. Fanell, gave two public, unclassified speeches in 2013 and 2014 that exposed the PLA's expansionist activities in the South and East China Seas. Navy leadership approved these speeches in part because Fanell presented them as his personal assessment. But his assessments countered the position of U.S. president Barack H. Obama's administration that the PRC was not a threat. Senior U.S. government officials immediately denigrated the speeches, and eventually Fanell was fired.[11] He was fired for doing his job: properly identifying a threat, analyzing what it means to U.S. national security, and exhib-

[8] Ben Blanchard, "U.S. Plays down Tension with China, Upbeat on Military Exchanges," Reuters (London), 22 February 2014.

[9] James E. Fanell and Kerry K. Gershaneck, "White Warships and Little Blue Men: The Looming 'Short, Sharp War' in the East China Sea over the Senkakus," *Marine Corps University Journal 8*, no. 2 (Fall 2017): 67–98, https://doi.org/10.21140/mcuj.2017080204.

[10] Paul D. Shinkman, "Chinese Army No Longer a Threat, Top U.S. General Says," U.S. News & World Report, 14 May 2013; and Shirley A. Kan, *U.S.-China Military Contacts: Issues for Congress* (Washington, DC: Congressional Research Service, 2014), 33–34.

[11] Erik Slavin, "What Happens When a Navy Officer Gets Real on China?," *Stars and Stripes*, 24 February 2014; and David B. Larter, "Senior Intel Officer Removed after Controversial Comments on China," *Navy Times*, 10 November 2014.

iting the moral courage to speak the truth despite pressure to back down.

It is no surprise that many Department of Defense education institutions downplayed the PRC threat for many years. One conversation I had with two then-recent U.S. Army War College (AWC) graduates at a July 2019 conference is reflective of many similar talks. The officers told me that the "Army War College is very soft on the China threat" and that students "don't learn anything about [PRC political warfare] there." Moreover, the AWC academic journal, *Parameters*, molds the thinking of future generals with highly lauded papers about "countering propaganda and misinformation" that fail to mention China even once.[12] The snowball effect of this bias also comes as no surprise. It may explain why senior U.S. Army officers, who are presumably AWC graduates, would contract the Rand Corporation to provide a 355-page study on modern political warfare in 2018 that intentionally avoided focus on the PRC threat. Remarkably, the report actually states that Rand and the Army had the option to include the PRC as a focus country for this one-year study but consciously chose to focus elsewhere.[13]

In *Stealth War*, Spalding describes how such willful acquiescence to the CCP's malign influence crosses many boundaries. On behalf of the NSC, Spalding sought to work with "leading think tanks, nongovernmental organizations, and law, auditing, and public relations firms that dealt with China" in the United States and was "eager to seek their help in exposing the Beijing government's influencing operations and sanctioning of illegal behavior."[14] Astonishingly, he was routinely rebuffed—but why? Spalding writes that "some of the more forthright people" said that assisting the NSC "might anger their Chinese funders or business accounts. The list of organizations that refused to engage with me publicly in my official capacity was stunning. Top white-shoe New York law firms. Organizations with mandates to promote democracy, freedom, and human rights would refuse to support my mission."[15] Many of those institutions and elites were profiting off China, and they did not want to have those ties exposed.

While working at a prestigious think tank in Hawaii, I witnessed firsthand much that Spalding describes in *Stealth War*: naïve acquiescence in some cases, but all too often the corruption of values and

---

[12] Michael Dhunjishah, "Countering Propaganda and Disinformation: Bring Back the Active Measures Working Group?," *War Room*, 7 July 2017.
[13] Linda Robinson et al., *Modern Political Warfare: Current Practices and Possible Responses* (Santa Monica, CA: Rand, 2018), https://doi.org/10.7249/RR1772.
[14] Spalding, *Stealth War*, 3.
[15] Spalding, *Stealth War*, 3.

willful blindness to PRC political warfare and espionage activities. I observed PRC successes in co-opting elected and government officials, businesses, academic institutions, nongovernmental organizations, and civic organizations, among others. This highly successful PRC political warfare campaign continues to this day.

These anecdotes reflect only a small part of the challenge the United States and its democratic friends and allies face when confronting PRC political warfare. Much more essential information lies within this book. Still more can be found in publications of the writers and organizations cited herein. It is my hope that this book stimulates readers' interest to seek out other references to expand their knowledge of PRC political warfare.

This book will help readers understand the nature of PRC political warfare to build the capacity to deter, confront, and defeat this existential threat. We face a perilous future if we fail to challenge the PRC's totalitarian rule and its plan to divide and destroy our nation. If we fail to do so, our children and their children will pay the savage price for our egregious negligence.

ACKNOWLEDGMENTS

M any individuals and organizations assisted me in the research and writing of this book. My vocabulary of wildly complimentary superlatives is quite extensive, but even it is insufficient to adequately express my gratitude to those who assisted me in this challenging endeavor. So, I will simply say, in gracious Hawaiian style, *mahalo nui loa* to those listed below whom I owe a special debt of gratitude and to those not listed who have asked to remain anonymous.

For their kind assistance and mentorship while I was in Taiwan, I am deeply indebted to Foreign Minister Jaushieh Joseph Wu; Ambassador Simon S. Y. Tu; Republic of China major general Tsung-Chi Yu (Ret), former commandant of Fu Hsing Kang College at National Defense University; Dr. I-Chung Lai, president of the Prospect Foundation; Associate Professor Chiung-Chiu Huang of the Graduate Institute of East Asian Studies at the College of International Affairs, National Chengchi University; and the ever-cheerful, ever-helpful staff at the National Central Library's Center for Chinese Studies.

From the Kingdom of Thailand, I am grateful to former Foreign Minister Kasit Piromya as well as many trusted associates in government, news media, business, and academia who, for understandable reasons, have asked to remain anonymous.

In the United States, my work was generously supported by Wallace C. Gregson, former U.S. assistant secretary of defense for Asian and Pacific security affairs; Matthew Pottinger, U.S. deputy national security advisor; James F. Moriarty, chairman of the American Institute in Taiwan; and Ivan Kanapathy, U.S. National Security Council deputy senior director for Asian affairs.

My research and analysis was strongly influenced by often-heroic experts such as Russell Hsiao, executive director of the Global Taiwan Institute in Washington, DC, and Mark Stokes, executive director of the Project 2049 Institute in Arlington, Virginia. I am also indebted to security experts Captain James Fanell (Ret); Dr. Anders Corr; Marine Corps Reserve colonel Grant Newsham (Ret); and Coast Guard Reserve captain Bernard Moreland (Ret). All have helped guide my thinking about PRC intentions, capabilities, and political warfare operations over the course of many years.

Finally, I sincerely thank Taiwan's Ministry of Foreign Affairs for generously providing me a Taiwan Fellowship to assist in the research and writing of this book.

SELECTED ABBREVIATIONS AND ACRONYMS

APWCE .... Asian Political Warfare Center of Excellence
ASEAN .... Association of Southeast Asian Nations
BRI .... Belt and Road Initiative
CAIFC .... China Association for International Friendly Contact
CCP .... Chinese Communist Party
CPPCC .... Chinese People's Political Consultative Conference
CPPRC .... Council for the Promotion of the
Peaceful Reunification of China
CPT .... Communist Party of Thailand
CSSA .... Chinese Students and Scholars Association
CUPP .... Chinese Unification Promotion Party
DPP .... Democratic Progressive Party
ETC .... Eastern Theater Command
KMT .... Kuomintang (Nationalist) Party
MSS .... Ministry of State Security
OCAO .... Overseas Chinese Affairs Office
PAD .... People's Alliance for Democracy
PLA .... People's Liberation Army
PLAT .... People's Liberation Army of Thailand
PRC .... People's Republic of China
PSC .... Politburo Standing Committee
ROC .... Republic of China
SSF .... Strategic Support Force
TALSG .... Taiwan Affairs Leading Small Group
TCP .... Taiwanese Communist Party
UFWD .... United Front Work Department
UN .... United Nations

POLITICAL WARFARE

CHAPTER ONE

An Introduction to PRC Political Warfare

Great victory at Niulan Hill, 1975. This painting depicts the Chinese perspective of the May 1841 Battle of Sanyuanli, a skirmish that led to an Anglo-Chinese "information war" that Cantonese scholars won.

The People's Republic of China (PRC) is at war with the world. It is a war fought mostly for control and influence, using coercion, corruption, and violent covert operations. The PRC prefers to win this war by never having to fire a shot, but its increasingly powerful military and paramilitary forces loom ominously in the background in support of its expanding war of influence.

To the leaders of the Chinese Communist Party (CCP), this war is meant to "rejuvenate" China to its former imperial grandeur as the "Middle Kingdom," to once again be "everything under the sun," the all-powerful hegemon power. It is a war to ensure the CCP's total control over China's population and resources, as well as those of foreign nations that the Chinese have historically called "barbarian states," both nearby and throughout the world.[1]

---

[1] Steven W. Mosher, *Hegemon: China's Plan to Dominate Asia and the World* (San Francisco, CA: Encounter Books, 2000), 1–2.

Much like the emperors of the Celestial Empire at its peak, the CCP classifies these barbarian nations as either tributary states that recognize the PRC's hegemony or potential enemies. Despite the lofty pretext of peaceful national rejuvenation reflected in PRC president Xi Jinping's "China Dream," the CCP has no desire for equality among nations. Rather, it seeks to impose its all-encompassing civilization on other, lesser states. The ideological foundation of Xi's China Dream is ultimately totalitarian, Leninist, and based on Marxist principles.[2]

For the CCP, this is a total war for regional and global supremacy, and it incorporates elements of military, economic, informational, and political warfare. PRC political warfare, especially, is both offensive and defensive in nature, taking the form of unrestricted warfare and being conducted on an international scale.[3]

As a prelude to this study, it is crucial to establish the answer to several key questions: Why does it matter that the PRC seeks regional and ultimately global hegemony? Why would the world not accept and tolerate a "rising China," a seemingly nonthreatening term so often used by PRC propaganda outlets and foreign advocates? Why should the world be concerned about China's long-term strategy to replace the United States as the global superpower? What is there to fear about "China's peaceful rise" and the CCP's goal of a "Chinese-led world order?"[4]

The answer is simple and stark: the PRC is a coercive, expansionist, hyper-nationalistic, militarily powerful, brutally repressive, fascist, and totalitarian state. According to retired U.S. Navy captain James E. Fanell, "The world has seen what happens when expansionist totalitarian regimes such as [the PRC] are left unchallenged and unchecked. In the world of this type of hegemon, people are subjects—simply property—of the state, and ideals such as democracy, inalienable rights, limited government, and rule of law have no place."[5]

It is useful here to establish a foundation regarding some general characteristics of totalitarianism, such as the identification of individuals as merely subjects of the state; control of media outlets,

[2] Mosher, *Hegemon*, 3; Xi Jingping, "Full Text of Xi Jinping's Report at 19th CPC National Congress," *China Daily* (Beijing), 4 November 2017; and Bill Birtles, "China's President Xi Jinping Is Pushing a Marxist Revival—but How Communist Is It Really?," Australian Broadcasting Corporation, 3 May 2018.

[3] Col Qiao Liang and Col Wang Xiangsui, *Unrestricted Warfare: Assumptions on War and Tactics in the Age of Globalization* (Beijing: PLA Literature and Arts Publishing House, 1999).

[4] Michael P. Pillsbury, *The Hundred-Year Marathon: China's Secret Strategy to Replace America as the Global Superpower* (New York: Henry Holt, 2015), 16; and *China's National Defense* (Beijing: State Council of the People's Republic of China, 1998).

[5] *Hearing on China's Worldwide Military Expansion, before the House Permanent Select Committee on Intelligence*, 115th Cong. (2018) (testimony by Capt James E. Fanell, USN [Ret]), hereafter Fanell testimony.

economic sectors, and educational institutions; control by a single political party with a separate chain of command alongside that of the government; a lack of checks and balances; personality cults and militarism; and a historical narrative of humiliation leading to hyper-nationalism and an entitlement to aggression. These defining characteristics were witnessed by the world during the twentieth century in countries such as Vladimir Lenin and Joseph Stalin's Soviet Union, Adolf Hitler's Germany, Benito Mussolini's Italy, Imperial Japan, and Pol Pot's Cambodia. Such political structures and narratives established a framework of governance for empires and dictatorships like the PRC long before the founding of the CCP. There is nothing new or inherently Chinese about totalitarian fascism.

The danger of contemporary totalitarian Sino-fascism, however, is unprecedented. The power of modern technology and the PRC's swift convergence of massive political, military, and economic power position it to be, according to Canada's prestigious Fraser Institute, "world freedom's greatest threat."[6]

The PRC has become a hegemon bent on controlling the world's resources ostensibly to benefit China—or, in reality, to benefit the approximately 90 million out of 1.4 billion Chinese who are CCP members. As merely one indicator of the PRC's wealth disparity, a 2016 Peking University study found that "the richest 1 percent of households held a third of the country's wealth, while the poorest 25 percent owned only 1 percent of its wealth."[7]

The CCP has proven that it can effectively leverage the openness of democratic systems to achieve hegemony over those democracies. It prefers to do this peacefully if possible, not entirely without a struggle but ideally without kinetic combat. But the PRC has continually indicated that it is now strong and confident enough to fight a war to achieve that hegemony, even if it must pay a very large price.[8]

As the PRC builds a navy that will be roughly twice the size of the U.S. Navy by 2030 and adds hypersonic missiles to its triad nuclear strike capability that now covers the entire U.S. mainland, Beijing defies international law and relies on corruption and coercion to achieve its diplomatic, economic, and military aims.[9] According to

---

[6] Fred McMahon, "China—World Freedom's Greatest Threat," Fraser Institute, 10 May 2019.

[7] Eleanor Albert, Beina Xu, and Lindsay Maizland, "The Chinese Communist Party," Council on Foreign Relations, 27 September 2019.

[8] Jonas Parello-Plesner and Belinda Li, *The Chinese Communist Party's Foreign Interference Operations: How the U.S. and Other Democracies Should Respond* (Washington, DC: Hudson Institute, 2018); Kerry K. Gershaneck, discussions with senior ROC political warfare officers, Fu Hsing Kang College, National Defense University, Taipei, Taiwan, 2018; and Tara Copp and Aaron Mehta, "New Defense Intelligence Assessment Warns China Nears Critical Military Milestone," *Defense News*, 15 January 2019.

[9] Fanell testimony; Nick Danby, "China's Navy Looms Larger," *Harvard Political Review*, 5 October 2019; and Liu Zhen, "China's Latest Display of Military Might Suggests Its 'Nuclear Triad' Is Complete," *South China Morning Post* (Hong Kong), 2 October 2019.

Ely Ratner at the Council on Foreign Relations, the PRC's strategies include "fracturing and capturing regional institutions that could otherwise raise collective concerns about China's behavior" and "intimidating countries in maritime Asia that seek to lawfully extract resources and defend their sovereignty."[10]

The PRC's political warfare apparatus is a key weapon in its quest for regional and global hegemony. Brutal internal repression is one well-documented form of its unique brand of political warfare. The PRC is criticized today by organizations such as Amnesty International and governments including that of the United States for imprisoning at least a million ethnic Uighurs in "re-education camps" under particularly cruel circumstances.[11] In fact, the repression of Uighurs and other Muslim sects is part of a much more insidious trend—according to *The Washington Post*, "China's systematic anti-Muslim campaign, and accompanying repression of Christians and Tibetan Buddhists, may represent the largest-scale official attack on religious freedom in the world."[12]

However, the PRC's internal political repression involves a brutality much more lethal than religious suppression and thought control. The CCP is responsible for the deaths of millions of Chinese during disastrous large-scale reigns of terror such as the Great Leap Forward (1958–62), the Cultural Revolution (1966–76), and smaller atrocities such as the 1989 Tiananmen Square massacre. Hong Kong-based historian Frank Dikötter has confirmed, based on findings in the PRC's archives, that during the Great Leap Forward alone, "systematic torture, brutality, starvation and killing of Chinese peasants" was the norm. More than 45 million people were "worked, starved or beaten to death" in China during those four years, while the Cultural Revolution resulted in the murder of at least 2 million more. Another 1–2 million were killed in "other campaigns, such as land-reform and 'anti-rightist' movements" in the 1950s.[13] This murderous repression also includes plausible reports that the PRC currently executes Falun Gong practitioners and other prisoners of conscience on a mass scale "in order to harvest organs that can be monetized for substantial profits by [CCP] officials."[14] Estimates of those killed directly or

---

[10] *Hearing on Strategic Competition with China, before the House Committee on Armed Services*, 115th Cong. (2018) (testimony by Ely Ratner, Maurice R. Greenburg Senior Fellow for China Studies, Council on Foreign Relations), hereafter Ratner testimony.

[11] "Up to One Million Detained in China's Mass 'Re-Education' Drive," Amnesty International, 24 September 2018.

[12] "China's Repressive Reach Is Growing," *Washington Post*, 27 September 2019.

[13] Arifa Akbar, "Mao's Great Leap Forward 'Killed 45 Million in Four Years'," *Independent* (London), 17 September 2010; Ian Buruma, "The Tenacity of Chinese Communism," *New York Times*, 28 September 2019; and Ian Johnson, "Who Killed More: Hitler, Stalin, or Mao?," *New York Review of Books*, 5 February 2018.

[14] Matthew P. Robertson, "Examining China's Organ Transplantation System: The Nexus of Security, Medicine, and Predation, Part 2: Evidence for the Harvesting of Organs from Prisoners of Conscience," Jamestown Foundation, China Brief 20, no. 9, 15 May 2020.

indirectly through CCP political warfare against the people of China are strongly debated, but during Mao Zedong's reign alone they range as high as 70 million.[15]

Though the CCP is responsible for what amounts to mass murder in its own country, it still tightly holds the reins of power in the PRC, and it idolizes the man who presided over its deadliest repression: Mao Zedong. Evidence of the CCP's continued admiration for Mao includes what the *China Daily* described as "unprecedented" respect and "piety" that Xi Jinping and the CCP displayed for Mao during celebrations for the 70th anniversary of the founding of the PRC in October 2019.[16] Unlike Russia, which eventually denounced Stalin's murderous reign, the CCP has proven ideologically incapable of acknowledging and atoning for its near-genocidal history.

The PRC's propaganda machine "has mastered the power of symbol and symbolism in the mass media and social media era," and many Chinese eagerly embrace its hyper-nationalistic "patriotic education" programs. Those residing in the PRC face censorship and thought control unimaginable to most citizens of liberal democracies.[17] Further, through its extensive propaganda and influence outlets, Beijing attacks rules or actions that, in the CCP's view, "contain China's power" or "hurt the feelings of the Chinese people." Meanwhile, PRC foreign ministry and propaganda organs lambast as "immoral" those who criticize its egregious human rights abuses and as "racist" those who object to overseas Chinese malign influence activities.[18]

In a May 2020 report to Congress, U.S. president Donald J. Trump highlighted this aspect of PRC political warfare: "China's party-state controls the world's most heavily resourced set of propaganda tools. Beijing communicates its narrative through state-run television, print, radio, and online organizations whose presence is proliferating in the United States and around the world."[19]

CCP censorship ensnares American institutions such as the National Basketball Association (NBA), recently chastised in *The Washington Post* for "essentially importing to the United States China's denial of free speech." In fact, the CCP routinely censors world-

[15] Johnson, "Who Killed More: Hitler, Stalin, or Mao?"

[16] Laurence Brahm, "Nothing Will Stop China's Progress," *China Daily* (Beijing), 2 October 2019.

[17] Li Yuan, "China Masters Political Propaganda for the Instagram Age," *New York Times*, 5 October 2019.

[18] Liu Chen, "U.S. Should Stop Posing as a 'Savior'," *PLA Daily* (Beijing), 27 September 2019; Amy King, "Hurting the Feelings of the Chinese People," *Sources and Methods* (blog), Wilson Center, 15 February 2017; Xinhua, "China Slams the Use of Bringing up Human Rights Issues with Political Motives as 'Immoral'," *Global Times* (Beijing), 12 December 2018; and Ben Blanchard, "China's Top Paper Says Australian Media Reports Are Racist," Reuters (London), 10 December 2017.

[19] Donald J. Trump, "United States Strategic Approach to the People's Republic of China," White House, 20 May 2020.

famous brands including Marriott, United Airlines, Cathay Pacific Airways, Givenchy, and Versace, as well.[20] Hollywood, too, has been co-opted "to avoid issues that the CCP would consider sensitive and produce soft propaganda movies that portray China in a positive light to global audiences."[21] Beijing is quite clear in conveying its coercive censorship requirements, as reflected in a *Global Times* headline: "Global Brands Better Stay Away from Politics." The article condemned "so-called 'freedom of speech'" and carried explicit and implicit threats to those who did not toe the CCP line.[22] Beijing also exports violent active measures to foreign countries in support of its political warfare activities abroad, as will be detailed in subsequent chapters of this book.

Economic coercion has become one particularly visible PRC political warfare tool. The CCP uses the promise of its global Belt and Road Initiative (BRI, also known as One Belt, One Road) to build what the *China Daily* describes as "a new platform for world economic cooperation."[23] U.S. assistant secretary of state for East Asia and Pacific affairs David R. Stilwell characterizes the BRI and other PRC economic coercion schemes less charitably, stating that Beijing employs "market-distorting economic inducements and penalties, influence operations, and intimidation to persuade other states to heed its political and security agenda."[24] Moreover, U.S. vice president Michael R. "Mike" Pence has specifically detailed American concerns regarding the PRC's use of destructive foreign direct investment, market access, and debt traps to compel foreign governments to acquiesce to its wishes.[25] Former U.S. National Security Council official Robert S. Spalding III describes the BRI as "infrastructure warfare." It may be, he writes, "the most subtle and most corrosive of China's unrestricted aggressions. Though it is always packaged as generous 'win-win' development deals, the ultimate goal is a bait-and-switch in which infrastructure is provided but full control of the platform is never fully given. It remains in the hands of Beijing."[26]

[20] "The Day the NBA Fluttered before China," *Washington Post*, 7 October 2019; and Amy Qin and Julie Creswell, "China Is a Minefield, and Foreign Firms Keep Hitting New Tripwires," *New York Times*, 8 October 2019.

[21] Ross Babbage, *Winning Without Fighting: Chinese and Russian Political Warfare Campaigns and How the West Can Prevail*, vol. I (Washington, DC: Center for Strategic and Budgetary Assessments, 2019), 36.

[22] "Global Brands Better Stay Away from Politics," *Global Times* (Beijing), 7 October 2019.

[23] Yang Han and Wen Zongduo, "Belt and Road Reaches out to the World," *China Daily* (Beijing), 30 September 2019.

[24] *Hearing on U.S. Policy in the Indo-Pacific Region: Hong Kong, Alliances and Partnerships, and Other Issues, before the Senate Foreign Relations Committee, Subcommittee on East Asia, the Pacific, and International Cyber Policy*, 116th Cong. (2019) (testimony by David R. Stilwell, Assistant Secretary of State for East Asian and Pacific Affairs, U.S. Department of State).

[25] Michael J. Pence, "Remarks by Vice President Pence on the Administration's Policy toward China" (speech, Hudson Institute, Washington, DC, 4 October 2018).

[26] BGen Robert Spalding, USAF (Ret), *Stealth War: How China Took Over while America's Elite Slept* (New York: Portfolio/Penguin, 2019), 162–63.

Of equal concern, the PRC shapes public opinion both inside and outside its borders "to undermine academic freedom, censor foreign media, restrict the free flow of information, and curb civil society."[27] As President Trump reported to Congress, "Beyond the media, the CCP uses a range of actors to advance its interests in the United States and other open democracies. CCP United Front organizations and agents target businesses, universities, think tanks, scholars, journalists, and local, state, and Federal officials in the United States and around the world, attempting to influence discourse and restrict external influence inside the PRC."[28]

Australia and New Zealand, Europe, Oceania and the Pacific Islands, South America, the Arctic nations, and Africa have all belatedly awoken to the remarkable degree to which the PRC's malign influence has infiltrated their regions in pursuit of Beijing's diplomatic, economic, and military interests.[29] Canada and the United States have had equally rude awakenings regarding the efficacy of PRC united front operations and other forms of coercion, repression, and violent attacks within their borders.[30] The COVID-19 pandemic has also alerted many nations to the PRCs harmful intentions and influence, despite an extraordinarily aggressive global propaganda campaign.[31]

John Garnaut, a former senior advisor to Australian prime minister Malcolm B. Turnbull, notes the nature of many countries' long-overdue awakenings concerning PRC political warfare as well as the lack of consensus on how they should respond: "Belatedly, and quite suddenly, political leaders, policy makers and civil society actors in a dozen nations around the world are scrambling to come to terms with a form of China's extraterritorial influence described variously as 'sharp power,' 'United Front work' and 'influence operations'." He adds that "a dozen [other nations] are entering the debate . . . but

[27] Ratner testimony.
[28] Trump, "United States Strategic Approach to the People's Republic of China."
[29] John Garnaut, "Australia's China Reset," *Monthly* (Victoria, Australia), August 2018; Didi Kirsten Tatlow, "Mapping China-in-Germany," *Sinopsis* (Prague), 2 October 2019; Austin Doehler, "How China Challenges the EU in the Western Balkans," *Diplomat*, 25 September 2019; Grant Newsham, "China 'Political Warfare' Targets U.S.-Affiliated Pacific Islands," *Asia Times* (Hong Kong), 5 August 2019; Derek Grossman et al., *America's Pacific Island Allies: The Freely Associated States and Chinese Influence* (Santa Monica, CA: Rand, 2019), https://doi.org/10.7249/RR2973; C. Todd Lopez, "Southcom Commander: Foreign Powers Pose Security Concerns," U.S. Southern Command, 6 October 2019; Heather A. Conley, "The Arctic Spring: Washington Is Sleeping through Changes at the Top of the World," *Foreign Affairs*, 24 September 2019; and Andrew McCormick, " 'Even If You Don't Think You Have a Relationship with China, China Has a Big Relationship with You'," *Columbia Journalism Review*, 20 June 2019.
[30] Tom Blackwell, "How China Uses Shadowy United Front as 'Magic Weapon' to Try to Extend Its Influence in Canada," *National Post* (Toronto), 28 January 2019; and Alexander Bowe, *China's Overseas United Front Work: Background and Implications for the United States* (Washington, DC: U.S.-China Economic and Security Review Commission, 2018).
[31] "World against the CCP: China Became the Target at the World Health Assembly," Chinascope, 21 May 2020.

none of these countries has sustained a vigorous conversation, let alone reached a political consensus."[32]

The use of political warfare, of course, is not unique to the PRC. All nation-states conduct influence operations such as traditional diplomacy and public diplomacy to impact the policies and actions of others in order to secure their own national interests. During the Cold War, for example, the United States and its partners and allies engaged in an ultimately successful political warfare effort to bring down the Soviet Union's Iron Curtain that divided much of the world. But the PRC's version of political warfare is different than that of other nations, and, according to Singaporean diplomat Bilahari Kausikan, it seeks to achieve much more through its influence and political warfare operations.

Kausikan, a highly respected expert on PRC malign influence, notes that the PRC is a totalitarian state that takes a "holistic approach which melds together the legal and the covert" in conjunction with "persuasion, inducement and coercion." Importantly, he argues that the aim of the PRC is not simply to "direct behavior but to condition behavior. . . . In other words, China does not just want you to comply with its wishes. Far more fundamentally, it wants you to think in such a way that you will of your own volition do what it wants without being told. It's a form of psychological manipulation."[33]

As it wages global political war to achieve its diplomatic, economic, and military goals, the PRC exports authoritarianism, as detailed in a study by the National Endowment for Democracy. Beijing intentionally undermines the credibility of democracy and individual freedoms to bolster support for its own totalitarian regime, which it calls the "China Model."[34] PRC political warfare has been especially effective in weakening U.S. status and alliances in Asia, such as when Beijing successfully exploited a growing rift between the United States and Thailand from 2014 to 2017 to consolidate its own political gains in this vital nation. Further, the PRC continues its work of more than 70 years to destroy the Republic of China on Taiwan, as well as Taiwan's ability to retain its hard-won democracy, sovereignty, and political and economic freedoms.

While there has been relatively recent bipartisan agreement in the United States regarding the need to confront the dangers posed by the PRC, there is still insufficient attention devoted to countering

---

[32] Garnaut, "Australia's China Reset."
[33] Bihahari Kausikan, "An Expose of How States Manipulate Other Countries' Citizens," *Straits Times* (Singapore), 1 July 2018.
[34] Juan Pablo Cardenal et al., *Sharp Power: Rising Authoritarian Influence* (Washington, DC: National Endowment for Democracy, 2017).

the political warfare threat. Based on this author's discussions with senior officials within the U.S. National Security Council, Department of State, and Department of Defense, there has existed a lack of will to identify and confront PRC political warfare. Consequently, there is no comprehensive approach at the strategic and operational levels that brings together the common vision, coherency, and resources needed to fight it. This situation was, until recently, further compounded by little inclination on the part of the U.S. government to even acknowledge the scope of PRC political warfare or its successes in Thailand and Taiwan. Accordingly, several chapters of this book will focus on PRC political warfare operations against these two nations.[35]

Related to this governmental-level inattention, and despite the vast importance of political warfare to the PRC and the existential threat it poses to virtually every nation in the world, there is relatively little open-source, English-language academic literature on the subject. Some organizations and individuals, however, have distinguished themselves in this fight by writing impressively, persistently, and heroically on PRC political warfare. Such organizations include the Project 2049 Institute, the Hudson Institute, the Jamestown Foundation, the U.S.-China Economic and Security Review Commission, and the Center for Strategic and Budgetary Assessments. Individual scholars and reporters include Anne-Marie Brady, J. Michael Cole, June Teufel Dreyer, John Garnaut, Bill Gertz, Clive Hamilton, Russell Hsiao, Peter Mattis, Robert Spalding, and Mark Stokes.

Nevertheless, there still remains a deficiency in academic research on PRC political warfare. Reasons for this paucity of academic focus include academic censorship and self-censorship, as well as a clear understanding by many scholars who might otherwise pursue this topic that such research will face severe opposition within their academic environments. But the failure is also due in part to the unwieldy and sometimes unhelpful terminology associated with influence operations. One objective of this book is to get the major terminology correct to clarify the scope of the political warfare threat and allow for better political and operational responses.

While this book seeks to break new ground on the topic of PRC political warfare, there are many more aspects of the subject that deserve additional in-depth research and analysis. One important topic not addressed herein is how to take the political war back to the PRC, to play offense as well as defense in this conflict. This and other

---

[35] Kerry K. Gershaneck, interview with a senior U.S. Department of State official, Bangkok, Thailand, 30 December 2016; and Kerry K. Gershaneck, interviews with a senior U.S. Department of State official, various locations, 2018–20.

related topics should be the focus of subsequent research at numerous private and public research and education institutions.

It is worth remembering that, at one time, the United States was quite good at conducting political warfare operations. During the Cold War, the U.S. government successfully waged political warfare against the Communist Bloc using an array of methods. These included overt actions such as building political alliances, initiating economic development, and spreading propaganda, as well as covert actions such as supporting friendly foreign elements and resistance factions in hostile states, conducting psychological operations, funding noncommunist political parties, organizing intellectuals and artists against Communism, and supporting dissenters and freedom fighters behind the Iron Curtain.[36]

The United States and like-minded nations must invest heavily and with great urgency to combat PRC political warfare to safeguard their freedoms and sovereignty. There is a massive challenge ahead to inoculate institutions and citizens against the existential threat posed by PRC political warfare and effectively counter that threat. It is time to stop losing the political warfare contest, intelligently engage in the fight, and ultimately win the war.

---

[36] Max Boot and Michael Scott Doran, "Political Warfare," Council on Foreign Relations, 28 June 2013.

CHAPTER TWO

Terms and Definitions

Criticize the old world and build a new world with Mao Zedong thought as a weapon. This 1966 propaganda poster was one of many produced during the Cultural Revolution (1966–76) to encourage young Chinese to study Mao in order to "scatter the old world and build a new world."

If, as Prussian military theorist Carl von Clausewitz wrote, "war is the continuation of politics by other means," then one could say that the People's Republic of China's (PRC) political warfare is the continuation of armed conflict by other means.[1] It provides an al-

---

[1] Kerry K. Gershaneck, "Taiwan's Future Depends on the Japan-America Security Alliance," *National Interest*, 7 June 2018.

ternative to open kinetic warfare and is a preferred instrument of national power, employed to win without fighting. This point was initially posited by American diplomat George F. Kennan, best known for his delineation of Western grand strategy during the Cold War as explicated in his famous "Long Telegram" of 22 February 1946.[2]

Two years after proposing the ultimately successful policy of "containing" the Soviet Empire to end its totalitarian regime, Kennan drafted another memorandum entitled "The Inauguration of Organized Political Warfare." His second landmark of strategic thinking states that, at that time, the United States was handicapped "by a popular attachment to the concept of a basic difference between peace and war, by a tendency to view war as a sort of sporting context outside of all political context . . . and by a reluctance to recognize the realities of international relations—the perpetual rhythm of [struggle, in and out of war]."[3]

Kennan also briefly laid out the nature of the threats from the Soviet Union and defined *political warfare* as "the employment of all the means at a nation's command, short of war, to achieve its national objectives. Such operations are both overt and covert. They range from such overt actions as political alliances, economic measures . . . and 'white' propaganda to such covert operations as clandestine support of 'friendly' foreign elements, 'black' psychological warfare and even encouragement of underground resistance in hostile states."[4]

This definition is as valid today as it was in 1948. However, the PRC's version of political warfare has evolved in ways not fully understood during Kennan's era, and new concepts and semantic battlegrounds have since emerged. Accordingly, it is useful to closely examine several key political warfare-related terms that are used in this book. Terms and definitions are, of course, crucially important. *Influence operations* and *political warfare*, for example, overlap extensively and are considered by many to be virtually interchangeable terms, but they differ in scope. Below is a short list of the vast collection of terms that civilian and military leaders must comprehend to effectively confront political warfare (table 1).

There are numerous definitions for these terms given by credible institutions, but each varies somewhat from the other, obscuring conceptual clarity. At a certain point, the dizzying array of terminology that government officials and academics accord to political warfare-related activities becomes counterproductive, consuming

[2] J. Y. Smith, "George F. Kennan, 1904–2005: Outsider Forged Cold War Strategy," *Washington Post*, 18 March 2005.
[3] George F. Kennan, "The Inauguration of Organized Political Warfare," Office of the Historian of the State Department, 4 May 1948.
[4] Kennan, "The Inauguration of Organized Political Warfare."

Table 1. Political warfare terms

assertive hegemony	fake news	information warfare	public opinion warfare
cyber warfare	false narratives	lawfare	sharp power
debt diplomacy	gray zone operations	liaison work	soft power
deception	hard power	malign influence	special measures
diplomacy	hybrid operations	psychological operations	subversion
disinformation	infiltration	public affairs	Three Warfares
engagement	influence operations	public diplomacy	united front

Compiled by the author, adapted by MCUP

time, intellect, and energy better invested in actually fighting the political warfare battle. Accordingly, for the purposes of this book, the following selected definitions apply.

Influence operations provide strategies and tactics used in support of broader political warfare campaigns. They are actions designed to influence foreign government leaders, businesses and industries, academia, media outlets, and other key elites in a manner that benefits the PRC. These operations are often, but not always, conducted at the expense of the self-interests of the countries at which the actions are directed.

Political warfare is all-encompassing, unrestricted warfare and a "critical component of PRC security strategy and foreign policy." According to a Project 2049 Institute study, political warfare is an alternative to armed conflict that "seeks to influence emotions, motives, objective reasoning, and behavior of foreign governments, organizations, groups, and individuals in a manner favorable to [the PRC's] own political-military-economic objectives." PRC political warfare goes beyond traditional united front and liaison work, such as building coalitions to support the PRC and "disintegrate" enemies, and the *Three Warfares*, which include public opinion/media warfare, psychological warfare, and legal warfare. Political warfare also involves active measures such as violence and other forms of coercive, destructive attacks.[5]

The term *political warfare* is precisely what government officials

---

[5] Mark Stokes and Russell Hsiao, *The People's Liberation Army General Political Department: Political Warfare with Chinese Characteristics* (Arlington, VA: Project 2049 Institute, 2013), 3, 5–6.

and academics should use to describe the PRC's extensive malign influence operations. Failure to name it as such blurs the fact that the PRC considers itself engaged in a political war with the United States and its partner nations and allies. Failure to understand the nature of this war severely undermines the ability to conceptualize the threat and to implement appropriate countermeasures. This failure ensures ultimate defeat.

It is important to recognize that political warfare is the normal way that the Chinese Communist Party (CCP) does business. Whereas in the United States such actions require special authorities and oversight for such operations, the CCP sees political warfare as everyday *modus operandi*. Its political warfare operations include both commonly recognized and nontraditional methods, combining typical influence operations with other state functions such as espionage, clandestine actions, and violent active measures.

The PRC's political warfare arsenal of influence includes operations identified previously, such as united front activities and the Three Warfares, as well as propaganda, diplomatic coercion, disinformation, overt and covert media manipulation, active measures, hybrid warfare, and soft power functions such as public diplomacy, public affairs, public relations, cultural affairs activities, and "indoctritainment."

Following is a brief overview of the PRC's primary political warfare concepts and weapons.

Unrestricted Warfare

The CCP conducts its political warfare activities under the rubric of *unrestricted warfare*, the underpinning of which was published in February 1999 by Qiao Liang and Wang Xiangsui, two senior People's Liberation Army (PLA) Air Force colonels with the Guangzhou Military District Political Department. Although perhaps not equal in academic stature to the PLA's *The Science of Military Strategy* and *The Science of Campaigns*, this book has great influence on the CCP's senior-level strategic thought.

The colonels wrote that unrestricted warfare "means that any methods can be prepared for use, information is everywhere, the battlefield is everywhere, . . . any technology might be combined with any other technology, and that the boundaries between war and non-war and between military and non-military affairs [have] systematically broken down."[6] Their book, *Unrestricted Warfare*, recommends that the PRC use "asymmetric warfare" to attack the United States and offers "non-military ways to defeat a stronger nation such as the United States through lawfare (that is, using international laws, bodies and courts to restrict America's freedom of movement and policy choices), economic warfare, biological and chemical warfare, cyberattacks, and even terrorism."[7]

The book received great attention and praise in the PRC, but after the 11 September 2001 terror attacks against the United States, many pro-Chinese academics and business leaders in America asserted that Qiao and Wang "were on the 'fringe' of Chinese thought and that their ideas should be dismissed." These assertions were disingenuous and supported PRC political warfare. Both colonels were subsequently promoted in rank and lauded by the PRC military and civilian news media.

Knowingly or unknowingly, those academics and business leaders in the United States were supporting a "carefully managed, secret, and audacious [public relations] and opinion-shaping operation" that was "supervised by the top leaders in Beijing."[8]

The Three Warfares

The Three Warfares, the traditional foundation of PRC political warfare, include public opinion/media warfare, psychological warfare, and legal warfare.[9] University of Cambridge professor Stefan A. Halper describes the Three Warfares as "a dynamic three dimensional warfighting process that constitutes war by other means. . . . Importantly, for U.S. planners, this weapon is highly deceptive."[10]

Elsa B. Kania at the Center for a New American Security states that the Three Warfares are "intended to control the prevailing discourse and influence perceptions in a way that advances China's interests, while compromising the capability of opponents to respond." Such operations conducted by the PRC against the United States and other countries are designed to "seize the 'decisive opportunity' for controlling public opinion, organize psychological offense and defense, engage in legal struggle, and fight for popular will and public opinion." This ultimately "requires efforts to unify military and

---

[6] Col Qiao Liang and Col Wang Xiangsui, *Unrestricted Warfare: Assumptions on War and Tactics in the Age of Globalization* (Beijing: PLA Literature and Arts Publishing House, 1999), 6–7.
[7] Michael P. Pillsbury, *The Hundred-Year Marathon: China's Secret Strategy to Replace America as the Global Superpower* (New York: Henry Holt, 2015), 116.
[8] Pillsbury, *The Hundred-Year Marathon*, 116–17, 138.
[9] Elsa B. Kania, "The PLA's Latest Strategic Thinking on the Three Warfares," Jamestown Foundation, China Brief 16, no. 13, 22 August 2016.
[10] Stefan A. Halper, *China: The Three Warfares* (Washington, DC: Office of the Secretary of Defense, 2013), 11.

civilian thinking, divide the enemy into factions, weaken the enemy's combat power, and organize legal offensives."[11]

According to Kania, key objectives of Three Warfares operations are: "control of public opinion, blunting an adversary's determination, transformation of emotion, psychological guidance, collapse of (an adversary's) organization, psychological defense, [and] restriction through law."[12] Halper cites an example of a possible PRC Three Warfares operation against the United States as follows: "If the U.S. objective is to gain port access for the [U.S. Navy] in a particular country . . . China would use the Three Warfares to adversely influence public opinion, to exert psychological pressure (i.e. threaten boycotts) and to mount legal challenges—all designed to render the environment inhospitable to U.S. objectives."[13]

Public Opinion/Media Warfare

Public opinion/media warfare uses overt and covert media manipulation to influence perceptions and attitudes. According to PLA National Defence University texts, it "involves using public opinion as a weapon by propagandizing through various forms of media in order to weaken the adversary's 'will to fight' while ensuring strength of will and unity among civilian and military views on one's own side."[14] Public opinion/media warfare "leverages all instruments that inform and influence public opinion including films, television programs, books, the internet, and the global media network" and is "directed against domestic populations in target countries."[15]

As Ross Babbage at the Center for Strategic and Budgetary Assessments writes, the PRC "operates the Voice of China, Xinhua News Agency, and hundreds of publications" that are "reinforced by the tailored use of local media outlets, strong social media capabilities, and cyber operations, all of which can be focused on current issues in particular countries." Moreover, "agencies of the Beijing regime fund the monthly publication of newspaper supplements [that contain] pro-Beijing news coverage in the major cities of many Western and developing countries, including the United States, Australia, and Britain."[16]

Public opinion/media warfare also employs "indoctritainment," which is exemplified in movies such as the propaganda blockbust-

---

[11] Kania, "The PLA's Latest Strategic Thinking on the Three Warfares."
[12] Kania, "The PLA's Latest Strategic Thinking on the Three Warfares."
[13] Halper, *China: The Three Warfares*, 12.
[14] Kania, "The PLA's Latest Strategic Thinking on the Three Warfares."
[15] Halper, *China: The Three Warfares*, 12–13.
[16] Ross Babbage, *Winning Without Fighting: Chinese and Russian Political Warfare Campaigns and How the West Can Prevail*, vol. I (Washington, DC: Center for Strategic and Budgetary Assessments, 2019), 35–36.

er *Wolf Warrior II* (2017). Further, Beijing has co-opted much of the Western film industry. According to U.S. vice president Michael R. "Mike" Pence, "Beijing routinely demands that Hollywood portray China in a strictly positive light" and "punishes studios and producers that don't. Beijing's censors are quick to edit or outlaw movies that criticize China, even in minor ways." The remake of *Red Dawn* (2012) "was digitally edited to make the villains North Korean, not Chinese," while *World War Z* (2013) saw the cutting of "the script's mention of a virus because it originated in China."[17] By virtue of "the scale of its domestic market," the PRC has ensured that Hollywood avoids "issues that the CCP would consider sensitive" and produces "soft propaganda movies that portray China in a positive light to global audiences," such as *The Great Wall* (2016).[18]

Psychological Warfare

Psychological warfare is defined by the U.S. Department of Defense as "planned operations to convey selected information and indicators to foreign audiences to influence their emotions, motives, objective reasoning, and ultimately the behavior of foreign governments, organizations, groups, and individuals. The purpose of psychological operations is to induce or reinforce foreign attitudes and behavior favorable to the originator's objectives."[19]

The PRC's use of psychological warfare includes employing "diplomatic pressure, rumor[s], false narratives and harassment to express displeasure, assert hegemony, and convey threats."[20] According to a variety of PLA National Defence University texts, Beijing's psychological warfare strategy includes "integrating [psychological attacks] and armed attacks . . . carrying out offense and defense at the same time, with offense as the priority . . . [and] synthetically using multiple forms of forces." During military operations, psychological warfare should be "closely integrated with all forms and stages" to "intensify the efficacy of conventional attacks" while "taking advantage of 'opportune moments' and 'striking first' to seize the initiative."[21]

Psychological warfare also involves military exercises and operations short of war, including the PLA Navy's transit of Taiwan's waterways, PLA Air Force overflights of Taiwan and Japan's territorial waters, military exercises near Taiwan designed to demoralize

---

[17] Michael J. Pence, "Remarks by Vice President Pence on the Administration's Policy toward China" (speech, Hudson Institute, Washington, DC, 4 October 2018).
[18] Babbage, *Winning Without Fighting*, vol. I, 36.
[19] *Psychological Operations*, Joint Publication 3-13.2 (Washington, DC: Joint Chiefs of Staff, 2010), GL-8.
[20] Halper, *China: The Three Warfares*, 12.
[21] Kania, "The PLA's Latest Strategic Thinking on the Three Warfares."

its citizenry and leadership, and joint training exercises between the PLA and Royal Thai Armed Forces.[22]

Legal Warfare

Legal warfare, or lawfare, exploits "all aspects of the law, including national law, international law, and the laws of war, in order to secure seizing 'legal principle superiority' and delegitimize an adversary."[23] Tools used in lawfare operations include "domestic legislation, international legislation, judicial law, legal pronouncement, and law enforcement," which are often used in combination with one another.[24]

In the PRC's efforts to assert control over the South China Sea, for example, lawfare "has involved the utilization of rather tortuous interpretations of international law to oppose the Philippines' position [in the dispute] and seek to delegitimize the arbitration process."[25] The PRC has also used lawfare to bolster its territorial claims in the South China Sea by designating the village of Sansha, located on the disputed Paracel Islands, as a Hainan Prefecture in an attempt to extend PRC control far into the region.[26] In addition, Beijing uses lawfare to block U.S. military activities in Japan and Pacific island territories.[27]

Beijing's use of legal warfare also includes its declaration of extraterritorial rights, which entails PRC security agencies to "extend their operations into the United States and other allied countries by attempting to operate with legal impunity and enforce their own domestic laws overseas." Such lawfare incursions include Operations Fox Hunt and Skynet, in which PRC agents penetrated foreign countries to "apprehend so-called corrupt ethnic Chinese and regime officials. As one example of these operations, Chinese agents attempted to kidnap an ethnic Chinese person in New York and smuggle him onto a China-bound aircraft."[28]

Active Measures

PRC political warfare campaigns include espionage and covert, Cold War-style *active measures*. As Kennan noted, the PRC refashions Clausewitz's famous dictum that "war is the continuation of politics

---

[22] Kasit Piromya, interview with the author, Bangkok, Thailand, 1 May 2018, hereafter Kasit interview.
[23] Kania, "The PLA's Latest Strategic Thinking on the Three Warfares."
[24] Halper, *China: The Three Warfares*, 13.
[25] Kania, "The PLA's Latest Strategic Thinking on the Three Warfares."
[26] Halper, *China: The Three Warfares*, 13.
[27] Ross Babbage, *Winning Without Fighting: Chinese and Russian Political Warfare Campaigns and How the West Can Prevail*, vol. II (Washington, DC: Center for Strategic and Budgetary Assessments, 2019), 17–25; and Kerry K. Gershaneck, " 'Faux Pacifists' Imperil Japan while Empowering China," *Asia Times* (Hong Kong), 10 June 2018.
[28] Babbage, *Winning Without Fighting*, vol. I, 30–31.

by other means" by conducting political warfare as an alternative to armed conflict by other means. Many policymakers and diplomats in the United States and its partner and allied countries fail to recognize such active measures, thereby imperiling their own national security.[29]

As will be detailed in subsequent chapters of this book, the PRC's active-measure tactics, techniques, and procedures include espionage, bribery, censorship, deception, subversion, blackmail, "enforced disappearances," street violence, assassination, and the use of proxy forces such as the People's Liberation Army of Thailand and the United Wa State Army in Myanmar.

These tools may be used for specific purposes, such as when an enforced disappearance is conducted in Thailand to silence an expatriate Chinese critic of the CCP. But the critics themselves are not the only political warfare targets. Once such a disappearance is publicized within the host nation, the overall impact is substantial. Thai citizens and Chinese seeking refuge in Thailand learn quickly that, to use a term that E. Perry Link is credited with coining, "the anaconda is indeed in the chandelier"—and the Thai government cannot protect them from it.[30]

United Front Work

United front work is a classic Leninist political warfare strategy, successfully employed by the Bolsheviks during the Russian Civil War. In a united front, Communists "cooperate with non-revolutionaries for practical purposes—for example, to defeat a common enemy—and [win] them over to the revolutionary cause." Following the CCP's effective use of a united front strategy to defeat the Chinese Nationalist faction, also known as the Kuomintang (KMT), in 1949 and force the Republic of China government from the mainland, this strategy came to be "an integral part of Chinese Communist thought and practice."[31]

As will be detailed in subsequent chapters, the united front strategy is one of Xi Jinping's "magic weapons" in achieving his China Dream.[32] It is a vital element of PRC political warfare, "not only

[29] Kerry K. Gershaneck, discussions with Thai and foreign academics, Thailand, 2013–18; Kerry K. Gershaneck, discussions with senior ROC political warfare officers, Fu Hsing Kang College, National Defense University, Taipei, Taiwan, 2018; and Kerry K. Gershaneck, interview with a senior U.S. Department of State official, Bangkok, Thailand, 30 December 2016.
[30] Kasit interview; and Perry Link, "China: The Anaconda in the Chandelier," *New York Review of Books*, 11 April 2002.
[31] Jonas Parello-Plesner and Belinda Li, *The Chinese Communist Party's Foreign Interference Operations: How the U.S. and Other Democracies Should Respond* (Washington, DC: Hudson Institute, 2018), 8–9.
[32] Parello-Plesner and Li, *The Chinese Communist Party's Foreign Interference Operations*, 8.

for maintaining control over potentially problematic groups, such as religious and ethnic minorities and overseas Chinese, but also as an important part of China's interference strategy abroad." According to University of Canterbury politics professor Anne-Marie Brady, the CCP employed united front work for decades in both its domestic and foreign policy, but Xi, whose own father directed political warfare operations for much of his career, has expanded the strategy greatly.[33]

While the CCP's United Front Work Department has functional responsibility for these operations and activities, PRC united front work is a task of all CCP agencies and members. Every CCP agency, from the International Liaison Department and the Central Propaganda Department to the Chinese People's Association for Friendship with Foreign Countries, is tasked with engaging in united front activities, as are all PRC government departments and local authorities. Executives of China's state-owned enterprises are CCP members, and as the CCP increasingly intrudes into the management of joint ventures, it is safe to assume that there exists intense PRC business engagement in united front work.[34]

A key element of united front work is to co-opt international organizations. For example, the PRC uses institutions such as the World Health Organization (WHO) and the International Criminal Police Organization (Interpol) to conduct its political warfare operations. Before the PRC admitted to detaining Interpol president Meng Hongwei in 2018, the U.S. Department of Justice was asked to investigate whether Meng, a former PRC vice minister of public safety, was abusing his position at Interpol to harass or persecute Chinese dissidents and activists abroad.[35] Concurrently, the WHO has been accused of turning a blind eye to the PRC's cover-up of the COVID-19 global pandemic, which has killed nearly 1.2 million people globally as of this writing. The WHO has also bowed to PRC direction by excluding Taiwan from the World Health Assembly during the past few years, in violation of its own charter.[36]

United front operations also target environmental activist groups, which have been compromised by PRC funding and influence. In May 2017, Greg Rushford at *The Wall Street Journal* exposed how multiple environmental organizations "are betraying their

---

[33] Anne-Marie Brady, "Exploit Every Rift: United Front Work Goes Global," in David Gitter et al., *Party Watch Annual Report*, 2018 (Washington, DC: Center for Advanced China Research, 2018), 34–40.

[34] Simon Denyer, "Command and Control: China's Communist Party Extends Reach into Foreign Companies," *Washington Post*, 28 January 2018.

[35] Bridget Johnson, "DOJ Asked to Probe China's Use of INTERPOL Notices to Persecute Dissidents," PJ Media, 30 April 2018.

[36] Kerry K. Gershaneck, "WHO Is the Latest Victim in Beijing's War on Taiwan," *Nation* (Thailand), 22 May 2018.

ideals in the pursuit of money and access in China." His research highlighted the unwillingness of multiple activist groups—Greenpeace most notable among them—to take a stand against Beijing's colossal environmental destruction in the South China Sea through its dredging-based artificial island-building program, as well as the silence of those activists regarding the PRC's massive overfishing in the South China Sea.[37] In October 2019, Michael K. Cohen exposed in the *Journal of Political Risk* several activist groups cooperating to ensure that the PRC maintains a total monopoly on the production of strategically vital rare earths, an advantage that the PRC has already used as a weapon against Japan and which, it has public stated, it will use against the United States, as well.[38]

Liaison Work

Liaison work, a phrase used primarily by the PLA, supports united front and other political warfare operations by vectoring military operations, intelligence, and finance "to amplify or attenuate the political effect of the military instrument of national power." Mark Stokes and Russell Hsiao, citing PLA references, provide the mission of liaison work as:

> Establishing military liaison work policies and regulations, organizing and executing Taiwan (subversion) work; researching and studying foreign military situations; leading All-Army enemy disintegration work; . . . organizing and leading psychological warfare education and training; . . . external military propaganda work; [and] assuming responsibility for relevant International Red Cross liaison and military-related overseas Chinese work.[39]

Regarding PLA liaison work focused on the United States, political warfare expert J. Michael Waller reports that "in an orchestrated campaign of good cop/bad cop, Chinese officials have gone directly to U.S. public opinion, trying to appeal to sentimental feelings of cooperation and partnership while literally threatening war. The operation is aimed at five levels: the American public at large, journalists

---

[37] Greg Rushford, "How China Tamed the Green Watchdogs: Too Many Environmental Organizations Are Betraying Their Ideals for the Love of the Yuan," *Wall Street Journal*, 29 May 2017.
[38] Michael K. Cohen, "Greenpeace Working to Close Rare Earth Processing Facility in Malaysia: The World's Only Major REE Processing Facility in Competition with China," *Journal of Political Risk* 7, no. 10 (October 2019).
[39] Stokes and Hsiao, *The People's Liberation Army General Political Department*, 14–15.

who influence the public and decision makers, business elites, Congress, and the president and his inner circle."[40]

Liaison work uses intelligence collection and analysis to create and exploit divisions within an opposing nation's government, particularly its defense establishment. To this end, it "develops and sustains rapport with foreign defense elites through exchanges" and "influences perceptions on Taiwan and with other external audiences through propaganda [as well as] strategic, operational, and tactical-level psychological operations." Finally, liaison work counters other nations' efforts to "shape perceptions within China."[41]

Subversion, more commonly referred to in PRC parlance as *disintegration work,* is the reverse side of friendly contact work. According to Stokes and Hsiao, ideological subversion targets the "political cohesion of coalitions, societies, and defense establishments." Political warfare operatives target individuals or groups to find and exploit political and psychological vulnerabilities. They then leverage propaganda, deception, and intelligence to "undermine an opponent's national will through [the] targeting of ideology, psychology, and morale."[42]

Liaison work is also directed at countersubversion against adversarial political warfare. The PRC views any external effort to "Westernize and weaken CCP control through peaceful evolution and [the] promotion of universal values" as subversion and responds by conducting psychological defense measures such as restricting media access and monitoring internet use.[43]

Public Diplomacy and Soft to Sharp Power

Some academics conflate political warfare with *public diplomacy,* but it is incorrect to do so. Public diplomacy is international political advocacy carried out in a transparent manner through routine media channels and public engagements. It differs from political warfare in terms of both target and intent. While public diplomacy seeks to influence the opinions of large audiences, political warfare involves a calculated manipulation of a target country's leaders, elites, and other influential citizens to undermine its strategies, defense policies, and broader international norms. Public diplomacy attracts, whereas political warfare compels.

Another way to view PRC political warfare is through the lens

---

[40] Stokes and Hsiao, *The People's Liberation Army General Political Department,* 14.
[41] Stokes and Hsiao, *The People's Liberation Army General Political Department,* 14–15.
[42] Stokes and Hsiao, *The People's Liberation Army General Political Department,* 15–16.
[43] Stokes and Hsiao, *The People's Liberation Army General Political Department,* 16.

of the terms *soft power, hard power, smart power,* and *sharp power.* The first two terms have been in the common lexicon of international relations and national security for about two decades, while the third became popular around 2009 and the fourth gained credence in the past several years.

Soft power, as attributed to Harvard University's Joseph S. Nye Jr., describes gentler, noncoercive means of cultural, ideological, and institutional influence. Nye hypothesized that much of the world would want to be like the United States, which would consequently help the United States shape the world. According to Eric X. Li, "for Nye, the basis of U.S. soft power was liberal democratic politics, free market economics, and fundamental values such as human rights."[44]

In the realm of international relations, soft power simply means the ability of one nation to affect another's government and people through attraction to the former's culture, political ideals, economy, and even military. Such actions are often conducted by persuasion rather than pressure. *Hard power,* on the other hand, involves coercive measures, such as the threat of military attack, blockade, or economic boycott. *Smart power* was later described by Nye to accommodate the use of "smart strategies that combine the tools of both hard and soft power"—that is, the use of both carrots and sticks to achieve foreign policy objectives.[45]

While PRC political warfare entails soft, hard, and smart power, some of its operations and techniques are neither *hard* in the openly kinetic or forcefully coercive sense nor *soft* in the gentle "attract and persuade" sense. The PRC's very aggressive influence operations and political warfare activities comprise what is now commonly referred to as *sharp power,* a form of asymmetric warfare that exploits the openness of democratic societies. Unlike soft power, sharp power "is not principally about attraction or even persuasion; instead, it centers on distraction and manipulation," according to a National Endowment for Democracy (NED) report.[46] In open and democratic systems, sharp power acts like a Trojan horse that covertly sabotages social harmony.

Sharp power can be defined as the aggressive use of media and institutions to shape public opinion abroad. It is "sharp" in that it is used to "pierce, penetrate, or perforate the information [and political environments] in the targeted countries." Those regimes that

---

44 Eric X. Li, "The Rise and Fall of Soft Power: Joseph Nye's Concept Lost Relevance, but China Could Bring It Back," *Foreign Policy,* 20 August 2018.

45 Joseph S. Nye Jr., "Get Smart: Combining Hard and Soft Power," *Foreign Affairs* 88, no. 4 (July/August 2009): 160–63.

46 Juan Pablo Cardenal et al., *Sharp Power: Rising Authoritarian Influence* (Washington, DC: National Endowment for Democracy, 2017), 6.

employ it "are not necessarily seeking to 'win hearts and minds,' the common frame of reference for 'soft power' efforts, but they are surely seeking to manage their target audiences by manipulating or poisoning the information that reaches them."[47]

The NED report cautions that Beijing's massive initiatives involving news media, culture, think tanks, and academia should not be misconstrued as "charm offensives" or efforts to "share alternative ideas" or "broaden the debate." Rather, through sharp power, "the generally unattractive values of authoritarian systems—which encourage a monopoly on power, top-down control, censorship, and coerced or purchased loyalty—are projected outward, and those affected are not so much audiences as [they are] victims."[48]

To some, sharp power represents a new front in the battle for public opinion. However, to those paying attention to the CCP's covert and overt operations dating as far back as the 1920s, sharp power is merely a standard element of PRC political warfare in fashionable new wrapping.

Hybrid Warfare

Hybrid warfare is defined by NATO political-military expert Chris Kremidas-Courtney as "the mix of conventional and unconventional, military and non-military, overt and covert actions employed in a coordinated manner to achieve specific objectives while remaining below the threshold of formally declared warfare."[49] Like Russia, the PRC successfully employs hybrid warfare—sometimes called *gray zone warfare*—to achieve its political aims.

In its hybrid operations, the PRC, like Russia, applies its "full spectrum of economic, legal, information, cyber, and paramilitary means to achieve [its] objectives in a slow and often ambiguous manner." Beijing is generally careful to "not cross any threshold which would trigger collective military action in response," thereby lowering the political price for its aggressive expansionism.[50] For example, Beijing has "gradually expanded its control and influence in the South China Sea by constructing artificial islands [and establishing military bases on them], sending armed fishermen to patrol claimed territorial waters, and declaring an air (defense) identification zone." It has exerted control over most of the South China Sea this way—

---

[47] Cardenal et al., *Sharp Power*, 6, 13.
[48] Cardenal et al., *Sharp Power*, 13.
[49] Chris Kremidas-Courtney, "Hybrid Warfare: The Comprehensive Approach in the Offense," Strategy International, 13 February 2019.
[50] Kremidas-Courtney, "Hybrid Warfare."

"without firing a shot."[51] Further, the PRC's employment of its coast guard and the People's Armed Forces Maritime Militia in coercive violent confrontations at sea with neighboring countries' ships and fishing boats is another example of its approach to hybrid warfare.[52] Moreover, the employment of proxy armies, such as the United Wa State Army and Kokang Army in Myanmar, is an example of gray zone warfare, as are difficult-to-attribute cyberattacks by the PLA Strategic Support Force cyber troops and the PRC's netizen "50 Cent Army."[53]

Self-Censorship, Totalitarianism, and Fascism

Finally, it is important to address self-censorship and how it relates to use of the terms *totalitarian* and *fascist* to characterize the CCP and the PRC as a society. Many government officials, academics, and business leaders in the United States and other democratic nations fall silent when these terms are used to describe the PRC, and some even attempt to deny it. This silence and denial reflects intellectual dishonesty at best. It is essential to use the terms that define the nature of the CCP regime, for failure to properly define the nature of the regime obscures necessary national-level response. Further, it allows the PRC's apologists and defenders to assert the "moral equivalence" defense of China's political warfare that the author has heard repeatedly: "Every country does it. So what?"

The "so what" is that the PRC is a fascist, totalitarian existential threat. Merriam-Webster defines *fascism* and *totalitarianism* as follows:

> *Fascism*: "a political philosophy, movement, or regime (such as that of the Fascisti) that exalts nation and often race above the individual and that stands for a centralized autocratic government headed by a dictatorial leader, severe economic and social regimentation, and forcible suppression of opposition; a tendency toward or actual exercise of strong autocratic or dictatorial control."[54]

---

[51] Kremidas-Courtney, "Hybrid Warfare."
[52] Conor M. Kennedy and Andrew S. Erickson, *China Maritime Report No. 1: China's Third Sea Force, the People's Armed Forces Maritime Militia: Tethered to the PLA* (Newport, RI: U.S. Naval War College, 2017); and James E. Fanell and Kerry K. Gershaneck, "White Warships and Little Blue Men: The Looming 'Short, Sharp War' in the East China Sea over the Senkakus," *Marine Corps University Journal* 8, no. 2 (Fall 2017): 67–98, https://doi.org/10.21140/mcuj.2017080204.
[53] Anthony Davis, "China's Loose Arms Still Fuel Myanmar's Civil Wars," *Asia Times* (Hong Kong), 28 January 2020; Bertil Lintner, "A Chinese War in Myanmar," *Asia Times* (Hong Kong), 5 April 2017; and Keoni Everington, "China's 'Troll Factory' Targeting Taiwan with Disinformation Prior to Election," *Taiwan News* (Taipei), 5 November 2018.
[54] "Dictionary: Fascism," *Merriam-Webster*, accessed 7 October 2019.

> *Totalitarianism*: "centralized control by an autocratic authority; the political concept that the citizen should be totally subject to an absolute state authority."[55]

By these definitions, the PRC is inarguably both totalitarian and fascist, based on the CCP's actions, laws, and culture. First, the CCP severely curbs the freedoms of its people, the people are allowed no rights to resist the will of their rulers, and dissent is crushed—violently, if necessary. Second, power is highly centralized, run on, as Xi Jingping claims, Marxist-Leninist tenets, and nominally Communist. Third, the nation is exalted above the people. Hypernationalism and jingoism are typically powered by a sense of historical grievance or victimhood. China is now overcoming its "century of humiliation" at the hands of Western imperialism, and every day Chinese children are exhorted to "never forget national humiliation."[56]

Additional justifications for labeling the PRC *totalitarian* are best explained by Chinese human rights lawyer Teng Biao and King's College London political science professor Stein Ringen. Teng writes that Xi Jinping's "new totalitarianism" and Mao Zedong's "old style of totalitarianism" are not all that different: "Under this kleptocratic system, the assets of regular citizens have never been afforded any institutionalized protection." Ideologically speaking, "the CCP has monopolized the media, created no-go zones in scholarship, instituted a brainwashing-style education system, established the Great Firewall, and persecuted intellectuals for their writing." Legally, "the [CCP] has always ridden roughshod over the law. Black jails, forced disappearances, torture, secret police, surveillance, judicial corruption, controlled elections, forced demolitions, and religious persecution have all been rampant." Teng concludes that "these abuses are a key element in the [CCP's] system of control," and that China is implementing a "sophisticated totalitarianism" that is "cruel and barbaric without being chaotic."[57]

Ringen wrote in a public letter to fellow China analysts in September 2018 that "the final straw has been the imposition of outright tyranny in Xinjiang, with extremes of surveillance, heavily intrusive thought-work, and mass detentions in 're-education' facilities." He also commented on "the relentless tightening of dictatorship during Xi Jinping's reign, culminating in the decimation of the community

[55] "Dictionary: Totalitarianism," *Merriam-Webster*, accessed 7 October 2019.
[56] Xi Jingping, "Full Text of Xi Jinping's Report at 19th CPC National Congress," *China Daily* (Beijing), 4 November 2017; and Zheng Wang, *Never Forget National Humiliation: Historical Memory in Chinese Politics and Foreign Relations* (New York: Columbia University Press, 2012).
[57] Teng Biao, "Has Xi Jinping Changed China? Not Really," ChinaFile, 16 April 2018.

of human rights lawyers that has stood as a bastion of courage and civility."[58]

According to Ringen, the chief features of totalitarianism are that "rule is upheld by terror," that "rule reaches into the regulation of natural human bonds in private spheres," that "rule is exercised through an extensive and impersonal bureaucracy," and that "the state operates under the authority of a commanding ideology." He continues, "The state is deep into the regulation of private lives, now intensified in the 'social credit system' by which rewards and punishments are distributed in the population according to patterns of private behaviour." Xi "has cast off pragmatism and clad his reign in the omnipresent China Dream ideology of nationalism and chauvinism. The result of totalitarian patterns of state rule is that social life is atomised and community crushed."[59]

Ringen concludes that he is aware of the "honest reluctance to [adopt] the language of totalitarianism. There has been hope and expectation of opening up. But in political life and civil society it is not happening. Far from it, the direction of travel is to shutting down. We should now [recognize] this in the language we use."[60]

While some argue that terms such as *totalitarian* and *fascist* do not apply to the PRC, most key government officials and many academics in democratic countries now realize that the terms are indeed accurate, even if they hesitate to use them for fear of retribution. To a degree, this fear is understandable, since the PRC employs a wide range of measures to ensure censorship and self-censorship. The Hudson Institute reports that these measures include coercive methods such as "denying visas to academics and blacklisting" as well as "subtler ways of inducing self-censorship. Publishers, for example, have an incentive to avoid books that might offend China's censors because China can retaliate by cutting off market access."

Economic links to the PRC may also prompt self-censorship since "many American universities receive significant donations from Chinese government entities, companies, and individuals." The U.S. Department of Education General Counsel asserts that "the evidence suggests massive investments of foreign money have bred dependency and distorted the decision making, mission, and values of too many institutions."[61] Universities in the United States were given more than $56 million from Chinese sources in 2017 alone. As

[58] Stein Ringen, "Totalitarianism: A Letter to Fellow China Analysts," *ThatsDemocracy* (blog), 19 September 2018.
[59] Ringen, "Totalitarianism."
[60] Ringen, "Totalitarianism."
[61] Tom Ciccotta, "Multiple Universities Refuse to Cooperate with Federal Investigations into Ties to China," Breitbart, 21 May 2020.

examples, Stanford University "received $32,244,826 in monetary gifts from China" during six years, while Harvard University "received $55,065,261 through a combination of contracts and monetary gifts."[62] Other American universities, meanwhile, have refused to cooperate with a federal investigation into their PRC income sources.[63]

Confucius reportedly said, "If names be not correct, language is not in accordance with the truth of things. If language be not in accordance with the truth of things, affairs cannot be carried on to success."[64] It is time to call the fight we are in by its right name: *political warfare*, the name the CCP calls it. In addition to adding this term to the daily lexicon, it is time for the U.S. government and academia to also use the terms *totalitarian* and *fascist* to describe the nature of the country posing the threat. It is also past time to counter the self-censorship that inhibits clear thinking about the implications of these terms as they pertain to the PRC.

[62] Parello-Plesner and Li, *The Chinese Communist Party's Foreign Interference Operations*, 35.
[63] Ciccotta, "Multiple Universities Refuse to Cooperate with Federal Investigations into Ties to China."
[64] Burton Watson, trans., *The Analects of Confucius* (New York: Columbia University Press, 2007).

CHAPTER THREE

A Brief History of PRC Political Warfare

Long live the great Marxism-Leninism-Mao Zedong thought. The foundations of Chinese political warfare were laid by the Soviet Union and the tenets of Karl Marx, Vladimir Lenin, and Joseph Stalin. Mao Zedong adapted the Soviet model to embody "Chinese characteristics." Pictured on the flag behind Mao, from left to right, are Stalin, Lenin, Friedrich Engels, and Marx.

> Attaining one hundred victories in one hundred battles is not the pinnacle of excellence. Subjugating the enemy's army without fighting is the true pinnacle of excellence. . . . The highest realization of warfare is to attack the enemy's plans; next is to attack their alliances; next to attack their army; and the lowest is to attack their fortified cities. . . . Thus one who excels at employing the military subjugates other people's armies without engaging in battle, captures other people's fortified cities without attacking them, and destroys other people's states without prolonged fighting.[1]
>
> ~Sun Tzu

---

[1] Sun Tzu, *The Complete Art of War*, trans. Ralph D. Sawyer (Boulder, CO: Westview Press, 1996).

The precepts of Chinese political warfare extend back to at least 500 BCE, as reflected by Chinese general and military strategist Sun Tzu's oft-quoted prescription above. However, the People's Republic of China (PRC) has rapidly developed formidable political warfare capabilities, and its potential to conduct such operations on a global scale is arguably unprecedented in world history. An understanding of how the PRC conducts political warfare requires a brief overview of China's unique historical context.

While the PRC is a newly modernized military and technological powerhouse, its current foreign and domestic policies have deep roots in China's ancient history. The bloody Warring States period (~475–221 BCE), leading to the unification of the seven feuding states under the Qin Dynasty, plays a particularly important role in defining the PRC's current approach to strategy, political warfare, deception, and stratagems with an emphasis on "overturning the old hegemon and exacting revenge."[2]

China expert Michael P. Pillsbury writes that the strategies used by Xi Jinping and his predecessors in the PRC's drive for supremacy are largely the result of lessons derived from the Warring States period. Resultant stratagems are based on the following principles:

- Induce complacency to avoid alerting your opponent.
- Manipulate your opponent's advisors.
- Be patient—for decades or longer—to achieve victory.
- Steal your opponent's ideas and technology for strategic purposes.
- Military might is not the critical factor for winning a long-term competition.
- Recognize that the hegemon will take extreme, even reckless action to maintain its dominant position.
- Never lose sight of *shi* . . . [which includes] deceiving others to do your bidding for you [and] waiting for the point of maximum opportunity to strike.
- Establish and employ metrics for measuring your status relative to other potential challengers.
- Always be vigilant to avoid being encircled and deceived by others.[3]

While acknowledging the impact of China's long history in laying a foundation for the PRC's current strategic culture, it is important to recognize that PRC political warfare has its strongest roots in the his-

---

[2] Michael P. Pillsbury, *The Hundred-Year Marathon: China's Secret Strategy to Replace America as the Global Superpower* (New York: Henry Holt, 2015), 31–51.
[3] Pillsbury, *The Hundred-Year Marathon*, 35–36.

tory of the Chinese Communist Party (CCP). The CCP's history includes deep-seated fears regarding the PRC's geostrategic situation and the relationship between the CCP and the Communist Party of the Soviet Union during the first half of the twentieth century.

A Tough Neighborhood Fosters Xenophobia

Apologists for the CCP's aggressive expansionist, repressive, and xenophobic policies often justify them due to China's long history of conflict and invasion. There is, indeed, historical basis for the regime's paranoia. According to a study published by the Center for Strategic and Budgetary Assessments (CSBA), "Chinese regimes have been forced to fight for their survival against powerful invaders that either swept across the Eurasian plains or assaulted across the eastern seaboard" for thousands of years. "The few geographical barriers on this vast land mass have provided only limited protection, and the resulting security challenges foster compelling historical narratives, a strong civilizational identity, and deep nationalism. Successive regimes mobilized these historical and cultural strengths to reinforce their legitimacy and periodically generate xenophobia."[4]

While the CCP was not the first tyrannical regime to wholly arouse xenophobia, it has exploited it with exceptional success. Today, it possesses a compelling ability to control the information, thoughts, and actions of both its own population and those of foreign countries through means unimaginable to early emperors.[5]

This totalitarian perspective, grounded in China's experiences during the Warring States period and the worldviews of its first emperor, Qin Shi Huang, provides the traditional strategic culture of centralized despotism, coercion, and persuasion that lays the foundation for contemporary CCP political warfare. From the earliest rulers of the Shang and Zhou Dynasties, autocracy has been the natural order of life, with no compact like the Magna Carta or Declaration of Independence or concepts such as post-Westphalian rights intervening between emperors and control over their subjects.

Ancient Despots as CCP Role Models

Emperor Qin Shi Huang imposed the first totalitarian state in China, ruling with an iron fist and regulating every aspect of his subjects'

---

[4] Thomas G. Mahnken, Ross Babbage, and Toshi Yoshihara, *Countering Comprehensive Coercion: Competitive Strategies against Authoritarian Political Warfare* (Washington, DC: Center for Strategic and Budgetary Assessments, 2018), 25.

[5] Yi-Zheng Lian, "China Has a Vast Influence Machine, and You Don't Even Know It," *New York Times*, 21 May 2018.

lives. He instituted a regime that would later be copied by Communists throughout the world, assigning political commissars to spy on governors and military leaders to make sure they did not diverge from or criticize his policies.[6]

According to China expert Steven W. Mosher, Qin exerted control over the Chinese population through every aspect of their daily existence. For example, severe punishment was the order of the day: "For major capital crimes, the offender and his entire family were annihilated. For even the most minor infractions, millions were sent to forced labor projects such as building imperial highways and canals." As the emperor "built his cult of personality to imbue himself with a godlike image and establish total supremacy both internal and external to his empire, [he] attempted to eradicate thought itself." This thought eradication included his order for "the burning of all books in the Imperial Archives except his own memoirs. Private ownership of books was prohibited. Soon, pyres of burning books lit up cities at night, but three million men were branded and sent to labor camps for owning books nonetheless."[7]

Qin's foreign policy was one of aggressive expansionism, intended to attain complete control over the region—and eventually the world—to achieve total hegemony. The natural extension of totalitarianism, hegemony would lead to order, ensuring that the Chinese empire avoided the chaos that characterized so much of its history.

That relentless quest for hegemony was also inspired by a sense of racial superiority and supremacist entitlement. Both concepts would later serve as the basis of many totalitarian regimes, with Adolf Hitler's Third Reich representing one of the most genocidal versions, that largely disappeared into the ashes of history following wars or other destructive forces. For the PRC, however, these factors still underpin the "China Dream," which outlines how the PRC will, through stealth and strength—or, in CCP parlance, "secrecy and stratagem"—become the "world's leading power, surpassing and then replacing" the United States.[8] The characters for China, 中国, literally mean "middle kingdom," and notions of China's centrality and the superiority of the Han race permeate Chinese literature and thought. Throughout history, China's rulers have encouraged a race-based nationalism and ethnocentrism to reinforce their legitimacy.

To become the hegemon, the dominant axis of power as well as the geographic and geopolitical center of the world, China required

[6] Steven W. Mosher, *Hegemon: China's Plan to Dominate Asia and the World* (San Francisco, CA: Encounter Books, 2000), 21.
[7] Mosher, *Hegemon*, 20–25.
[8] Pillsbury, *The Hundred-Year Marathon*, 28–29; and Thomas G. Mahnken, *Strategy & Stratagem: Understanding Chinese Strategic Culture* (Sydney, Australia: Lowy Institute for International Policy, 2011), 3, 18, 24–26.

that all other states become vassal or tributary states. Mosher writes that Chinese elites "believed their emperor to be the only legitimate political authority" in the world and "regarded themselves as the highest expression of civilized humanity."[9] Accordingly, the Chinese treated "barbarian" nations as a powerful suzerain would, by imposing unequal conditions, exacting tribute, and influencing their leaders and peoples through cultural, economic, and military power. For two millennia, China's hegemony in the region lasted, sustained by powerful armies and political warfare.[10]

The CSBA study notes that "there have been strong incentives for China's rulers . . . to not only harness all of the resources of the society but also to do so in innovative ways." As noted at the beginning of this chapter, Sun Tzu "argued strongly for political, psychological, and other non-combat operations to subdue enemies prior to committing armies to combat.[11]

In the early twentieth century, Chinese Communists such as Mao Zedong adapted Sun Tzu's strategic analyses and Qin Shi Huang's totalitarian tactics to the inspiration they found in Marxist-Leninist ideology. During that same time, the particularly virulent views that Soviet Union leaders Vladimir Lenin and Joseph Stalin held on attaining and maintaining power greatly influenced the fledgling CCP.

Soviet Influence on the CCP

In nearly all aspects, the Soviet Union initially provided the role model for Chinese Communist policy, organization, and operation. Mao and his followers learned operational arts, such as political warfare, from the Moscow-led Communist International (Comintern). As they adapted those Soviet operational arts to China's own unique historical context, they merged Western revolutionary theory and practice with their own version of what might be termed "total war with Chinese characteristics."[12]

Mao combined China's historical strategic culture with Comintern instruction as well as individual insights from Carl von Clausewitz, Lenin, Stalin, Leon Trotsky, and others. He then developed a new concept of revolutionary war to defeat Chiang Kai-shek's Na-

---

[9] Steven W. Mosher, *Bully of Asia: Why China's Dream Is the New Threat to World Order* (Washington, DC: Regnery Publishing, 2017), 10.

[10] Mosher, *Hegemon*, 2–5; and Mohan Malik, "Historical Fiction: China's South China Sea Claims," *World Affairs* 176, no. 1 (May/June 2013): 83–90.

[11] Mahnken, Babbage, and Yoshihara, *Countering Comprehensive Coercion*, 25.

[12] Mark Stokes and Russell Hsiao, *The People's Liberation Army General Political Department: Political Warfare with Chinese Characteristics* (Arlington, VA: Project 2049 Institute, 2013), 6–7.

tionalist Kuomintang (KMT) government in the Chinese Civil War and force it into exile on Taiwan. Mao had also used his concept in more limited efforts to fight Japanese forces that had invaded China during the Second Sino-Japanese War.

As the CSBA study on political warfare notes, "The importance of early political operations throughout the theatre of operations . . . became a key foundation of Chinese military doctrine for revolutionary and unconventional war, as well as for a broader range of operations." Twentieth-century Chinese leaders "saw these political campaigns as being critically important not only on home territory but also in enemy countries."[13] Like the Soviets, Mao envisioned his revolution as eventually engulfing other lands. He wrote that "Lenin teaches us that the world revolution can succeed only if the proletariat of the capitalist countries supports the struggle for liberation of the people of the colonies and semi-colonies. . . . We must unite with the proletarians of . . . Britain, the United States, Germany, Italy, and all other capitalist countries; only then can we overthrow Imperialism . . . and liberate the nations and the peoples of the world."[14]

Today, the PRC continues to use its Soviet-based political warfare concepts to "promote the rise of China within a new international order and defend against perceived threats to state security."[15]

The United Front: The PRC's Magic Weapon

As introduced in the previous chapter, the united front is a critical weapon in the PRC political warfare arsenal. Under the principle of "uniting with friends and disintegrating enemies," Mao called for worldwide revolution, using united fronts "to mobilize [the CCP's] friends to strike at [its] enemies." He described the united front as a "magic weapon" that could match the military power of the Chinese Red Army, the precursor to the People's Liberation Army (PLA).[16]

United front strategy was originally developed by the Bolsheviks during the Russian Civil War. It called for cooperating with nonrevolutionaries for practical purposes—for example, to defeat a common enemy—and winning them over to the revolutionary cause. In China, the strategy was first used in the 1920s to form an alliance between the CCP and KMT to end warlordism.[17] Since then,

[13] Mahnken, Babbage, and Yoshihara, *Countering Comprehensive Coercion*, 26.
[14] Mao Zedong, *Selected Works of Mao Tse-Tung* (Beijing: Foreign Language Press, 1965), 104.
[15] Stokes and Hsiao, *The People's Liberation Army General Political Department*, 3.
[16] Peter Mattis, "An American Lens on China's Interference and Influence-Building Abroad," *Open Forum*, Asan Forum, 30 April 2018.
[17] Lyman P. Van Slyke, *Enemies and Friends: The United Front in Chinese Communist History* (Stanford, CA: Stanford University Press, 1967), 3.

this focus on influencing, co-opting, demoralizing, and subverting enemy elites and military forces has remained consistent for almost 100 years. Co-option of non-Communist forces remains its essence today, although exporting revolution is less important now than exporting the totalitarian China Model.[18]

In the early CCP, underground political work was divided into numerous systems. According to Mark Stokes and Russell Hsiao, the Urban Work Department "focused on ordinary citizens, minorities, students, factory workers, and urban residents," while the Social Work Department "concentrated on the upper social elite of enemy civilian authorities, security of senior CCP leaders, and Comintern liaison" and the General Political Department "was responsible for political warfare against opposing military forces," employing what is termed "enemy work and liaison work."[19]

A second united front between the CCP and KMT was established to fight the Japanese invaders during the Second Sino-Japanese War, but it broke down during the war. During the Chinese Civil War, CCP enemy work and liaison work were critical to undermining KMT morale and building domestic and international support to win the war on the mainland. The CCP prevailed over the KMT on mainland China in 1949 and founded the PRC.

The CCP "established its first organ responsible specifically for liaising with overseas Chinese communities" in 1940, and by the 1950s the strategy came to be "an integral part of Chinese Communist thought and practice."[20]

The success of PRC united front operations has fluctuated from the founding of the PRC, to the devastating Great Leap Forward of the 1950s, to the chaotic Cultural Revolution of the 1960s and 1970s, to the Charm Offensive of the 1990s, and finally to the Belt and Road-aligned political warfare battle for global dominance that is underway today. Some of those successes will be explored in detail in subsequent chapters.

Active Measures in the Political Warfare Fight

One key to the PRC's political warfare success is its relentless use of active measures, which the CCP learned from the Soviet Union's employment of "black" and "gray" tools and tactics. Active measures

---

[18] *Hearing on Strategic Competition with China, before the House Committee on Armed Services*, 115th Cong. (2018) (testimony by Aaron L. Friedberg, Professor of Politics and International Affairs, Woodrow Wilson School, Princeton University), hereafter Friedberg testimony.

[19] Stokes and Hsiao, *The People's Liberation Army General Political Department*, 6–7.

[20] Alexander Bowe, *China's Overseas United Front Work: Background and Implications for the United States* (Washington, DC: U.S.-China Economic and Security Review Commission, 2018); and Van Slyke, *Enemies and Friends*, 3.

involve "manipulative use of slogans, distorted arguments, disinformation, and carefully selected true information [to] influence the attitudes and actions of foreign publics and governments." Black active measures employ "agents of influence, covert media manipulation, and forgeries [to] shape foreign public perception and attitudes of senior leaders," while gray active measures leverage "united front entities, think tanks, institutes, and other non-governmental organizations that [enable] an ostensibly independent line from the Soviet party-state." Conversely, "attributable statements of the Communist Party Propaganda Department" are referred to as "white," or overt, propaganda.[21]

While the Republic of China (ROC) on Taiwan has been the historic primary target of PRC political warfare, the CCP has extended its political warfare objectives well beyond its traditional ROC enemy. Since regional and global hegemony is the PRC's ultimate objective, the entire international community is now the target. The PRC has employed massive resources to its active-measure operations since 1949, both regionally as well as across the globe.

The PRC's support of its proxy United Wa State Army (UWSA) in Myanmar seems an anomaly to many contemporary diplomats, academics, and journalists, but such support has always been the norm for the PRC. For more than four decades during the Cold War, Beijing's "national liberation armies" waged revolutionary war throughout Southeast Asia and cost the United States and its allies dearly while severely undermining nation-building there.

Robert Taber, a leading counterinsurgency analyst, wrote that a "typical revolutionary political organization will have two branches: one subterranean and illegal, the other visible and quasi-legitimate." The former comprises "activists . . . saboteurs, terrorists, arms runners, fabricators of explosive devices, operators of a clandestine press, distributors of political pamphlets, and couriers to carry messages from one guerrilla sector to another." The latter includes "intellectuals, tradesmen, clerks, students, [and] professionals," who are "capable of promoting funds, circulating petitions, organizing boycotts, raising popular demonstrations, informing friendly journalists, spreading rumors, and in every way conceivable waging a massive propaganda campaign aimed at two objectives: the strengthening and brightening of the rebel 'image,' and the discrediting of the regime."[22]

Using these and related techniques, the PRC has funded, sup-

---

[21] Stokes and Hsiao, *The People's Liberation Army General Political Department*, 6.
[22] Robert Taber, *The War of the Flea: A Study of Guerrilla Warfare Theory and Practice* (New York: Citadel Press, 1965), 32–33.

plied, and trained forces engaged in independence movements and insurgencies from the 1950s to the present day. Its focus was primarily on the newly developing nations of Southeast Asia, with some additional support given in South Asia, Africa, and Latin America.[23] In Southeast Asia, insurgent forces proxy armies were the sharpest weapon in Beijing's political warfare arsenal. These armies were ultimately successful in Vietnam, Cambodia, and Laos, while countries like Thailand and Malaysia held the line only with massive support from the United States and United Kingdom, respectively, and innovative counterinsurgency concepts.

Today, the PRC continues its use of proxy armies, such as the UWSA in Myanmar. The UWSA was founded in 1989 when it emerged from the collapse of the PRC-backed Communist Party of Burma. It now administers a region the size of Belgium on the Sino-Myanmar border, a major hub in the Asian narcotics trade. With direct support from the PRC, the UWSA is at present the largest nonstate military actor in Asia, a well-equipped and well-led force that has achieved a serious measure of deterrence in relation to Myanmar's armed forces. It is also the major power broker in Myanmar today, influencing the nation's stalled peace process. The PRC-equipped Kokang rebels, of Chinese descent, are also viewed as proxies of Beijing in its reported efforts to annex the Kokang region of Myanmar, similar to the Russian annexation of Crimea in 2014.[24]

China's Charm Offensive and Rejuvenated United Front

As late as the 1980s, the PRC was considered a pariah in much of the international community, seen as a Communist threat that had sponsored vicious revolutions exemplified by Cambodia's genocidal Pol Pot regime. The massive starvation and ultimate failure of the Great Leap Forward (1958–62) and subsequent brutal anarchy of the Cultural Revolution (1966–76) damaged the PRC's global image and greatly weakened the effectiveness of its political warfare and other influence operations.[25]

The 1989 Tiananmen Square massacre further diminished the PRC's influence. Of particular note, the international backlash of the massacre served as a turning point for the CCP in terms of both internal propaganda and suppression and the refinement of its

---

[23] Joshua Kurlantzick. *Charm Offensive: How China's Soft Power Is Transforming the World* (New Haven, CT: Yale University Press, 2008), 1–15.
[24] Bertil Lintner, "A Chinese War in Myanmar," *Asia Times* (Hong Kong), 5 April 2017.
[25] Kurlantzick, *Charm Offensive*, 16–20.

external influence capabilities.[26] The PRC has since advanced to a remarkable degree in its ability to use soft power in its global political warfare operations, as reflected in its Charm Offensive campaign that began in the late 1990s.

Despite missteps in the 1990s that generated even more international pushback, such as military actions against Vietnam and threats against Taiwan, by the end of the decade the PRC had initiated its very sophisticated global Charm Offensive campaign. It was based on a systematic, coherent soft power strategy which supported its overall political warfare objectives. Beijing employed a wide range of influence-related reforms, such as significantly upgrading the quality and sophistication of its diplomatic corps, to successfully engage the international community. The end of the Cold War in 1991 helped cloak its advances.

The PRC was assisted greatly in its progress by the United States' retreat from the world stage under President William J. "Bill" Clinton. The United States dismantled its main public diplomacy and counterpolitical warfare organization, the U.S. Information Agency, in 1999, a victim of victory in the Cold War. Further, the Clinton administration neglected many of the multilateral institutions that were built after World War II and failed to intercede in either the 1994 Rwandan genocide or the 1997 Asian financial crisis.[27]

Consequently, the foundation was laid for a "rising China" to assert itself on the world stage as the United States' influence appeared to wane. As the CCP watched Washington "retreat from the world, consumed with its own economic boom, with the Internet, and with American culture wars," its rulers felt confident that it now could surpass the United States. Accordingly, it set about "shaping its regional environment" by focusing its soft power tools to portray itself as "a benign, peaceful, and constructive actor in the world."[28] The PRC has since "adopted an increasingly active and pragmatic diplomatic approach around the world that emphasizes complementary economic interests." In addition to a more sophisticated diplomatic corps bolstering influence and image, Beijing has funded infrastructure, public works, and economic investment projects in many developing countries."[29]

[26] Kurlantzick, *Charm Offensive*, 25–48.
[27] Kurlantzick. *Charm Offensive*, 43–44.
[28] Kurlantzick. *Charm Offensive*, 43, 51–52.
[29] Thomas Lum et al., *Comparing Global Influence: China's and U.S. Diplomacy, Foreign Aid, Trade, and Investment in the Developing World* (Washington, DC: Congressional Research Service, 2008).

Political Warfare in the Xi Era

Since 2012, the PRC has become even more sophisticated and ambitious in its use of political warfare to achieve its broad strategic objectives. According to Princeton University professor Aaron L. Friedberg, "Beijing is employing a variety of techniques to shape the perceptions of both leaders and elites in the advanced industrial nations (including the United States) as well as in much of the developing world."[30] Friedberg continues that the PRC's methods include:

> the funding of university chairs and think tank research programs; offers of lucrative employment to former government officials who have demonstrated that they are reliable "friends of China;" all-expenses-paid junkets to China for foreign legislators and journalists; expulsion of foreign media that present unfavorable views of China to overseas audiences; increasingly sophisticated use of well-funded official, quasi-official and nominally unofficial media platforms that deliver Beijing's message to the world; pressure on movie studios and media companies to ensure continued access to the vast Chinese market by avoiding politically sensitive content; [and] mobilization and exploitation of overseas students and local ethnic Chinese communities to support Beijing's aims.[31]

The CCP has long employed propaganda and disinformation against its enemies, but in recent years it has found a "fertile information environment" in the new world of social media to "amplify its time-honed tactics of political and psychological warfare." The added benefit of using social media to flood its adversaries' societies with propaganda and disinformation is that it ultimately weakens people's faith in democracy and can create political instability.[32] In pursuit of social media dominance, the PRC has established PLA cyber force of as many as 300,000 soldiers as well as a netizen "50 Cent Army" of perhaps 2 million individuals who "are paid a nominal fee to make comments on social media sites in favor of [CCP] propaganda."[33]

---

[30] Friedberg testimony.
[31] Friedberg testimony.
[32] Russell Hsiao, "CCP Propaganda against Taiwan Enters the Social Age," Jamestown Foundation, China Brief 18, no. 7, 24 April 2018.
[33] Keoni Everington, "China's 'Troll Factory' Targeting Taiwan with Disinformation Prior to Election," *Taiwan News* (Taipei), 5 November 2018.

PLA Reform and the "Omnipresent Struggle"

The PLA's evolving role in political warfare and use of information and cyber operations rate special note. According to a U.S. National Defense University study, in late 2015, the PLA "initiated reforms that have brought dramatic changes to its structure, model of warfighting, and organizational culture."[34] These reforms include the creation of a Strategic Support Force (SSF) that consolidates most PLA cyber, electronic, psychological, and space warfare capabilities.

Specifically, the role of the SSF is significant to how the PLA plans to conduct information operations and fight informationized wars. The SSF "appears to have incorporated elements of the PLA's psychological and political warfare missions," which comes as a result of a "subtle yet consequential PLA-wide reorganization of China's political warfare forces. This may portend a more operational role for psychological operations in the future."[35]

The PLA sees the SSF as essential for "anticipating adversary action, setting the terms of conflict in peacetime, and achieving battlefield dominance in wartime." The SSF supports the overal political warfare goal of "winning without fighting" by "shaping an adversary's decisionmaking through actions below the threshold of outright war, accomplishing strategic objectives without escalating to open conflict." The PRC does not adhere to "Western models of conflict, in which peace and war are distinct stages." Contrawise, the CCP model is the "spectrum of omnipresent 'struggle,' a Maoist-Marxist-Leninist paradigm that sees a broad political front in an enduring clash of political systems and ideologies, with military competition and conflict being merely one part of that whole."[36]

As another key result of PLA reform was the establishment of the Eastern Theater Command (ETC) in February 2016, to replace the Nanjing Military Region. The ETC plays a major role in "directing political-military coercion against Taiwan," and its reorganization into an expanded theater command increases its operational capacity.[37] The founding of the SSF in combination with the establishment of the ETC offers the PLA the organization and resources needed to advance its capabilites beyond that allowed by its previous Mao-era political warfare support structure.

---

[34] John Costello and Joe McReynolds, *China's Strategic Support Force: A Force for a New Era* (Washington, DC: National Defense University Press, 2018), 1–2.
[35] Costello and McReynolds, *China's Strategic Support Force*, 2.
[36] Costello and McReynolds, *China's Strategic Support Force*, 45.
[37] Rachael Burton and Mark Stokes, "The People's Liberation Army Theater Command Leadership: The Eastern Theater Command," Project 2049 Institute, 13 August 2018.

Bringing the United Front to the Forefront

While the CCP's use of political warfare goes back to the party's beginnings, the significance of those operations—particularly efforts to build what amounts to fifth columns overseas through the United Front Work Department—took on new impetus with Xi Jinping's ascension to the leadership of the CCP and PRC in 2012 and 2013, respectively. Xi's father, Xi Zhongxun, a Chinese Communist revolutionary and PRC official, led united front and other political warfare operations through much of his career, which clearly impacted Xi Jingping's understanding of their value.

In Xi's view, the time had come for a strong and confident China to move beyond former PRC leader Deng Xiaoping's advice to hide its assets and bide its time. Arguably, Xi was elevated to implement the long-term strategy of no longer hiding the PRC's capabilities or intentions, which Deng had not-so-subtly telegraphed and most Western poititicans and analysts chose to ignore. Delegates to the CCP's 18th Party Congress were lectured on the importance of united front work, and the bureaucracy hastened to comply.[38]

In February 2018, Xi "issued a directive to cultivate greater support amongst the estimated 60 million-strong Chinese diaspora worldwide." He encouraged "closely uniting" with Chinese living overseas in support of the China Dream and emphasized that "to realize the great rejuvenation of the Chinese nation, we must work together with our sons and daughters at home and abroad." Xi continued that "it is an important task for the party and the state to unite the vast number of overseas Chinese and returned overseas Chinese and their families in the country and play their positive role in the great rejuvenation of the Chinese nation."[39]

The CCP's united front work aimed at the outside world has consolidated since the 19th Party Congress, carrying on trends established during the previous five years. University of Centerbury professor Anne-Marie Brady reports that since then, "Xi has removed any veneer of separation between the [CCP] and the Chinese state. So while the United Front Work Department does indeed play an important role in CCP united front work, comprehending China's modern political warfare tactics requires a deep understanding of all the CCP's agencies, their policies, their leadership, their methodology, and the way the party-state system works in China."[40]

---

[38] Gerry Groot, "The Rise and Rise of the United Front Work Department under Xi," Jamestown Foundation, China Brief 18, no. 7, 24 April 2018.

[39] *Hearing on China's Worldwide Military Expansion, before the House Permanent Select Committee on Intelligence,* 115th Cong. (2018) (testimony by Capt James E. Fanell, USN [Ret]), hereafter Fanell testimony.

[40] Anne-Marie Brady, "Exploit Every Rift: United Front Work Goes Global," in David Gitter et al., *Party Watch Annual Report, 2018* (Washington, DC: Center for Advanced China Research, 2018), 35.

Brady projects that future Xi-era united front activities will focus on four key areas: first, "stepped-up efforts to manage and guide the Chinese diaspora—both Han Chinese and ethnic minorities such as Uighurs and Tibetans—so as to utilize them as agents of Chinese foreign policy while meting out increasingly harsh treatment do those who do not cooperate"; second, "co-opting and cultivating foreign economic and political elites in the nations of the world to support and promote the [CCP's] global foreign policy goals"; third, "a global, multi-platform, strategic communication strategy to promote the [CCP's] agenda"; and finally, "the formation of a China-centered economic and strategic bloc"—the Belt and Road Initiative (BRI).[41]

Regarding the BRI, Brady describes Xi's initiative as "a classic united front activity." She notes that it is "pitched as 'beyond ideology' and designed to create a new global order, which [CCP] analysts describe as 'Globalization 2.0'." United front work supports the BRI, and vice versa. "The [CCP] has seeded allies and clients throughout the economic and political elite of many countries at the national as well as the local level and is getting them to promote acceptance for the [BRI] in their respective countries."[42]

To influence the Chinese diaspora, much of the PRC's propaganda effort targets overseas Chinese students and communities, who often feel a strong sense of patriotism toward their homeland. To build on and exploit these sentiments, the Chinese ministry of education declared in 2016 a priority to further spread the China Dream abroad by "harness[ing] the patriotic capabilities of overseas students" and "establish[ing] an overseas propaganda model which uses people as its medium."[43] With its increasing control of both Chinese-language and foreign news media organizaions abroad, the PRC attempts to whip overseas Chinese into a hyper-nationalistic frenzy, and employ them to influence, obstruct, and politically paralyze any nation that opposes the PRC's actions.[44]

During his congressional testimony in 2018, retired U.S. Navy captain James E. Fanell assessed that Xi and the CCP "will exploit these overseas Chinese to undermine military and political adversaries worldwide, and to advance [their own] political and military objectives. Prime among these will very likely be be lobbying for the establishment of more PRC military access" for PLA forces operating globally. With an operational base already established in

---

41 Brady, "Exploit Every Rift," 36.
41 Brady, "Exploit Every Rift," 36.
43 Jonas Parello-Plesner and Belinda Li, *The Chinese Communist Party's Foreign Interference Operations: How the U.S. and Other Democracies Should Respond* (Washington, DC: Hudson Institute, 2018), 16.
44 Julie Makinen, "Chinese Social Media Platform Plays a Role in U.S. Rallies for NYPD Officer," *Los Angeles (CA) Times*, 24 February 2016.

Djibouti in the Horn of Africa, the PLA Navy now operates in the Indian Ocean and the Mediterranean, Baltic, and Arctic Seas. The PRC has sealed long-term port deals that span the globe, including in Indonesia, Pakistan, Bangladesh, Tanzania, Myanmar, Malaysia, Australia, Sri Lanka, Cambodia, Greece, Namibia, Mauritius, Djibouti, Brunei, and the Strait of Malacca. These ports "have already started to provide critical berthing and logistics" to the PLA Navy, including maintenance, provisions, and refueling.[45] The PRC is also attempting to acquire berthing in the Azores and is currently negotiating port deals in the Maldives, Scandinavia, and Greenland.

PRC Political Warfare on the Offensive

Anne-Marie Brady warns that despite worldwide revelations regarding PRC politcal warfare and influence operations, the PRC has not backed off. "Conversely," she continues, CCP united front work "aimed at the outside world has gone on the offensive, fighting on all fronts, indicating that the [CCP] leadership believes it is in a position of strength and has no reason to hide its efforts."[46]

As described by Nadège Rolland at the National Bureau of Asian Research, the PRC has established a layered defense, starting with the protection of its domestic perimeter and incrementally extending outward. It stifles the inward flow of liberal democratic values and ideals within its territory through a "Great Firewall around China's cyberspace" and by "strengthening party control over domestic media and information circulation." The CCP has also intensified domestic propaganda and so-called patriotic education to inoculate its people against dangerous ideas that might slip through the first line of defense. In its "counterattack mode," the CCP targets "audiences outside of the Chinese diaspora, striking deeper into the adversary's territory, and hitting hard." The PRC "is actively targeting foreign media, academia and business communities through the deployment of front organisations" to co-opt foreigners and is retaliating against those who it sees threatening its core interests at any level.[47]

Due to their belief that the PRC now enjoys superior strength, Xi and CCP leaders no longer care as much about public exposure of their attempts to, for example, "leverage overseas Chinese as agents of influence, pressure foreign universities and movie studios to accept Chinese censorship guidelines, and co-opt foreign elites into

---

[45] Fanell testimony.
[46] Brady, "Exploit Every Rift," 34.
[47] Nadège Rolland, "China's Counteroffensive in the War of Ideas," Real Clear Defense, 24 February 2020.

supporting Beijing's goals," reports Brady. She concludes that "Xi is exploiting every rift and is fighting on all fronts—at the same time as continuing to seek partners to unite with against the chief enemy: the [United States] and other Western democracies. . . . For Xi Jinping, the Western democracies represent the 'Old Era' of the global order, which the 19th Party Congress has declared is officially over."[48]

---

[48] Brady, "Exploit Every Rift," 39.

CHAPTER FOUR

PRC Political Warfare Goals, Ways, Means, and Wartime Support

Chineseposters.net

Long live the victory of the Korean People's Army and the Chinese People's Army. This 1951 propaganda poster depicts Chinese and North Korean forces defeating U.S. Army general Douglas MacArthur and the United Nations armed forces during the Korean War.

I n 2019, Ross Babbage at the Center for Strategic and Budgetary Assessments identified four strategic goals of the People's Republic of China's (PRC) political warfare operations, the first and most significant of which is "the maintenance of uncontested Communist Party rule." To achieve that aim, the Chinese Communist Party (CCP) "employs sophisticated political warfare operations to suppress domestic dissent and reinforce Party loyalty as well as to undermine China's international rivals."[1]

The second strategic goal is to achieve Xi Jinping's "China Dream" to "restore China to what it sees as its rightful place as the preponderant power in the Indo-Asia-Pacific [region], in both

[1] Ross Babbage, *Winning Without Fighting: Chinese and Russian Political Warfare Campaigns and How the West Can Prevail*, vol. I (Washington, DC: Center for Strategic and Budgetary Assessments, 2019), 24.

its continental and maritime domains." To this end, the CCP "has propagated a powerful narrative that emphasizes the leadership's determination to overcome the 'century of China's humiliation' and restore the nation's power, wealth, and influence." The CCP employs proven-but-updated political warfare methods to achieve this goal: to "penetrate deeply into the opponent's camps, gather intelligence, plant disinformation, recruit sympathizers and spies, sow disruption, undermine morale, and seize effective control of strategically important infrastructure."[2]

The CCP's third goal is to "build China's influence and prestige" so that it will be "respected as equal, if not superior, to the United States." It conducts political warfare operations to "push the United States and its democratic allies from their predominant role in the Western Pacific and Eastern Indian Ocean" and to "build strategic strength in hitherto non-aligned parts of Central Asia, the Middle East, Africa, and South America."[3]

Finally, the CCP's fourth goal is to "export its model of tight authoritarian political control coupled with a managed but relatively open economy."[4] Its political warfare narrative is that the PRC approach to governance and development is a far more attractive option to that offered by the liberal democracies of the West. Princeton University professor Aaron L. Friedberg states that "China now seeks to present itself as providing an alternative model for development to that offered by the West, one that combines market-driven economic growth with authoritarian politics."[5] Notable for its relevance to the CCP's global intentions, Babbage assesses that "part of Xi's vision is the fostering of a growing group of like-minded revisionist countries that, over time, may constitute an inter-national partnership, alliance, or even a China-centered empire."[6]

Subsequent chapters in the book will provide detailed discussions of the specific strategies and tactics the PRC employs in its political warfare operations, but a 2018 Hudson Institute study provides an apt, if somewhat informal, description of PRC political warfare goals, target audiences, and strategies: "With the United States, whose geostrategic power the CCP perceives as the ultimate threat, the goal is a long-term interference and influence campaign that tames American power and freedoms . . . such as freedom of expres-

---

[2] Babbage, *Winning Without Fighting*, vol. I, 24.
[3] Babbage, *Winning Without Fighting*, vol. I, 24.
[4] Babbage, *Winning Without Fighting*, vol. I, 25.
[5] *Hearing on Strategic Competition with China, before the House Committee on Armed Services*, 115th Cong. (2018) (testimony by Aaron L. Friedberg, Professor of Politics and International Affairs, Woodrow Wilson School, Princeton University), hereafter Friedberg testimony.
[6] Babbage, *Winning Without Fighting*, vol. I, 25.

sion, individual rights, and academic freedom." Target audiences include politicians, academics, businesspeople, students, and the general public. "With deep coffers and the help of Western enablers, the CCP uses money, rather than Communist ideology, as a powerful source of influence, creating parasitic relationships of long-term dependence." By changing how the United States and other democratic nations think and speak about the PRC, the CCP is "making the 'world safe' for its continued reign."[7]

However, PRC political warfare goals extend well beyond CCP self-preservation. They include restoring China to what the CCP sees as its rightful place as the Middle Kingdom, particularly in eastern Eurasia but also across more distant continental and maritime domains. Moreover, closely related to driving the United States from the Asia-Pacific region is the PRC's goal of seizing—or, as the CCP describes it, "reunifying with"—Taiwan.

Taiwan remains a central focus of PRC political warfare. Mark Stokes and Russell Hsiao write that "from Beijing's perspective, Taiwan's democratic government—an alternative to mainland China's authoritarian model—presents an existential challenge to the [CCP's] monopoly on domestic political power."[8] The CCP's desired final resolution to the Chinese Civil War entails the destruction of the Republic of China (ROC) as a political entity and the absorption of Taiwan as a province of the PRC. Consequently, seizing Taiwan represents a key milestone in what Xi describes as "national reunification," and he has clearly stated that he will use all means—including force—to achieve that goal.[9]

Regarding the United States and other advanced industrial nations, Friedberg identifies two additional PRC political warfare aims: "to gain or maintain access to markets, technology, ideas, information and capital deemed essential to China's continuing economic success" and "to discourage foreign governments, acting separately or in concert, from pursuing policies that might impede China's rise or interfere with the achievement of its strategic objectives."[10]

Friedberg also notes that Beijing seeks to attain its objectives by delivering two messages: that "China is a peaceful, non-threatening and still-developing nation that is interested in 'win-win cooperation'" and that "China is a fast-growing power whose rise is inevi-

---

[7] Jonas Parello-Plesner and Belinda Li, *The Chinese Communist Party's Foreign Interference Operations: How the U.S. and Other Democracies Should Respond* (Washington, DC: Hudson Institute, 2018), 3–4.
[8] Mark Stokes and Russell Hsiao, *The People's Liberation Army General Political Department: Political Warfare with Chinese Characteristics* (Arlington, VA: Project 2049 Institute, 2013), 41.
[9] Chris Buckley and Chris Horton, "Xi Jinping Warns Taiwan that Unification Is the Goal and Force Is an Option," *New York Times*, 1 January 2019.
[10] Friedberg testimony.

table and unstoppable," meaning that "prudent leaders [should] seek to curry favor by getting on board 'the China train' rather than incurring its wrath by opposing its wishes." Friedberg concludes that the PRC is "using a combination of its rapidly growing military, economic and political or information warfare capabilities to try to weaken the U.S. position in Asia with the aim of displacing it as the preponderant regional power."[11]

A brief examination of how the PRC structures its political warfare efforts to achieve these goals follows, including a brief overview of PRC political warfare traits, ways and means, and organization, as well as how political warfare supports the PRC's wartime and other military operations.

PRC Political Warfare Traits

The Center for Strategic and Budgetary Assessments identifies common traits of PRC political warfare as follows:

- A powerful centralized command of political warfare operations by the CCP through organizations such as the United Front Work Department (UFWD) and the People's Liberation Army (PLA).
- A "clear vision, ideology, and strategy" for the employment of political warfare.
- The employment of overt and covert means to influence, coerce, intimidate, divide, and subvert rival countries to force their compliance or collapse.
- Tight bureaucratic control over the domestic populace.
- A thorough understanding of rival nations being targeted by political warfare.
- The use of a comprehensive array of political warfare tools in coordinated actions.
- A willingness to accept high levels of risk resulting from the exposure of political warfare activities.[12]

---

[11] Friedberg testimony.
[12] Thomas G. Mahnken, Ross Babbage, and Toshi Yoshihara, *Countering Comprehensive Coercion: Competitive Strategies against Authoritarian Political Warfare* (Washington, DC: Center for Strategic and Budgetary Assessments, 2018), 54–57.

Ways and Means: Funding and Economic Aspects

The PRC is the world's second-largest economy, and the CCP has invested enormous resources into influence operations abroad, estimated in 2015 to reach $10 billion a year and certainly much higher by 2020.[13] Further, the PRC's Belt and Road Initiative (BRI) programs provide access to massive additional resources to support political warfare, since the BRI is rightly viewed as a global UFWD strategy.[14]

Cash rules in this global political war, augmented as needed by threats of overt or covert military, economic, or other attacks. Unlike the Cold War, ideology plays a very small role in this current political conflict with the PRC. As the authors of *China and the U.S.: Comparing Global Influence* explain, "At hardly any time did countries aspire to adopt the Chinese model. Mao's disastrous Great Leap Forward, Cultural Revolution, collective farms, state owned enterprises, egalitarian poverty (except for Party insiders), and repressive government had little appeal except to other dictatorial regimes."[15]

However, Beijing's phenomenal economic growth during the past three decades has now provided a different model. Further, the new Chinese model is based on the "Beijing Consensus," which largely rejects most Western economic and political values and models. The main attribute of this PRC model is for "people to be brought out of poverty, not necessarily to have legal freedoms."[16]

With the scale and relatively rapid growth of the Chinese economy and seeming largess, the CCP is indeed helping many political, news media, and other influential elites worldwide come out of poverty. Cash has proven to be the most compelling motivator for those supporting and enabling the PRC's global ambitions, especially when combined with a massive expansion of both the PRC's military capabilities and its ever-watchful political warfare and intelligence apparatuses.

Beijing also frequently employs economic instruments in its political warfare campaigns. The PRC is the largest trading partner for nearly all countries in the western Pacific, and its goodwill is important for their development and prosperity. "Hence," notes Babbage, "if the Chinese regime wishes to apply pressure on a regional country or on key corporate leaders, it has many economic levers it can pull and, periodically, it does. One notable case was China's

[13] David Shambaugh, "China's Soft-Power Push: The Search for Respect," *Foreign Affairs* 94, no. 4 (July/August 2015): 99–107.

[14] Anne-Marie Brady, "Exploit Every Rift: United Front Work Goes Global," in David Gitter et al., *Party Watch Annual Report, 2018* (Washington, DC: Center for Advanced China Research, 2018), 36.

[15] Thomas Lum et al., *China and the U.S.: Comparing Global Influence* (Hauppauge, NY: Nova Science Publishers, 2010), 7.

[16] Lum et al., *China and the U.S.*, 9–10.

tourism sanctions, boycott of the Lotte retail chain, and other re-
prisals against South Korea following Seoul's commitment to host
American missile defense systems."[17]

Organization

All party and state organizations support the CCP's political warfare
operations, and it is useful to examine how some of these key elements interrelate. Peter Mattis at the Jamestown Foundation writes
that there are three layers within this system: CCP officials, executive
and implementing agencies, and supporting agencies that "bring
platforms or capabilities to bear in support of united front and propaganda work." According to Mattis, several CCP officials supervise
the party divisions responsible for political warfare and other influence operations. That organization flows down from the Politburo
Standing Committee (PSC). The top united front official serves as
chairman of the Chinese People's Political Consultative Conference
(CPPCC) and is the fourth highest-ranking member of the PSC. Two
additional top Politburo members direct the Propaganda Department (now called the Publicity Department) and the UFWD, respectively, and also sit on the CCP Secretariat, "which is empowered to
make day-to-day decisions for the routine functioning of the party-
state."[18]

Mattis describes the UFWD as "the executive agency for united
front work" both within the PRC and abroad. It "operates at all levels
of the party system," and its purview includes "Hong Kong, Macao,
and Taiwan affairs; ethnic and religious affairs; domestic and external propaganda; entrepreneurs and non-party personages; intellectuals; and people-to-people exchanges," as well as the Overseas
Chinese Affairs Office (OCAO). The UFWD also leads the establishment of party committees in both Chinese and foreign businesses.[19]

The OCAO is particularly important in rallying the worldwide
diaspora. Its mission is to "enhance unity and friendship in overseas
Chinese communities; to maintain contact with and support overseas Chinese media and Chinese language schools; [and] to increase
cooperation and exchanges" between overseas Chinese and China's
domestic population in matters relating "to the economy, science,
culture and education."[20] To this end, it routinely brings researchers,

---

[17] Babbage, *Winning Without Fighting*, vol. I, 38–39.
[18] *Hearing on U.S. Responses to China's Foreign Influence Operations*, before the House Committee on Foreign Affairs, Subcommittee on Asia and the Pacific, 115th Cong. (2018) (testimony by Peter Mattis, Fellow, Jamestown Foundation),
hereafter Mattis testimony.
[19] Mattis testimony.
[20] Mattis testimony.

media figures, and community leaders from Chinese communities in foreign nations back to China to attend conferences and meetings.

Alexander Bowe at the U.S.-China Economic and Security Review Commission writes that the UFWD is organized into nine major bureaus and four additional offices:

- Party Work Bureau: deals with China's eight non-Communist political parties.
- Ethnic and Religious Work Bureau: concerns China's ethnic minorities.
- Hong Kong, Macau, Taiwan, and Overseas Liaison Bureau: deals with those areas and the international Chinese diaspora.
- Cadre Bureau: cultivates United Front operatives.
- Economics Bureau: liaises with less developed regions of China.
- Independent and Non-Party Intellectuals Work Bureau: liaises with Chinese intellectuals.
- Tibet Bureau: cultivates loyalty and suppresses separatism in Tibet.
- New Social Class Representatives Work Bureau: cultivates political support of the Chinese middle class.
- Xinjiang Bureau: cultivates loyalty and suppresses separatism in Xinjiang.
- General Office: coordinates business and administrative work.
- Party Committee: responsible for ideological and disciplinary matters.
- Policy Research Office: researches United Front theory and policy and coordinates propaganda.
- Retired Cadres Office: implements policy concerning departing/retired personnel.[21]

Bowe adds that "a range of CCP military and civilian organizations are [also] active in carrying out United Front work, either working directly for the UFWD or under the broader leadership of the CPPCC." The Council for the Promotion of the Peaceful Reunification of China (CPPRC), which promotes the reunification of the PRC and ROC on Taiwan, has "at least 200 chapters in 90 countries, in-

[21] Alexander Bowe, *China's Overseas United Front Work: Background and Implications for the United States* (Washington, DC: U.S.-China Economic and Security Review Commission, 2018), 5.

cluding 33 chapters in the United States registered as the National Association for China's Peaceful Unification."[22]

Mattis writes that the CCP's Propaganda/Publicity Department is responsible for conducting the "party's theoretical research; guiding public opinion; guiding and coordinating the work of the central news agencies [and] guiding the propaganda and cultural systems; and administering the Cyberspace Administration of China and the State Administration of Press, Publication, Radio, Film, and Television."[23]

Numerous party-state organizations also contribute to the CCP's influence operations. Although they do not focus on united front or propaganda work specifically, they can be used for those purposes. "Many of these agencies share cover or front organizations when they are involved in influence operations," Mattis reports, "and such platforms are sometimes lent to other agencies when appropriate."

Examples of these party-state organizations include the Ministry of Civil Affairs, Ministry of Culture, Ministry of Education, Ministry of Foreign Affairs, Ministry of State Security, State Administration of Foreign Expert Affairs, Xinhua News Agency, and Liaison Bureau of the PLA's Political Work Department.[24]

The PLA plays a significant role in the PRC's political warfare organization. Under the leadership of the CCP's Central Military Commission, the Political Work Department serves as the PLA's principle political warfare command. J. Michael Cole at the Global Taiwan Institute describes its predecessor, the PLA General Political Department, as "an interlocking directorate that operates at the nexus of politics, finance, military operations, and intelligence."[25]

Stokes and Hsiao note that Political Work Department liaison work "augments traditional state diplomacy and formal military-to-military relations, which are normally considered to be the most important aspects of international relations."[26] The Political Work Department, the UFWD, and other influence organizations play a major role in establishing and facilitating the activities of a multitude of friendship and cultural associations such as the China Association for International Friendly Contact, a central organization in coopting foreign military officers.

Unlike the Soviet and current Russian models of political war-

[22] Bowe, *China's Overseas United Front Work*, 8.
[23] Mattis testimony.
[24] Mattis testimony.
[25] J. Michael Cole, "Unstoppable: China's Secret Plan to Subvert Taiwan," *National Interest*, 23 March 2015. The People's Liberation Army General Political Department was reorganized as the Political Work Department of the Central Military Commission in 2016.
[26] Stokes and Hsiao, *The People's Liberation Army General Political Department*, 3.

fare, PRC intelligence agencies such as the Chinese Intelligence Service and Ministry of State Security seem to play a subordinate role in foreign influence operations. Individuals assigned to these influence operations are rarely intelligence officers themselves, but are generally party elite who understand the CCP's international objectives and are skilled in managing foreigners. Nevertheless, the Chinese Intelligence Service and Ministry of State Security are certainly engaged in PRC active measures, for intelligence collection is always an integral part of political warfare work as a foundation for both the successful execution and outcome of political warfare operations.[27]

Political Warfare in Support of PLA Combat Operations

Through the use of political warfare and deception, the PRC has achieved notable strategic victories without fighting. However, if the PRC's rulers perceive that political warfare alone will not deliver the results they desire—in, for example, Taiwan, the East or South China Seas, or India—they may choose to achieve their goals through conventional and unconventional combat operations, or a war could ignite inadvertently from their actions.[28]

Retired U.S. Navy captain James E. Fanell argues that in any armed conflict within the Asia-Pacific Region or elsewhere in the world, "the PRC's fight for public opinion will be [its] second battlefield," on which it will conduct a "wide range" of political warfare operations.[29] The PRC has used political warfare to support numerous military operations in the past, to include its intervention in the Korean War in 1950, its annexation of Tibet in 1951, the Sino-Indian War in 1962, the Sino-Soviet Union border conflict in 1969, its battle for Vietnam's Paracel Islands in 1974, the Sino-Vietnam War in 1979, its attack on Vietnam's Spratly Islands in 1988, its occupation of the Philippines' Mischief Reef in 1995, the standoff with India and Bhutan at Doklam in 2017, and its skirmish with Indian forces at Ladakh in 2020.

The PRC's principle of "uniting with friends and disintegrating enemies" will guide its active political warfare measures during armed conflict, as the CCP devises its narrative of events, actions,

[27] Peter Mattis, "A Guide to Chinese Intelligence Operations," *War on the Rocks*, 18 August 2015.
[28] Cortez A. Cooper III, "China's Military Is Ready for War: Everything You Need to Know," *Buzz* (blog), National Interest, 18 August 2019.
[29] *Hearing on China's Worldwide Military Expansion, before the House Permanent Select Committee on Intelligence*, 115th Cong. (2018) (testimony by Capt James E. Fanell, USN [Ret]), hereafter Fanell testimony.

and policies to lead international discourse and impact the policies of both its friends and adversaries.[30]

Chinese strategic literature particularly emphasizes the role of the Three Warfares—public opinion/media warfare, psychological warfare, and legal warfare—to subdue an enemy before conflict can break out or ensure victory if conflict does occur. According to Elsa B. Kania at the Center for a New American Security, the Three Warfares establish "a perceptual preparation of the battlefield that is seen as critical to advancing [PRC] interests during both peace and war." PLA officers become acquainted with political warfare early in their careers, and as they rise in rank they study the concept in depth in various texts on military strategy, including the PLA Academy of Military Science and PLA National Defence University editions of *Science of Military Strategy* as well as *An Introduction to Public Opinion Warfare, Psychological Warfare, and Legal Warfare.*[31]

In addition to employing the Three Warfares, it is likely that the PRC will engage in "hybrid warfare" actions comparable to those used by Russia in its 2014 annexation of Crimea.[32] Cortez A. Cooper III writes that its political warfare doctrine and capabilities involve "military and para-military forces that operate below the threshold of war, such as increased presence in contested waters of fishing fleets and supporting maritime militia and navy vessels," which may "spark conflict when an opposing claimant such as the Philippines, Vietnam, or Japan responds."[33] The PRC is already engaged in hybrid warfare against Taiwan, so this type of operations would likely increase in preparation for an attack against that nation.[34] Once armed conflict ignites, the CCP would quite likely continue its hybird warfare.

In addition, Fanell contends that the PRC "will augment conventional military operations with non-conventional operations, such as subversion, disinformation and misinformation (now commonly referred to as 'fake news'), and cyberattacks. The operationalization of [psychological warfare] with cyber is key to this strategy." The PRC has enlarged its psychological warfare forces, especially at the 311 Base in Fuzhou in Fujian Province, which is subordinate to the PLA's Strategic Support Force and works closely with the nation's cyberforces.[35]

[30] Stokes and Hsiao, *The People's Liberation Army General Political Department*, 3.
[31] Elsa B. Kania, "The PLA's Latest Strategic Thinking on the Three Warfares," Jamestown Foundation, China Brief 16, no. 13, 22 August 2016.
[32] Fanell testimony.
[33] Cooper, "China's Military Is Ready for War."
[34] David R. Ignatius, "China's Hybrid Warfare against Taiwan," *Washington Post*, 14 December 2018.
[35] Fanell testimony.

The PRC will conduct political warfare operations before, during, and after any hostilities that it initiates. Prior to military confrontation, it will initiate a worldwide political warfare campaign that employs united front organizations and other supporters to initiate protests, support rallies, and use the internet, television, and radio to conduct propaganda and psychological operations. History proves that political warfare actions are often tied to the PRC's strategic deception operations, which are designed to confuse or delay adversaries' defensive actions until it is too late to effectively respond.[36]

The PLA will likely seize the initiative in the opening phase of war by "striking the first blow." PRC policy stipulates that "the first strike that triggers a Chinese military response need not be military; actions in the political and strategic realm may also justify a Chinese military reaction."[37] Such a trigger could be a perceived slight, diplomatic miscommunication, or statement by a government official that upsets China enough to warrant a response.

As the PLA engages in kinetic combat against its targeted enemy forces, the PRC will fight for worldwide public opinion on the "second battlefield." Influence operations will be employed to confuse and discourage the enemy while also attempting to win support for the PRC's position from initially undecided nations. Fanell states, "In addition to standard propaganda, disinformation and deception will be employed, such as false reports of surrender of national governments and/or forces, atrocities and other violations of international law, and other reports intended to distract or paralyze decision making by the [United States] and it friends and allies." This political warfare campaign, helping to rally mass support for the PRC's "righteous" actions, will continue during and after the military operation itself, regardless of the operation's success.[38]

---

[36] Fanell testimony.
[37] Anthony H. Cordesman and Steven Colley, *Chinese Strategy and Military Modernization in 2015: A Comparative Analysis* (Washington, DC: Center for Strategic and International Studies, 2015), 109.
[38] Fanell testimony.

CHAPTER FIVE

PRC Political Warfare against Thailand: An Overview

The people do not fear the American imperialists, but the American imperialists fear the people. This propaganda poster highlights the PRC's support for national liberation forces in Southeast Asia, including Thailand, Laos, Cambodia, and Vietnam. The PRC provided political warfare, military personnel, and material support that led to Vietnam, Cambodia, and Laos falling to Communist forces.

A historical overview of Thailand's relationship with China is necessary to understand the relative ease with which the People's Republic of China (PRC) has been able to infiltrate and influence the thinking and conduct of the Royal Thai government and other Thai institutions, as well as significantly multiply the impact of its influence operations, in recent years.

Relations between Thailand and China have strong historical roots, alternating between periods of Thai tributary-state status in deference to Chinese domination, Thai indifference toward China as the latter's hegemony weakened, and extreme tension and open (albeit proxy) warfare. Key factors impacting the relationship between these two nations include their close geographic proximity to one another, their relations with neighboring states, and the influence of external powers with interests in the region, such as the United States and Soviet Union. Other important factors include Thailand's historic "Bamboo Diplomacy," which allowed it to largely fend off imperialist advances, the economically powerful Chinese community in Thailand, and the ideological compulsions of communism, especially after World War II.[1]

In historical documents and analyses contained in R. K. Jain's *China and Thailand, 1949–1983* (1984), the geographical, social, and historical factors that bound Sino-Thai relations during the mid-twentieth century are examined. Jain's edited volume is uniquely valuable, as it appends copies of original key documents and reports and offers a near-contemporaneous account that does not suffer from revisionism reflected in much present-day writing regarding the PRC and Thailand. Benjamin Zawacki's *Thailand: Shifting Ground Between the U.S. and a Rising China* (2017) is also very useful. Based primarily on diplomatic cables and other documents obtained by Wikileaks and an impressive array of interviews, Zawacki's book defines the key events and decisions that led to the near-collapse of Thai-U.S. relations during the 2014–17 timeframe.

Origins of the Sino-Thai Relationship

Jain establishes that the Thai kingdom of Nanchao existed in what is now China's Yunnan Province for several centuries before becoming a vassal state of China around 900 ACE. However, the ethnic Thais were forced south following the Mongol invasion of China in the thirteenth century and soon founded the Kingdom of Sukhothai. The kingdom sent a tributary mission to China in 1294 ACE, thereby submitting to the Middle Kingdom's "family of nations." When the Ayutthaya Dynasty came into power in 1350, it secured recognition from the Ming Dynasty in China and began sending systematic tributary missions to Beijing, which continued through 1853. After the 1853 tribute mission, China and Thailand ceased diplomatic relations.[2]

For hundreds of years following the Thai movement south, large numbers of people of Chinese origin moved into what is now Thailand, particularly during the nineteenth and twentieth centuries. Many left homelands in China's Fujian and Guangdong Provinces due to poor living conditions. They also came by sea from Hainan and coastal mainland ports. Among the Chinese immigrants

---

[1] R. K. Jain, ed., *China and Thailand, 1949–1983* (New Dehli: Radiant, 1984), xxi.
[2] Gungwu Wang and Chin-Keong Ng, eds., *Maritime China in Transition, 1750–1850* (Wiesbaden, Germany: Harrassowitz Verlag, 2004), 33–38.

to Thailand were many Teochew, Hakka, Hailamese, Hokkien, and Cantonese people.[3]

The late Southeast Asia scholar Benedict Anderson noted that the exodus from China directly impacted Thailand's present monarchy. The modern history of Thailand begins in 1767, when a Burmese army sacked, looted, and burned the ancient capital of the Ayutthaya Kingdom. Much of the vanquished realm then fell under Burmese occupation, its aristocracy annihilated. The subsequent Siamese Kingdom of Thonburi went through years of chaos and devastation. In time, King Taksin of Thonburi drove the Burmese out. Taksin was a Sino-Thai who, Anderson asserted, defeated the Burmese by "making use of experienced Chinese sailors who had settled in southeastern Siam."[4] Taksin the Great is revered in Thailand to this day, but after a 14-year reign, he was overthrown in a palace coup and executed along with his entire family. Maha Ksatriyaseuk, better known as Rama I, succeeded Taskin and founded the Chakri Dynasty in 1782, which has lasted in Thailand to this day.[5]

Both Taksin and Rama I were of ethnic Teochew stock. Toechew had become the dominant group among overseas Chinese in Siam, marrying into high-status families and being given important jobs at the court. Anderson wrote, "Only with the rise of [Thai and Chinese] nationalism did it become embarrassing to admit that the king might be an immigrant, and the Chakri began to conceal the Sino-Thai origins of their dynasty."[6]

Increased Migration and Rising Nationalism

In addition to hundreds of years of Chinese migration to Siam (what is now Thailand), many Chinese men intermarried with Thai women and appeared to assimilate.[7] During the reign of King Rama V, the Thai government encouraged the "immigration of poor, illiterate Chinese to work on commercial sugar plantations, or to build port facilities and a new transport network of roads and railways."[8] The government did not restrict Chinese immigration, permitted free movement, and imposed low taxes. However, there were occasional revolts by Chinese migrants against Siamese authorities, such as a rebellion in 1848 resulting from a tax increase. Government retribu-

---

[3] Chee Kiong Tong and Kwok B. Chan, *Alternate Identities: The Chinese of Contemporary Thailand* (Leiden, Netherlands: Brill, 2001), 189–91.
[4] Joseph P. L. Jiang, "The Chinese in Thailand: Past and Present," *Journal of Southeast Asian History* 7, no. 1 (March 1966): 40, https://doi.org/10.1017/S0217781100003112.
[5] Benedict Anderson, "Riddles of Yellow and Red," *New Left Review* 97 (January/February 2016): 11.
[6] Anderson, "Riddles of Yellow and Red," 12.
[7] Jiang, "The Chinese in Thailand," 48–49.
[8] Anderson, "Riddles of Yellow and Red," 13.

tion was severe, to include "a general massacre" of 10,000 Chinese men, women, and children at one battle site.[9]

Ultimately, the failure of Chinese to assimilate with Thais, combined with growing Thai nationalism and Chinese nationalism fostered by the Qing Dynasty, led to negative outcomes. Such nationalism manifested itself in the promulgation of the Chinese nationality law in 1909, a "tool that could maintain the affiliation of those beyond territorial sovereignty, either overseas or in extraterritorial zones, with the Qing state."[10] In effect, this law enlisted support for China from overseas Chinese and was arguably a forerunner of the PRC's united front operations that employ overseas Chinese organizations today. Calls for Chinese abroad to support China strongly influenced the thinking of the Chinese population in Siam.

In 1910, a three-day strike coordinated by Chinese secret societies in Bangkok brought economic life in the kingdom's capital to a halt. The reason for the strike was that the Chinese were protesting the fact that they had to pay the same annual tax required of Thai citizens. The Thai government was shocked by such a brazen demonstration of Chinese economic power within the kingdom. More ominously, the Thais perceived that the Chinese saw themselves as not subject to Thai law within Thailand, and they began to understand that an unassimilated mass that felt above Thai law could potentially rise up against the government.

The next 40 years would be trying times, as both Chinese and Thais sparred over issues of race, ethnicity, economics, and wartime alliances. The collapse of the Qing Dynasty and establishment of the Republic of China (ROC) in 1912 created a greater awareness of Chinese nationality among overseas Chinese, many of whom began establishing Chinese schools and newspapers to preserve their separate cultural identify and, in effect, resist assimilation. Thailand passed various laws to ensure the assimilation of all Chinese living in the kingdom, including the Thai Nationality Act of 1913. The following year, however, King Rama VI wrote a treatise under the pen name of "Asvabahu" that deemed the Chinese inassimilable because of their "racial loyalty and sense of superiority."[11]

The ROC attempted to establish diplomatic relations with Thailand early after the Kuomintang (KMT) took control of China in 1911. However, because a treaty drafted for that purpose referred to Thai-

[9] Jiang, "The Chinese in Thailand," 52.

[10] Jiang, "The Chinese in Thailand," 55–58; and Shao Dan, "Chinese by Definition: Nationality Law, Jus Sanguinis, and State Succession, 1909–1980," *Twentieth-Century China* 35, no. 1 (2009): 4–28, https://doi.org/10.1179/tcc.2009.35.1.4.

[11] Jiang, "The Chinese in Thailand," 56.

land as a "vassal" state to China, the effort failed, as did others in the 1920s and 1930s. Thailand refused China's diplomatic overtures out of fear that formal relations would allow China the opportunity to interfere in Thailand's internal affairs via its Chinese population.

While the Communist Party of Siam reportedly existed in Thailand by the late 1920s, the Communist Party of Thailand (CPT) would not be officially founded until 1942. The organization initially took its ideological lead from the Soviet Union, though it was aided significantly by Chinese leftists who had fled China following the KMT-Chinese Communist Party (CCP) split in 1927 and would eventually side with China's Maoists during the Soviet-Sino split in the early 1960s. Following a June 1932 coup that replaced Thailand's absolute monarchy with a constitutional monarchy, the ruling oligarchy was sufficiently concerned with the Chinese Communist threat that it enacted an Anti-Communist Act in 1933.

The War Years

In 1938, Phibun Songgram became prime minister of Thailand, establishing a military dictatorship and changing the country's official name from Siam to Thailand the following year. A supporter of Imperial Japan, he approved of the Japanese invasion of China and took actions to suppress the anti-Japanese Chinese population within Thailand. As the Chinese community supported anti-Japanese boycotts in response to Japan's aggression against China, the Thai government shut down many Chinese businesses, schools, and newspapers and deported politically active Chinese, despite China's protests.[12]

During World War II, Thailand allied with Japan, declaring war on the United Kingdom and the United States and increasing restrictions on the ethnic Chinese population within its borders. Chinese were excluded from certain professions and forced out of many areas of the country deemed "military zones." Further, Chinese who cooperated with the Nationalists in China were imprisoned.[13] Restrictions on Chinese nationals lightened slightly after the ouster of Prime Minister Phibun in 1944. Meanwhile, as the Thai government worked with Japan and the Free Thai Movement endeavored to end that alliance, other Thais working with both the Soviet Union and Mao Zedong's CCP established the CPT in 1942.

Following the defeat of Imperial Japan and the end of World

---

[12] E. Bruce Reynolds, "'International Orphans': The Chinese in Thailand during World War II," *Journal of Southeastern Asian Studies* 28, no. 2 (September 1997): 365–88, https://doi.org/10.1017/S0022463400014508.
[13] Jiang, "The Chinese in Thailand," 58.

War II in September 1945, Thai prime ministers Seni Pramoj and Pridi Banomyong worked to restore Thailand's international status and curried favor with China and the Soviet Union to support Thailand's joining of the United Nations (UN) in 1946. To this end, Thailand restored most of the rights enjoyed by Sino-Thais prior to 1939 and repealed the Anti-Communist Act.[14]

Formal Relations and Falling Out

In January 1946, Thailand and the China signed the Siamese-Chinese Treaty of Amity and Commerce to establish diplomatic relations based on "the principles of equality and mutual respect of sovereignty."[15] The first Chinese ambassador to Thailand arrived in Bangkok in September 1946, and the Thai-Chinese Friendship Society was established in 1947 with former prime minister Pridi Banomyong as a prominent member. After losing a power struggle with former wartime dictator Phibun Songgram, Pridi would later flee to China and set up a "Free (Greater) Thai Autonomous Region" in Yunnan.[16]

In 1948, Phibun once again became prime minister of Thailand. When the CCP emerged victorious in China's long civil war the following year and established the PRC, the ROC government retreated to Taiwan. The ROC closed its five consulates in Thailand, and its embassy in Bangkok lost much of its influence. Nevertheless, Thailand refused to recognize the Communist PRC until 1 July 1975.

In the interim, Sino-Thai relations were fraught with distrust, suspicion, and bloodshed. The PRC rapidly began sponsoring national liberation movements and wars throughout the region. Out of concern for the Communist threat, the Thai government took steps against both Communists and the Chinese minority in general. Hundreds of Chinese union leaders were arrested, and schools and associations were raided.[17] By 1949, Thai officials were worried that the PRC would assist Vietnamese and Laotian Communists working with secessionist elements in northeast Thailand and use the 50,000 Vietnamese refugees in Thailand for subversion. Although the PRC protested, the Thai government curbed the activities of ethnic Chinese Communities in Thailand, as most Communists in the country at that time were Chinese.

After the Korean War broke out in August 1950, Thailand be-

[14] Jiang, "The Chinese in Thailand," 58–59.
[15] Jiang, "The Chinese in Thailand," 58–59.
[16] Jain, *China and Thailand*, xiii.
[17] Jiang, "The Chinese in Thailand," 59.

came the second country in Asia to offer ground forces to the UN, which was fighting against PRC- and Soviet-backed North Korean forces. By entering into an economic and military assistance agreement with the United States that year, Thailand clearly aligned itself with the U.S.-led "free world" against the PRC and the Soviet Union. Also in 1950, China Radio International, a PRC state-run radio station, began broadcasting anti-American and pro-PRC propaganda in the Thai language to help lay the foundation for what would become a 30-year civil war waged by the CPT.

Despite a significant international PRC propaganda campaign, aided by former Thai prime minister Pridi, who was then living in exile in China, in 1954 Thailand became a founding member of the Southeast Asia Treaty Organization, which was designed to align non-Communist countries to combat the Communist threat.[18]

PRC propaganda in Thailand during this era focused on themes of anti-Americanism, neutralism, the PRC's "peaceful intentions" under the "five principles of peaceful co-existence" as espoused at the 1955 Bandung Conference, and formal recognition of the PRC. The Bandung Conference allowed the PRC to commence what might be called an early version of its 1990s-era Charm Offensive as part of its political warfare arsenal.[19] Among other activities, a "Thai Peoples' Mission for the Promotion of Friendship," led by a former minister and leader of Thailand's socialist opposition, visited Mao Zedong and PRC premier Zhou Enlai in Beijing in January 1956. Further, the PRC began a "people's diplomacy" campaign and other efforts to develop foreign trade contacts. One result of these influence operations was a softening of Bangkok's opposition to recognition of the PRC.[20] But that softening would not last long.

While working to cultivate and neutralize Thailand, the PRC dubbed Thailand's monarchy and military leadership as "fascist reactionaries," "lackeys of imperialism," and other pejorative names familiar to those who study terminology employed by the Communist International (Comintern). Other propaganda tactics employed by the PRC were to constantly blame the United States for "inciting Thailand and South Vietnam" against it and to support North Vietnamese attacks against the Thai government regarding the treatment of Vietnamese residents in the kingdom.[21]

In 1958, Cambodia, with which Thailand shares a long border, shocked Bangkok's elites by formally recognizing the PRC. Thai

---

[18] Jain, *China and Thailand*, xiv.
[19] Jiang, "The Chinese in Thailand," 60.
[20] Jain, *China and Thailand*, xiv–xlvii.
[21] Jain, *China and Thailand*, xlix, lxxii.

leaders assumed that the opening of a PRC embassy in the Cambodian capital of Phnom Penh would increase subversive activity in Thailand as well as Cambodia. Their suspicions were justified, as the PRC strengthened its support for the Viet Minh and Pathet Lao Communist forces in Vietnam and Laos. This served as a prelude to a period of intense Sino-Thai hostility that lasted a decade. By 1959, the PRC-initiated "Thai Autonomous People's Government" in Yunnan was infiltrating northern Thailand and inciting unrest among the population there. As a result, Bangkok banned all trade with and personal travel to the PRC and strengthened relations with the ROC on Taiwan to give its Chinese community an alternate focus of loyalty.

As the PRC-backed Pathet Lao forces seized the eastern half of Laos, Thai leaders worked closely with the United States to fight Communist internal subversion and external aggression in their country. Following Thai-U.S. agreements in May 1962, U.S. military units began being stationed in Thailand to be used primarily for operations against the National Liberation Front of South Vietnam. Predictably, the PRC lambasted Thailand through propaganda organs such as *People's Daily* for becoming "an active accomplice of U.S. imperialism in their aggression against the people of Indo-China" and for "interference in Laos' internal affairs."[22] The stationing of U.S. forces in Thailand was portrayed by the PRC as American imperialism meant "to occupy Thailand" as well as "a serious threat to the security of China" against which the Chinese people had to react.

A PRC-Backed Guerrilla War in Thailand

In January 1965, PRC foreign minister Chen Yi effectively declared war on Thailand, in the eyes of Thai leaders and key nations supporting Thailand, when he told a visiting European diplomat that he hoped for "a guerilla [sic] war in Thailand within the year."[23] The Australia-New Zealand-United States (ANZUS) alliance determined that the PRC had identified Thailand as its next target, and fears of a "Chinese Korea-style invasion, most probably knifing through Northern Thailand" became very real.[24]

The PRC and Thailand waged political warfare against each other on propaganda battlefields such as the UN and news media outlets. One of the PRC's chief propaganda organs was the Voice of

[22] Jain, *China and Thailand*, li.
[23] Jain, *China and Thailand*, lii–liii.
[24] Benjamin Zawacki, *Thailand: Shifting Ground between the U.S. and a Rising China* (London: Zed Books, 2017), 40.

the People of Thailand radio station, established in Yunnan in 1962. PRC propaganda stressed that Thailand had become "the advance post for U.S. aggression in Indochina," criticizing Thai military incursions into Laos and Cambodia and its provision of ground, air, and naval units to fight in South Vietnam during the Vietnam War. Thailand's response to the latter was that it was merely defending "South Vietnam's rights as well as [its] own vital interest against the encroachments resulting from Communist conspiracies against free nations."[25]

Meanwhile, the PRC-supported Thai Patriotic Front was established by the CPT in January 1965 to fill the role of the united front in the triangular "party-army-front" strategy. It conducted training in Yunnan camps located about 120 kilometers north of the Thai border and allowed the CPT to increase combat operations against the Thai government.[26] Beijing made no secret of its support for the CPT's armed struggle, openly congratulating it in its successes through such venues as the *Peking Review* and *People's Daily*. PRC media outlets also worked to "arouse the masses and develop armed struggle in rural areas."[27]

Beijing's target audience for this propaganda included Thailand's Chinese population. In 1965, roughly half of Bangkok's population was ethnic Chinese and comprised the largest "overseas Chinese" community in Southeast Asia. While this population posed a serious fifth column threat, Thai officials stressed that it was politics rather than ethnicity that formed the basis of their efforts to cut the CPT off from Thai-Chinese funding and other support. The Thai government implemented some measures, such as requiring that the Thai language be used to teach in Chinese schools and taking down Chinese-language signs in Bangkok's Chinatown, but it did not apply population control measures, and it even began to allow Thais of Chinese ancestry to enter the Royal Thai Armed Forces.[28]

Thailand did, however, rightfully target the PRC for its hostile actions. As a result of Beijing's "open aggression, indirect aggression, and subversive activities," Thailand voted against the PRC's admission into the UN from 1966 to 1971.[29] By this point, Mao's Cultural Revolution, in which up to 2 million Chinese reportedly perished, was disrupting the PRC's foreign policy to a point that would eventually greatly erode its influence within Southeast Asia. But the zeal

[25] Jain, *China and Thailand*, liii, liv.
[26] Zawacki, *Thailand*, 40.
[27] Jain, *China and Thailand*, liv.
[28] Zawacki, *Thailand*, 39–40.
[29] Jain, *China and Thailand*, liii–lvi.

of "cultural revolutionaries" elsewhere in the world nevertheless translated into even more enthusiastic PRC support for Communist revolutionary movements, including those in Thailand.

As part of regional "collective political defense" efforts against increased PRC aggression, Thailand helped found the Association of Southeast Asian Nations (ASEAN) in 1966.[30] Subsequent PRC political warfare against ASEAN was based in part on the assertion that the organization was "an instrument fashioned by U.S. imperialism and Soviet revisionism for pursuing neo-colonial ends in Asia."[31] The injection of the term "Soviet revisionism" reflected the then-deepening Sino-Soviet rivalry that would ultimately result in a complete rift between the two major competing Communist systems.

Through 1969, King Bhumipol and the Thai bureaucracy stood united in fighting the Communist insurgency in Thailand and resisting PRC aggression, even as the CPT announced the establishment of the People's Liberation Army of Thailand (PLAT) that year. The Thais were confident in U.S. support, which was key to the government's ability to succeed on both military and informational battlefields. At this time, roughly half a million American troops were in Southeast Asia, including some 48,000 operating out of seven airbases in Thailand, and the U.S. Department of State, the U.S. Information Agency, and the Central Intelligence Agency (CIA) were supporting Thai counterinsurgency operations.[32] However, in the United States, a combination of successful political warfare operations conducted by North Vietnam and other nations and organizations fueled legitimate public concern about how the war in Vietnam was being waged. This led to increasing political division, social breakdown, and erosion of public and Congressional support in America for the defense of South Vietnam.

The Nixon Doctrine and Sino-Thai Reassessment

In 1969, newly elected U.S. president Richard M. Nixon announced the Nixon Doctrine. Also known as the Guam Doctrine, the policy principle mandated turning over responsibility for combat operations in Southeast Asia from the United States to its partner nations then at war, albeit with continued American material, training, and other support. Nixon subsequently began a partial withdrawal of U.S. forces from Vietnam and signaled his intent to normalize rela-

---

[30] Zawacki, *Thailand*, 41.
[31] Jain, *China and Thailand*, lv.
[32] William P. Rogers, *United States Foreign Policy, 1969–1970: A Report of the Secretary of State*, General Foreign Policy Series (Washington, DC: U.S. Department of State, 1971), 57–59.

tions with the PRC.[33] In reaction, Thailand's prime minister Thanom Kittikachorn and his government reassessed their country's relations with the PRC and began reaching out to Beijing. According to Thanom's foreign minister, "Communist China will become pivotal to peace, security and freedom in Asia as it turns from internal preoccupations to outside interests and as the United States tries to sneak out of the Asian scene."[34]

In 1971, Nixon announced he would visit the PRC, a move that "shocked and shook" the Thai government, which had received no forewarning. Further efforts were made to enhance Thai-Sino relations in search of a "peaceful co-existence," but those efforts were rebuffed by the PRC. During the vote that year for the PRC's admission to the UN, Thailand offered verbal support for the PRC but ultimately abstained from voting because it wanted to vote separately to keep Taiwan in the UN, though that option was taken off the table.[35]

By 1973, the Thai government publicly announced that its Communist insurgency had been "effectively contained" and offered to trade with the PRC as a way to ease tensions between the two nations and reduce PRC support for the CPT. By the end of the year, an oil deal had been penned, and in 1974 the Thai legislature passed authorization for "normal trade," which had been prohibited since 1959. However, a brutal and bloody internal crackdown by Thailand's military rulers in 1973 resulted in 3,000 university students, intellectuals, labor leaders, and others fleeing Bangkok to join CPT ranks in the jungles, forming a united front and providing better leadership and technical capabilities to both the CPT and the PLAT.[36]

Seismic Realignment: From Hot War to Cold Peace

In June 1975, and Thailand's prime minister Kukrit Pramoj visited the PRC, and Bangkok established formal relations with Beijing the following month.[37] While normal relations did not lead to an immediate end to PRC support for the CPT, it did lead to Thailand's trade with the PRC increasing from $4.7 million (USD) in 1974 to $169 million in 1977.

The fall of Saigon in South Vietnam, Phnom Penh in Cambodia, and Vientiane in Laos to Communist forces in April 1975 led to a seis-

---

33 Jain, *China and Thailand*, lv.
34 Zawacki, *Thailand*, 43.
35 Jain, *China and Thailand*, lvi; and Zawacki, *Thailand*, 44.
36 Jain, *China and Thailand*, ix.
37 Jain, *China and Thailand*, lvii.

mic realignment in Asia. The North Vietnamese victory in the Vietnam War, though supported and applauded by Beijing, proved to be a liability for it as well, since the new Socialist Republic of Vietnam (SRV) pursued a strengthened relationship with the Soviet Union. To counter the SRV-Soviet alignment and to contest growing concerns about Soviet influence in Asia, Thailand and the PRC aligned more closely together. Among the PRC's steps taken toward alignment with Thailand by mid-1975 was a promise to stop supporting CPT insurgents.[38]

While the PRC dealt with a violent leadership transition from Mao to Deng Xiaoping and confronted a hostile Soviet Union and Vietnam, with some irony it encouraged Thailand to keep a U.S. military presence there. The PRC's rulers saw the United States as essential for regional security—including its own. With Communist victories to the north and east and without knowing how long the Cold War would last, King Bhumibol of Thailand strongly supported continued close relations with the United States.[39]

Nonetheless, under conditions established by Prime Minister Kukrit, within a year the last American bases in Thailand were returned to the Thais and U.S. operational forces left the country. In yet one more ironic twist, the PRC received credit for ending the Communist insurgency in Thailand that it had helped start and sustained for nearly 30 years.[40] Further, Kukrit agreed that Thailand would sever diplomatic ties with Taiwan in support of the PRC's "One China" principle.[41]

Following Kukrit's loss in the 1976 election and a subsequent military coup, Sino-Thai relations again soured. The staunch anti-Communist Thanin Kraivichien was installed as prime minister, and he immediately took steps to reduce interaction with Beijing. This led to an increase in PRC support for the CPT and a resumption of PRC political warfare operations such as anti-Thai radio broadcasts assailing Bangkok's "reactionary ruling clique" and the expansion of the CPT's united front to include the Socialist Party of Thailand.[42] However, Royal Thai Army general Kriangsak Chamanan replaced Thanin just one year later in 1977. Although anti-Communist, Kriangsak wanted to use the PRC to improve Thai-Cambodian relations in the face of a threatening Vietnam.

---

[38] Zawacki, *Thailand*, 53.
[39] Zawacki, *Thailand*, 49.
[40] Although it claimed to have cut off aid for the CPT, the PRC sustained CPT bases in Laos and Cambodia and continued radio propaganda operations in Yunnan through 1979. It also maintained party-to-party relations between the CCP and CPT.
[41] Zawacki, *Thailand*, 53.
[42] Jain, *China and Thailand*, xi.

Kriangsak met with Deng Xiaoping twice in 1977 and allowed previously banned Chinese-language newspapers in Thailand to begin publication again. He then visited Beijing in March 1978 to sign a trade agreement. There, he was informed that the CCP would continue relations with the CPT but that Beijing considered the Communist insurgency in Thailand to be an "internal problem." Kriangsak was also asked to join the PRC's "opposition to imperialism and hegemonism."[43]

In December 1978, Vietnamese forces invaded Cambodia, then called Democratic Kampuchea, and in January ousted the genocidal PRC-supported, Pol Pot-led Khmer Rouge regime that had taken control three years before. That same month, the PRC and the United States established formal relations, and in February, with Thailand's support, the PRC invaded Vietnam.[44] Cooperation between Bangkok and Beijing accelerated rapidly, because the Thai government feared its forces would be no match for the Vietnamese. Thai military officers believed that if Vietnamese troops crossed the Thai-Cambodian border in the morning, they would "reach Bangkok in time for lunch." The PRC invasion was designed to be brief and "teach [Vietnam] a lesson."[45]

During the Sino-Vietnamese and Cambodian-Vietnamese Wars, the latter of which pushed against Thailand's eastern border, the Thai government allowed the PRC to use air and land routes across its territory to support Pol Pot's Cambodian forces, which were also being supported by the CPT.[46] According to Southeast Asia scholar Gregory Vincent Raymond, the Royal Thai Armed Forces supported the Cambodians by "conducting cross-border intelligence gathering missions," by "initiating and developing contacts with Cambodian and PRC leaders," and by "channeling significant amounts of military aid to the Khmer Rouge." He concludes that transforming "what had been a very antagonistic relationship with China into a quasi-alliance against Vietnam [was] Thailand's most telling and important manouevre."[47]

The PRC made concessions to Thailand to secure its support against Vietnam during the Sino-Vietnamese War. For example, the same PRC political warfare organs that had vilified Royal Thai Government leaders for nearly 30 years as "fascist reactionaries" and "lackeys of imperialism," including the *Peking Review* and the *People's*

[43] Jain, *China and Thailand*, ix.
[44] Zawacki, *Thailand*, 59–60.
[45] Zawacki, *Thailand*, 60.
[46] Jain, *China and Thailand*, lxiii.
[47] Gregory Vincent Raymond, *Thai Military Power: A Culture of Strategic Accommodation* (Copenhagen, Denmark: NIAS Press, 2018), 161–65, 174.

Daily, now glowingly emphasized Thailand's readiness "to fight to safeguard its security, sovereignty, and integrity" against Vietnamese aggression. Further, senior PRC officials vowed to support Thailand "in its efforts to protect itself from aggression and expansion," and asserted that the PRC would place "first priority" on Thailand in its efforts to strengthen its relations with ASEAN nations. Beijing also claimed to shut down its Voice of the People of Thailand and Radio Yunnan radio stations, though other reports contradicted such claims.[48]

Of greater importance, the ending of Chinese support to the CPT reduced Thailand's internal security challenges. The PRC vowed to stop providing weapons to the PLAT, and Thai leaders in return continued to allow arms shipments to the Khmer Rouge to pass through Thai territory despite Bangkok's official stance of "strict neutrality" concerning the fighting in Cambodia. Vietnamese attacks into Thailand in mid-1980 further solidified Sino-Thai relations. Although Thai-U.S. relations revived following these incursions with such cooperation as antitank weapons training and large-scale combined exercises, Thailand also dramatically increased its cooperation with the PRC, and it was ultimately the PRC that was credited with helping block the Vietnamese from conducting a full-scale invasion of Thailand.[49]

Economic and Political Convergence: The Rise of the Sino-Thais

Through the mid-1980s, Prime Minister Prem Tinsulanonda and the all-important Thai monarchy greatly strengthened relations with one another, which would pay off significantly in the coming decades. Further, Thailand's ethnic Chinese community began being viewed as the country's "most valuable economic resource."[50]

Although Thailand's food industry Charoen Pokphand (CP) Group had first established a presence in the PRC in 1949, it was in the early 1980s that the Thai leadership began encouraging larger business expansion into China. Prem tapped the CP Group to help lead the way, and its Thai-Chinese directors gained significant influence in the Thai government after being appointed as advisors to the foreign ministry.[51] Through the present day, the CP Group continues to greatly influence Thailand's government in the interests of

[48] Jain, *China and Thailand*, lxiv, lxxv.
[49] Raymond, *Thai Military Power*, 163–64.
[50] Zawacki, *Thailand*, 70.
[51] Zawacki, *Thailand*, 70.

its business with the PRC, both directly through such activities as lobbying officials and other business leaders and indirectly through such means of directing advertising purchases.

Of equal importance during this era, Thais of Chinese origin leveraged business connections and their skills to not only influence politics but also become politicians. Chinese-Thai businessmen bought their way into what was dubbed the "Network Monarchy," a "para-political institution" including the monarchy, the military, and other elites. Thai military officers were placed on boards of directors to curb the influence of Chinese business leaders, but many were co-opted by the very businesses they helped oversee.[52] Other officers, however, resisted PRC business influence, the co-opting of their peers, and the warming of Sino-Thai relations, which ultimately led to the unsuccessful "Young Turks" coup attempt in 1981.

By the end of the 1980s, the PRC had ended CPT radio broadcasts from Yunnan and established a communications link between the People's Liberation Army and the Royal Thai Supreme Command Headquarters. Senior-level civilian and military official visits between the two nations were routine, and PRC weaponry and munitions, often of dubious quality, were flowing into the Thai military units.[53] Trade protocols calling for the PRC's import of Thai agricultural products and Thailand's import of PRC oil and machinery were in place. Although Thai leaders were wary of the PRC's continued support of the Khmer Rouge in the Cambodian-Vietnamese War and took close note of the CCP's wonton brutality during the June 1989 Tiananmen Square massacre, Sino-Thai relations continued to improve. Between 1989 and 2001, various Thai leaders sought to balance Thailand's relations between the United States and the PRC. Chief among them was Chuan Leekpai, who as prime minister sought to maintain good relations with the United States as a "countervailing power to an ambitious and expansionist China."[54]

A military coup in 1991 led to the brutal suppression of political protests the following May and resultant intervention by King Bhumipol himself. Subsequently, Thailand experienced a "Thai Spring," which spurred the birth of a modern, democratic Thai civil society that did not lend popular support to close relations with the PRC. But the 1997 Asian financial crisis, which began in Thailand, resulted in a dramatic shift in Thailand's perspectives as to whether the United States or the PRC provided the most enduring friendship and benefit. As Thailand's economy imploded, the United States of-

[52] Zawacki, *Thailand*, 68–71.
[53] Zawacki, *Thailand*, 74.
[54] Zawacki, *Thailand*, 77.

fered austerity measures while the PRC provided offers of seed capital, a move that would reap tremendous political dividends several years later.[55]

While King Bhumipol was suspicious that the PRC had geopolitical designs on Thailand, he allowed his daughter, Crown Princess Maha Chakri Sirindhorn, to visit the PRC as often as once a month and Queen Sirikit to visit in 2000. Further, Thai citizens of Chinese ancestry, comprising approximately 10–14 percent of the population, continued to advance to previously unachievable levels in business, civil service, and the military through "money politics." Benjamin Zawacki writes that during this period, Sino-Thais "advanced in prominence and power in Thailand just as China was doing so in the world outside."[56]

Regarding money politics, the rich and powerful CP Group, which had investments in every PRC province, assisted in the formation of a new political party in Thailand and lobbied on behalf of the PRC. According to a senior Thai official, the CP Group "was the only company that stood to gain from our close relations with China. It recruited the best brains. Diplomats were working for CP, everyone was working for the China lobby." One example of the level of interaction between the CP Group and the PRC is that the former assisted the latter in its suppression the Falun Gong spiritual practice in Thailand after the CCP's campaign against Falun Gong began in 1998.[57]

The 1997 Financial Crisis and the Rise of Thaksin

The 1997 Asian financial crisis marked a significant turning point in Thai history. The crisis, largely the result of Thailand's mismanagement of its economy, was pivotal in changing Thai perceptions about the PRC and the United States, for it turned into a regional economic emergency that drew contrasting responses from both nations. Washington and Beijing planted the seeds for their subsequent decline and rise, respectively, in Thailand's twenty-first-century foreign policy calculation. While the United States was perceived as "dogmatic, arrogant, and wrong," China offered unconditional assistance. Ultimately, Thais perceived the U.S. response under President William J. "Bill" Clinton to be inappropriate and "too little, too late,"

[55] Zawacki, *Thailand*, 77.
[56] Zawacki, *Thailand*, 80.
[57] Zawacki, *Thailand*, 81–83.

while the PRC's offer of $1 billion (USD) was perceived as timely and useful—even though the aid never actually materialized.[58]

The political impact of the PRC's unconditional-yet-never-fulfilled offer of financial assistance was very significant in Thailand. According to one senior Thai politician, "everybody was saying 'Oh, thank you China'." Japan, which actually provided significant help to Thailand, did not receive much public credit, which was perceived to be the result of the PRC's "clever marketing." In part because of that perception, Sino-Thais, who were perhaps hit hardest by the crisis, continued to expand their power and influence.[59]

In February 1999, Thailand and the PRC agreed upon a Sino-Thai "Plan of Action for the 21st Century," the first such agreement that the PRC would sign with any ASEAN nation. The plan reflected the PRC's "desire for a decline in American power" and "outlined cooperation in trade and investment, defense and security, judicial affairs, science and technology, diplomacy, and culture."[60] By the start of the new millennium, Thai prime minister Chuan Leekpai had facilitated a vast increase in substantive exchanges with the PRC, with more than 1,500 Sino-Thai meetings—the most Thailand had with any other nation—occurring between 1998 and 2000.

Another largely overlooked focus of Sino-Thai interaction during this era is the idea for the Kra Canal. The concept, which has been discussed for hundreds of years, calls for digging a 50- to 100-kilometer canal across Thailand's narrow Kra Isthmus to connect the Gulf of Thailand to the east with the Andaman Sea to the west. According to Zawacki, the canal would "render ancillary" the Straits of Malacca, thereby reducing the threat that U.S. military forces could pose to PRC energy and trade interests that transit them. From 1997 through the present day, Thai prime ministers have reexamined the feasibility of the concept, with increasing incentives from the PRC that align with its interest in the project.[61]

In January 2001, Thaksin Shinawatra, a former Royal Thai Police lieutenant colonel from the Thai Rak Thai (Thais Love Thais) Party, which he founded three years earlier, won 41 percent of the ballots cast in Thailand's general election, securing the largest electoral victory in Thai history. Thaksin was from a wealthy Sino-Thai family, reportedly of Hakka origin.[62] That September, several commercial airplanes hijacked by Islamofascist terrorists brought down the

---

[58] Zawacki, *Thailand*, 90–92.
[59] Zawacki, *Thailand*, 94.
[60] Zawacki, *Thailand*, 97.
[61] Benjamin Zawacki, "America's Biggest Southeast Asian Ally Is Drifting toward China," *Foreign Policy*, 29 September 2017; and Zawacki, *Thailand*, 100.
[62] Anderson, "Riddles of Yellow and Red," 17.

United States' World Trade Center and part of the Pentagon, initiating America's lengthy distraction from Asia as it became consumed by its Global War on Terrorism. Both events shaped the increasing tilt of Thailand's rulers and elites from the United States to the PRC.

Also shaping Thailand's tectonically shifting landscape at the turn of the twenty-first century was what has been described as a "vacuum of competence" within the U.S. embassy in Bangkok and the U.S. Department of State's Bureau of East Asian and Pacific Affairs in maintaining the Thai-U.S. alliance. This vacuum contrasted greatly with the professional operatives within the PRC's embassy in Bangkok and its Ministry of Foreign Affairs. Beijing assigned influential senior CCP operatives, most of who spoke fluent Thai, to its diplomatic posts in Thailand. According to former U.S. Ambassador to Thailand Ralph L. Boyce, they did a "masterful job of reaching out to Sino-Thais." The PRC's increasingly sophisticated approach to Thailand included soft power tools such as "panda diplomacy," which involved Beijing gifting giant pandas to Thailand zoos and was very popular with the Thai people.[63]

Prime Minister Thaksin was key to Thailand's shift to the PRC. Benedict Anderson wrote that he "had become one of Thailand's richest men thanks to a near-monopolistic mobile-phone concession, which he obtained under the last military regime." After founding the Thai Rak Thai party, Thaksin "recruited a batch of ex-leftists" who were "eager to become leaders at long last."[64] In the end, Thaksin would tear Thailand apart and be deposed in a coup, but not before he gave first priority to enhancing relations with the PRC and dramatically shifted Thailand's strategic focus from the west to the north.

Under Thaksin's rule, Sino-Thai engagement became more comprehensive and geostrategic, all at the expense of interaction between Thailand and both the United States and Taiwan. As Beijing worked to establish the diplomatic, economic, and propaganda environment for this shift, Thaksin was backed by an increasingly dominant Sino-Thai population, which made up the "critical mass" of his Thai Rak Thai Party. These Sino-Thais focused on their ethnic Chinese identity rather than their "Thai-Chinese" identity as Thailand accepted the narrative that the PRC was to be "most important."

At a commemoration of the 30th anniversary of Sino-Thai relations, Thaksin boasted that there were more Chinese in his cabinet than Thais. Encouraged and enticed by Beijing, he developed a

[63] Zawacki, *Thailand*, 106–7, 114–15.
[64] Anderson, "Riddles of Yellow and Red," 13.

strong strategic relationship with the PRC, designed a new regional architecture that featured the PRC and excluded the United States, and signed an unprecedented Sino-Thai trade agreement in 2003. He also appointed as his first minister of defense the pro-PRC general Chavalit Yongchaiyudh and vastly increased military sales and exchanges with Beijing. The PRC, meanwhile, initiated military training exercises with Thailand, its first with any Southeast Asian country, during the Thaksin era.[65]

Thaksin's professed commitment to democracy was limited to his own hold on power. He adopted the "China Model" of an authoritarian government and a "liberal" economy, while Beijing's influence on his security policies was strong. Thaksin would ultimately "preside over Thailand's worst human rights record since that of Field Marshal Sarit in 1957–1963," waging a war on drugs that led to the deaths of at least 2,500 people, most of whom were killed extrajudicially and many of whom were simply political opponents or business competitors. In response to a continued Islamic terrorist insurgency in southern Thailand, the Thais began consulting the PRC on internal security issues as early as 2004, drawing especially from the PRC's experience repressing Uighurs in western China. Thaksin responded to the Islamic insurgents' war crimes with war crimes of his own, employing ruthless tactics similar to those used by the PRC, including enforced disappearances, systematic torture, extrajudicial executions, and arbitrary detention. The prime minister attacked individual journalists and the news media in general, initiating a steep decline in press freedom that is seen in all PRC-affiliated regimes.[66]

On the propaganda front, Beijing dramatically increased its media presence in Thailand during Thaksin's reign, impacting the nation as well as the larger region. Through its various organs, the CCP's Propaganda Department developed close relations with Thai media outlets and funded trips for Thai journalists to the PRC, as it did in many other countries. The English-language China Central Television became quite popular in Thailand, and Mandarin-language broadcasts were made readily available. Xinhua News Agency, operating out of Bangkok since 1975, was joined in 2005 by the English-language *China Daily* newspaper, which established a regional hub there. Shortly thereafter, the *People's Daily* newspaper, the *Guangming Daily* media group, and the China Radio International network were operating out of Thailand. The patterns of news coverage in Thailand shifted accordingly. For example, while PRC

---

[65] Zawacki, *Thailand*, 105–32.
[66] Zawacki, *Thailand*, 125–29.

"news agencies" routinely ran CCP propaganda regarding the suppression of "splittists" in Xinjiang and Tibet, Thai media outlets ran similar stories after a PRC-sponsored Thai journalist visited Tibet in 2004.[67]

In conjunction with these overt intrusions in Thailand by the PRC state-run media, Thai media outlets progressively succumbed to the lure of PRC funding and influence, which was offered both directly and indirectly. Through "carrot and stick" methods directed by PRC-affiliated businesses, for example, Thai media outlets that toed the PRC line received advertising funding from those businesses or the PRC directly, while those that did not were refused any advertising support.[68]

Thailand's "China Model"

By the early 2000s, many Thai-Chinese who had refrained from speaking Chinese dialects began using Mandarin publicly, while others sought to learn to speak the language. Chinese schools and associations proliferated, with the assistance of the PRC embassy and consulates. In support of the PRC's rapidly expanding Confucius Institute language programs, Beijing flooded Thailand with hundreds of professors. Eventually, there would be more Confucius Institutes in Thailand than in all other ASEAN countries combined.[69]

By the time Royal Thai Army troops rolled through the streets of Bangkok to oust Prime Minister Thaksin in a *coup d'état* on 19 September 2006, the China Model was thoroughly ingrained in the psyche of competing Thai elites. The People's Alliance for Democracy (PAD) "yellow shirt" leadership, comprised in part by Maoist guerrilla leaders from the 1970s who admired the PRC, were every bit as enamored with the China Model as were Thaksin's Thai Rak Thai Party "red shirt" followers. Although it was caught off guard, Beijing assessed that it had nothing to fear from the coup against its most effective Thai partner in modern history. The PRC embassy in Bangkok "advised Beijing that China's influence in Thailand remains strong for a variety of reasons," including "growing commercial links, cultural ties, collegial diplomatic relations, and growing military cooperation programs."[70]

According to former Thai foreign minister Kasit Piromya, the

[67] Zawacki, *Thailand*, 116, 127–28.
[68] Kerry K. Gershaneck, discussions with Thai and foreign academics, Thailand, 2013–18.
[69] Kerry K. Gershaneck, interview with a senior U.S. Department of State official, Bangkok, Thailand, 30 December 2016; and Zawacki, *Thailand*, 111–16.
[70] Zawacki, *Thailand*, 130–31.

PRC began exerting even greater influence around this time by "buying up government and political leadership" and showing increasing sophistication in conducting influence operations, such as providing advisors to Thai businesses. "A lot of PRC students came [to Thailand] to influence the thinking of the Thai populace and build anti-U.S. sentiment," Kasit stated. "You see this in editorials that appease PRC activities and criticize American and Western behavior."[71]

The Role of the United States

The only viable counter to the dramatic increase of PRC influence in Thailand during this period was the United States. As elites across Thailand's political spectrum embraced the China Model and its implicit authoritarianism, American leadership routinely failed to act effectively.

In a pattern repeated all too often during the past two decades, the United States was ill-prepared to identify and counter PRC political warfare and largely failed to recognize the rapidly shifting ground beneath them. Two U.S. ambassadors were knowledgeable of the country, but three others were considered "out of their professional depth." All were left adrift policy-wise, while sensitive Wikileaks cables that were leaked further damaged trust. The influence of Thailand's king, the most steadfast American ally in Southeast Asia for seven decades, gave way to factions that favored the PRC.[72]

Ambassador Darryl N. Johnson, who served in Thailand from 2001–4, brought great cultural understanding to the post but displayed "surprisingly limited" appreciation for the PRC's increasing power and influence. Compounding this, the U.S. embassy closed its consulates in northern and southern Thailand. The U.S. Information Service, with its counterpropaganda mandate, had been closed in 1997, and there were far fewer seasoned Thailand hands assigned to the American embassy. Consequently, the embassy's view toward Thailand became "centralized" and "myopic." While Ambassador Ralph L. Boyce, who succeeded Johnson from 2005–7, had exceptional Thai language ability and "strong connections with the military, Privy Council, business leaders, academics, and politicians from all sides," he was hamstrung by narrow-minded State Department direction and a staff that did not possess his depth.[73]

This lack of institutional strength and inability to focus on the

---

[71] Kasit Piromya, interview with the author, Bangkok, Thailand, 1 May 2018, hereafter Kasit interview.
[72] Benjamin Zawacki, interview with the author, 4 April 2016, hereafter Zawacki interview.
[73] Zawacki, *Thailand*, 147.

PRC's rapidly escalating influence toward Thailand would continue during the tenure of Ambassador Kristie A. Kenney, who served from 2011–14. In a speech given in Honolulu, Hawaii, in 2013, she admitted to a "lack of energy" in the alliance and to the fact that relations between Thailand and the United States would "never be the same."[74] When asked what steps she was taking to improve the relationship, she did not offer an answer. Kenney's vision of public diplomacy was perhaps hampered by the increasingly troubled political breakdown in Thailand, but it was perceived as weak. Meanwhile, her PRC counterpart was speaking in public about $12.5 billion (USD) railway development deals. During Kenney's tenure, influential Thais concluded that the United States had lost the ability to "connect, explain, and push a complicated set of interests, rather than only the security interests shared during the Cold War." As a result, the U.S. relationship with Thailand was "slipping without any good coordination or good sense of direction."[75]

U.S. presidents George W. Bush and Barack H. Obama paid varying degrees of attention to Thailand during their administrations, but even with Bush designating Thailand as a "major non-NATO ally" in 2003 and Obama paying a highly publicized visit to the country in 2012, their actions seemed insufficient. An issue that drew special attention was Obama's "pivot"—later called a "rebalance"—to Asia in 2012. The president's move was an appropriate response to an evolving world situation, particularly with an increasingly threatening PRC. However, it was never backed by substantial security, economic, or political investment. In reality, it was the PRC which "pivoted" in response to Obama's "non-pivot."[76]

A significant event occurred in another Southeast Asia country in 2012 that severely damaged Thai perceptions of the value of the Kingdom's alliance with Washington. This was the Scarborough Shoal incident of April–June 2012. The shoal, 193 kilometers west of Subic Bay, is contested by many claimants including the PRC and the Philippines, but the Philippines held effective control in late May 2012. When Chinese vessels were discovered fishing illegally there, Manila responded, which ultimately led to a lengthy standoff with a fleet of PRC maritime enforcement vessels and PLA Navy vessels. The PRC employed economic coercion as well, slowing entry of Philippine agricultural products to China and drastically reducing the number of Chinese tourists allowed to visit the Philippines. After the U.S. Department of State brokered a compromise between the PRC and the Philippines and both sides pulled back, the PRC immediately ignored the agreement and abruptly seized the Shoal. Philippine president Benigno Simeon Cojuangco Aquino III flew to Washington to personally request the help of President Barack H. Obama, but received no specific statements of support.[77] The PRC seized sovereign rights at Scarborough Shoal from a U.S. treaty ally without firing a shot, and all Southeast Asian nations took close note.

The head of the PRC's Leading Group that orchestrated the seizure was at that time not well-known in the West: a man named Xi Jinping. This event made him a national hero just when he most needed the political legitimacy. The acquiescence of the United States became a significant turning point—the real "pivot"—for Xi and his vision to "restore" China's territorial claims and destroy the system of alliances that had long contained its expansionism. While the Scarborough seizure was downplayed by the Obama administration and treated as a minor fisheries dispute, Chinese scholars recognized the significance of Xi's template for mooting U.S. alliances by undercutting confidence in the agreements, calling it the "Scarborough Model."[78] The senior Thai civilian and military officials with whom the author worked at the Royal Thai Military Academy and Thammasat University in subsequent years, many of whom were pro-American, would refer to the Scarborough Model as a compelling reason why Thailand must focus on improving relations with Beijing and away from an unreliable Washington.[79]

This inability or unwillingness on the part of U.S. diplomats to pay attention to PRC political warfare in Thailand continued after Kenny's departure in November 2014. A subsequent American chargé d'affaires confidently asserted during an interview with this author that PRC political warfare in Thailand "is not a problem," and the real threat was "Russian political inference."[80]

The 2014 Coup and Another Tectonic Shift

Thailand's shift into China's growing sphere of influence and away from that of the United States continued unabated under the five prime ministers who succeeded Thaksin, including Thaksin's sister Yingluck Shinawatra, military leaders, and members of the main

[77] *Hearing on Strategic Competition with China, before the House Committee on Armed Services*, 115th Cong. (2018) (testimony by Ely Ratner, Maurice R. Greenburg Senior Fellow for China Studies, Council on Foreign Relations).
[78] James E. Fanell and Kerry K. Gershaneck, "White Warships and Little Blue Men: The Looming 'Short, Sharp War' in the East China Sea over the Senkakus," *Marine Corps University Journal* 8, no. 2 (Fall 2017): 67–98, https://doi.org/10.21140/mcuj.2017080204.
[79] Gershaneck, discussions with Thai and foreign academics; and Kerry K. Gershaneck, discussions with Thai military officers, Thailand, 2013–18.
[80] Gershaneck, interview with a senior U.S. Department of State official.

opposition party. By 2012, the PAD routinely touted the PRC's anti-American propaganda by claiming the United States was attempting to overthrow the Thai monarchy, was hoping "to create instability so that it can install its military bases to block China's influence," and had developed space weapons that could cause natural disasters, which forced the PLA "to hold talks with its Thai counterparts."[81]

Perhaps coincidentally, the *People's Daily*, the official newspaper of the CCP, established its first "overseas" edition in Thailand in 2012. It was launched with great fanfare, as the inauguration event in Bangkok was attended by more than 300 representatives from Thai and PRC academic, business, cultural, and political circles.[82]

In 2013, Thailand's Democrat Party, in an apparent bid to not be outdone by the PAD in making anti-American allegations, imitated a PRC propaganda narrative attacking the United States. The party accused the United States of conspiring with Thai government officials to establish a U.S. naval base in exchange for better trade deals. This occurred as Thailand and the PRC completed their first Sino-Thai Strategic Dialogue. Thailand continued to act on behalf of PRC interests that year, when, for example, it interceded with ASEAN on behalf of Beijing to separate the South China Sea dispute from the wider ASEAN-PRC relationship. Further, Thailand became increasingly enthralled with high-speed rail and other plans, such as the Kra Canal concept, that benefit the PRC's Belt and Road initiative.[83] In the March 2014 parliamentary elections, "78 percent of the seats in Thailand's parliament were occupied by ethnic Chinese, even though they accounted for just 14 per cent of the population."[84]

On 7 May 2014, after months of mass protests, violence, and political and legal maneuverings, Thai prime minister Yingluck Shinawatra was removed from her post after Thailand's constitutional court found her guilty of legal violations. A week later, the Royal Thai Armed Forces declared martial law. After General Prayut Chan-ocha, commander in chief of the Royal Thai Army, was unable to obtain an agreement with legislators on a way to end longstanding violence and demonstrations in Bangkok, he led a coup against the government on 22 May. Unlike 2006, it was the U.S. embassy that was caught by surprise this time. Subsequent failures by both Thai and American politicians and diplomats led to a severe rift between

[81] Zawacki, *Thailand*, 289.
[82] Kornphanat Tungkeunkunt, "China's Soft Power in Thailand," Institute of Southeast Asian Studies (Singapore), 3 June 2013.
[83] Zawacki, *Thailand*, 289–91.
[84] Anderson, "Riddles of Yellow and Red," 19.

Thailand and the United States that amounted to a significant geo-political victory for the PRC.[85]

As the United States condemned the coup according to its law and traditions, which was expected by the Thai military junta leaders, it did so in inept and inexperienced ways. According to one U.S. State Department official, this amateurish response "took a lot of our closest friends, people who had been admirers of the U.S. role in Thailand for the last 30 or 40 years, aback." Conversely, the PRC ambassador to Thailand met with the junta leaders in early June and assured them of the PRC's commitment to a good relationship, while Prayut, who had become prime minister on 22 May, gave a public speech in which he stated his commitment to "strategic partnership 'at all levels' with China."[86]

As noted by Thammasat University's Thitinan Pongsudhirak, "Washington's hardline reaction in 2014 was so conspicuous, Beijing's embrace of the coup-makers became that much more salient. As the chorus of Western criticism against the junta gathered sound and fury, Thailand's top brass sought and received succor from Beijing."[87] The PRC continued to exploit the Thai coup and American missteps, both real and alleged, as the junta accelerated trade and other ties with Beijing. Prime Minister Prayuth insisted that "Thailand remains committed as ever to its strategic partnership 'at all levels' with China."[88] Thailand's civic and other organizations chimed in, supporting Beijing's narratives and lambasting American "colonialism" and the United States' response to the coup.[89]

After Ambassador Kenney left her post in Thailand in November 2014, it took the United States nearly a year to replace her. Thailand and the PRC read much in the inability of the Obama administration to fulfill this most basic requirement at such a critical juncture. Since the 2014 coup, Sino-Thai engagement at the political, economic, military and security, educational, and cultural levels increased dramatically.

By 2017, the cumulative impact of PRC political warfare and other actions toward Thailand had produced an outcome unthinkable during the height of the Cold War: the majority of Thai military officers perceived the PRC, not the United States, to be Thailand's most useful and reliable ally. This finding is of massive significance.

---

[85] Zawacki interview; and Zawacki, *Thailand*, 293.
[86] Zawacki, *Thailand*, 293–94.
[87] Thitinan Pongsudhirak, "A Recalibration between Thailand and the Outside World," *Bangkok Post* (Thailand), 2 October 2015.
[88] Wassana Nanuam, Patsara Jikkham, and Anucha Charoenpo, "NCPO Boosts China Trade Ties," *Bangkok Post* (Thailand), 7 June 2014.
[89] "Uni Alumni Blast U.S. 'Meddling' in Coup," *Bangkok Post* (Thailand), 2 June 2014.

In the modern Thai state since 1932, the military forms a central pillar of governance and has often been the government's most important political actor. It has also been one of the most pro-American factions of the Thai government because of its close working relationship with the U.S. military, which includes its use of common doctrine, weapons, and equipment and extensive education in the United States.

An Australian National University report for the U.S. Department of Defense, conducted during three years and surveying approximately 1,800 Thai military officers and defense officials, indicates a stunning shift in Thai perceptions toward the United States and the PRC. While the Thai military "still places great store on the United States for security" and prefers the use of English language and American military doctrine and procedures, the PRC has eclipsed the United States in influence and in terms of perceived power. The report notes that "Thai historical memory omits U.S. protection and largesse during the Cold War" and "downplays hostile Sino-Thai relations when China actively supported armed insurgents of the Communist Party of Thailand." Equally disturbing is that despite those Thai officials' "unease about China's growing military capabilities" and views that "the U.S. security guarantee is still important for Thailand, there is significant ambivalence to the United States." Offering a striking testament to the power of the PRC political warfare narrative and the failure of the United States and Thailand to properly reply, the respondents judged the military threat from the United States as greater than any other great power, including the PRC.[90]

Thailand's prime minister Prayuth Chan-ocha confirmed the tectonic shift of Thailand's relations with China and the United States in a June 2018 interview with *Time*. "The friendship between Thailand and China has been over thousands of years, and with [the United States] for around 200 years," he said. "China is the number one partner of Thailand, along with other countries in the second and third place like the U.S. and others."[91]

Thailand, according to former Foreign Minister Kasit, prides itself on its Bamboo Diplomacy, balancing foreign nations and "bending with the wind." Right now, he says, the strong wind is blowing from Beijing.[92]

---

[90] John Blaxland and Greg Raymond, *Tipping the Balance in Southeast Asia?: Thailand, the United States and China* (Washington, DC: Center for Strategic & International Studies; Canberra, Australia: Strategic & Defence Studies Centre, Australian National University, 2017), 3–6.
[91] Charlie Campbell, "Thailand PM Prayuth Chan-ocha on Turning to China over the U.S.," *Time*, 21 June 2018.
[92] The term *Bamboo Diplomacy* refers to a flexible foreign policy. Kasit interview.

CHAPTER SIX

PRC Political Warfare against Thailand: A Contemporary Analysis

Chineseposters.net

Down with Imperialism! This 1965 poster reflects a PRC propaganda theme that was used across Southeast Asia and globally: that U.S. defense of its friends and allies is "imperialism" and must be defeated.

The following analysis is a detailed examination of current People's Republic of China (PRC) political warfare operations directed against Thailand, including its goals, objectives, strategies, tactics, and themes. Much of it is based on extensive discussions between this author and current and former Thai and

U.S. officials, academics, and journalists, many of whom agreed to be interviewed on the condition that they not be identified by name or position. Each interviewee was asked a series of questions, their answers to which are summarized below. This analysis is also based on the examination of many documents, books, and reports cited herein, as well as on this author's own personal experience while working in Thailand for more than six years at Thammasat University, the Royal Thai Military Academy, and the Royal Thai Naval Academy.

PRC Goals and Strategies for Conducting Political Warfare against Thailand

The PRC's chief political warfare goal is to ensure that the Thai government is a compliant, reliable, and supportive ally.[1] Strategies include:

- Employing traditional united front operations, liaison work, and other political warfare tools in conjunction with violence, economic pressure, military intimidation, and diplomacy as needed.
- Engaging Thailand on all fronts—including its economy, politics, diplomacy, military, monarchy, and membership in the Association of Southeast Asian Nations (ASEAN)—both comprehensively and concomitantly, so that ebbs in any one area are offset by flows in others.
- Utilizing themes that exploit historical ethnic, ideological, trade, and security ties, as well as highlighting the "inevitable PRC victory bandwagon" that suggests it is best to join the PRC since it is now in its strongest position and the United States is growing weaker and increasingly irrelevant and unreliable.
- Encouraging Thailand's rulers to adopt authoritarian governance based on the PRC model, to include resistance to "corrupt western ideals" such as democracy, freedom of the press, and freedom of expression.

---

[1] Kasit Piromya, interview with the author, Bangkok, Thailand, 1 May 2018, hereafter Kasit interview. Some Thais argue that the PRC's actual goal is to make Thailand a vassal state or even southern province, as they perceive Cambodia and Laos to currently be, but Kasit believes that the PRC understands the latent anti-Chinese sentiment in Thailand and is therefore not striving to make Thailand a vassal state.

- Through increased military engagement and sales, relegating U.S. military presence irrelevant and persuading Thailand to support the PRC's efforts to push the United States from the region.[2]

Desired Outcomes of PRC Political Warfare in Thailand

Thailand becomes essentially a tributary state in full compliance with PRC strategic goals and supportive of PRC diplomatic, security, and economic objectives regarding ASEAN, the South China Sea, and other issues. Specifically, the PRC seeks to ensure that:

- Thailand offers its support or neutrality on contentious issues such as the PRC's propaganda campaign to counter international outrage over its role in the COVID-19 pandemic and disputes in the Indian Ocean and East and South China Seas, its adherence to the PRC's "One China" policy calling for the absorption of Taiwan and control of Tibet and Hong Kong, and its compliance regarding the PRC's use of the Upper Mekong River and its regional Belt and Road Initiative (BRI).
- Thailand acts as an "enforcer" for the PRC and assists PRC political warfare efforts. If Thailand's direct support is not feasible, then it will at least offer no resistance or interference.
- The Thailand-United States alliance is split completely.[3]
- Thailand supports the PRC achieving unchallenged political, military, economic, diplomatic, and cultural dominance throughout the region.

---

[2] Kasit interview.
[3] Kasit interview. While Kasit believes that the PRC wants to minimize the Thailand-United States alliance rather than completely terminate it, others argue that the destruction of American alliances in the Asia-Pacific region has long been a goal of PRC foreign and security policy.

Themes and Audiences
of PRC Political Warfare in Thailand

The PRC's primary political warfare themes include the following:

- The PRC is a nonthreat and a noncompetitor, but rather a partner in economic growth, to Thailand.
- The Chinese and Thai people are more than mere friends—they are as close as family.
- The PRC is strong, while the United States is weak and undependable.
- "Asia is for Asians," as exemplified by the PRC, while archaic western values do not apply in the region.[4]
- The political and economic policies of the "China Model" should be adopted by Thailand as a "Thai Model."

The PRC's primary audiences in Thailand include national- and local-level elected officials, royal family members who are close to Beijing, senior military officials, the nation's privy council, and elites across all sectors who are of Sino-Thai ethnicity. Secondary audiences comprise influential journalists and social media users as well as academics, while tertiary audiences include students and average Thai citizens. It is interesting to note that the PRC does not seem to place much emphasis on religious leaders, despite the strong influence of Buddhism in Thailand.

Tools, Tactics, Techniques, and Procedures
for PRC Political Warfare in Thailand

China specialist Peter Mattis notes that the PRC uses many actions to "influence and shape the world, and Beijing leverages all means of national power to do so. Diplomatic and economic tools are at least as much of the party's toolkit as united front work and propaganda."[5] This is a form of total war that employs active measures such as violence and other forms of coercive, destructive attacks.

Below is a brief overview of some of the political warfare activities that the PRC uses to shape Thailand. These examples are provided to demonstrate that even within a country that is quite favorably disposed toward the PRC, the PRC still wages political warfare operations on a routine basis. The outcome in Thailand is similar to that of many other countries throughout the world: the Thai govern-

---

4 Kasit interview.
5 Peter Mattis, "An American Lens on China's Interference and Influence-Building Abroad," *Open Forum*, Asan Forum, 30 April 2018.

ment routinely submits to PRC demands for compliance across all spectrums, Thai academics avoid topics that Beijing deems sensitive, Thai students are intimidated from speaking freely, Thai media outlets and scholars self-censor themselves, Thai business and influential institutions curb their speech to placate the PRC, and the nearly 70 million Thai citizens are subjected daily to PRC propaganda disseminated through online, television, print, and radio media outlets run by the Chinese Communist Party (CCP).

Censorship

The Thai government's well-documented willingness to censor on behalf of the PRC includes supporting the PRC narrative regarding the COVID-19 pandemic, as reported by Sophie Boisseau du Rocher of the French Institute of International Relations. Boisseau du Rocher writes of concerns that "angry voices emanating from civil society toward (the government) that . . . failed to take strong action to fight the virus (in a bid not to offend China, among other reasons) may end up in jails for 'subversion' or being sued with repressive methods on charges of conspiracy or incitement."[6] She also notes that, in support of the PRC propaganda campaign to blame countries other than China for the pandemic outbreak, "Thailand was first to blame 'dirty Caucasian tourists' for infecting Thailand 'because they don't shower and do not wear masks'."[7]

The Thai government's censorship for the PRC is also reflected in such wide-ranging actions as the detention and expulsion of Hong Kong democracy activist Joshua Wong in October 2016 and Prime Minister Prayut Chan-ocha's threat to ban the film *Operation Mekong* (2016), which depicts a drug-running-related massacre involving murky PRC-affiliated organizations and Thai military forces, if it included scenes that would offend Beijing or the Thai junta in any way.

Thailand has arguably copied PRC censorship and restrictions on freedom of speech through such vehicles as the internet "Single Portal" (similar to the PRC's "Golden Shield Project," colloquially known as the "Great Firewall") and reeducation camps for reporters and others who cover issues that displease the junta, as well as intimidation of journalists to force them to self-censor.[8] Some publications, such as *The Bangkok Post* and *The Nation*, retain some editorial freedom regarding the PRC, but that latitude appears to be disappearing.

---

[6] Sophie Boisseau du Rocher, "What COVID-19 Reveals about China-Southeast Asia Relations," *Diplomat*, 8 April 2020.
[7] Boisseau du Rocher, "What COVID-19 Reveals about China-Southeast Asia Relations."
[8] Kerry K. Gershaneck, discussions with Thai and foreign academics, Thailand, 2013–18.

Academics routinely self-censor because they are often under pressure from their administration and other faculty members, as well as the PRC and Sino-Thais, to do so.[9] The PRC embassy in Bangkok does not hesitate to try to censor criticism from current or former senior Thai officials. For example, after a former Thai foreign minister gave a speech in Taiwan regarding the prospects of PRC regional domination in October 2017, the PRC embassy lambasted Thailand's Ministry of Foreign Affairs to force it to silence the official.[10]

Intimidation

PRC agents and those acting on behalf of the PRC quietly intimidate Thai academics and other citizens, who then act as de facto PRC agents of influence. One public example of this observed by the author was an emotional insistence by a senior Huachiew Chalermprakiet University law professor during a June 2016 forum at Thammasat University that Thailand must support the PRC's claim to most of the South China Sea. The professor's rationale was that they had been informed by a PRC representative that if Thailand did not support the PRC's position in the South China Sea, the PRC might choose to claim the Gulf of Thailand and designate it a "core interest," due to China's historic presence there.

Other Thai scholars report that PRC academics have told them that Thailand must support the PRC plan for the Kra Canal across Thailand's Kra Isthmus, as it is important to both PRC trade and security and offers a way for the PRC to punish Singapore for its failure to support PRC positions. Those Thai scholars understood such comments to imply that the PRC could inflict similar punishment on Thailand if it failed to support PRC policies and actions.[11]

Detention, Expulsion, and Kidnapping

The Thai government is reportedly complicit in blacklisting, expelling, and assisting in the abduction of PRC critics.[12] One prominent example is the detention and expulsion of Hong Kong activist Joshua Wong from Thailand at PRC request in October 2016, when Wong had been invited to speak at Chulalongkorn University in Bangkok. Two days after his expulsion from the country, Thai authorities allowed Wong to make a Skype call to a Chulalongkorn University audience—but only if he agreed to not criticize the PRC in the call. Armed police were in the room filled with students when

---

[9] Gershaneck, discussions with Thai and foreign academics.
[10] Kasit interview.
[11] Gershaneck, discussions with Thai and foreign academics.
[12] Kerry K. Gershaneck, interviews with a senior U.S. Department of State official, various locations, 2018.

Wong called to ensure his compliance.[13] Other examples include the case of a dissident Hong Kong bookseller, a naturalized Swedish citizen, who was abducted in Thailand and taken to the PRC for trial, as well as ethnic Uighurs whose forced return to the PRC was condemned by Amnesty International.[14] Regarding the bookseller, one of five individuals allegedly abducted by the PRC from the same bookstore, Human Rights Watch commented that "China's willingness to snatch people in Thailand and Hong Kong with the apparent involvement of their governments adds to the concerns."

Many critics of the PRC in Thailand today are convinced that there are "Chinese agents everywhere" and that they are not safe. This indicates a very significant psychological warfare victory for the PRC, as it sends the strong message: "If you displease us, Thailand is with us, and we can get you any place and any time."[15]

Bribery, Blackmail, and Extortion

Allegations of and questions about corruption regarding Thailand's $1.2 billion (USD) purchase of a Chinese *Yuan*-class ST26-T submarine in 2017 have often been made on social and news media, well as in private conversations between this author and various sources.[16] While there is ample anecdotal evidence regarding the impact of bribery, blackmail, and extortion as tools of PRC political warfare operations in Thailand, this information is not used in this book for numerous reasons. These reasons include privacy issues and legal ramifications under Thailand's severe Article 44, *lèse majeste* (insulting a ruler; treason), and other laws that have been used to prosecute journalists, researchers, and citizens alike.

News Media: Coopting, Manipulation, and Ownership

The PRC has assumed an increasingly dominant position in Thai, Chinese, and English-language news media regarding content and perspective in what has been dubbed "the Sinicization of Thai news." The PRC's news dominance precedes the COVID-19 pandemic but, as one news outlet reported, "Thai media is outsourcing much of its coronavirus coverage to Beijing."[17]

---

[13] Alan Wong and Edward Wong, "Joshua Wong, Hong Kong Democracy Leader, Is Detained at Bangkok Airport," *New York Times*, 4 October 2016.
[14] "China: Release Abducted Swedish Bookseller," Human Rights Watch, 17 October 2016; and "Nowhere Feels Safe: Uyghurs Tell of China-led Intimidation Campaign Abroad," Amnesty International, accessed 19 June 2020.
[15] Gershaneck, discussions with Thai and foreign academics.
[16] Wasamon Audjarint, "Submarine Deal Shows Thailand's Growing Reliance on China," *Nation* (Thailand), 1 June 2017. The purchase of two more ST26 submarines has been "put on hold" due to the COVID-19 pandemic. See Nontarat Phaicharoen and Wilawan Watcharasakwet, "Thai Military Suspends Deals on Foreign Weapons while Nation Battles COVID-19," *BenarNews* (Bangkok), 22 April 2020.
[17] Jasmine Chia, "Thai Media Is Outsourcing Much of Its Coronavirus Coverage to Beijing and That's Just the Start," *Thai Enquirer* (Thailand), 31 January 2020.

PRC news media expanded its already imposing presence in Thailand during 2019, the year was christened by the Thai government as the "ASEAN-China Year of Media Exchanges." Since then, the PRC "has been making tremendous inroads into Thai-language news and is beginning to make its appearance in English-language Thai newspapers." At least 12 of Thailand's most popular news agencies are provided, free of charge, between 60 and 100 articles from China Xinhua News, all translated into Thai. Readers often do not realize these articles are provided by the PRC. Of even greater impact, the Thai "China Xinhua News" Facebook page has 70 million followers.[18]

Thai news media personnel are often afforded all-expenses-paid trips to the PRC, a program not unlike those run by other countries' embassies. In conjunction with grooming Thai reporters and editorial staff, PRC propaganda organs purchase newspaper inserts with themes such as Sino-Thai friendship, increasing infrastructure and military cooperation between the two nations, and the growing importance of PRC tourism and investment in Thailand. The PRC embassy also offered grants to Thai media organizations, with conditions that the recipients attend workshops and training on topics important to China.

A weekly *China Daily* insert in the Thai newspaper *The Nation* in October 2018, for example, led its front page with a story headlined "Resisting Risks from the U.S.: Improper U.S. Practices Escalate Trade Tension with China and Pose Uncertainties for Asia's Healthy Growth." The 31-page insert was filled with anti-American articles whose headlines included "Beijing Report Defends Trade Practices," "Tariffs Harmful, Says Former U.S. Envoy," "U.S. Levies Challenge Global Commerce," "America Reverting to Its Past, says Jacques," and "U.S. Retailers Brace for an Uncertain Future." Along with that heavy dose of propaganda, the insert was filled with fluff pieces on Chinese art, culture, and dining.[19]

The same issue of *The Nation* also included a full-page story headlined "Trump's 'Meddling' Claim Plays into China's Trade Narrative," which had originally run in *The Wall Street Journal* several days before. It read, "By claiming without offering proof that China is interfering in the U.S. midterm elections, President Trump not only escalated bilateral tensions, but he also provided ammunition to senior Communist Party members who say his real intention is to stop China's ascent as a global power."[20] *The Nation's* "Opinion Anal-

---

[18] Chia, "Thai Media Is Outsourcing Much of Its Coronavirus Coverage to Beijing and That's Just the Start."

[19] Gershaneck, discussions with Thai and foreign academics.

[20] Josh Chin, "Trump's 'Meddling' Claim Plays into China's Trade Narrative," *Wall Street Journal*, 27 September 2018.

ysis" section also ran a quarter-page article under the column "What Others Say" titled, "America's Unilateral Trade Policies Could Slow Growth." Unsurprisingly, the source is the *China Daily.*[21]

The PRC embassy in Bangkok and its consulate generals in the cities of Chiang Mai, Songkhla, and Khon Kaen have engaged in increasingly sophisticated media relations activities during the past decade, taking direct action to persuade or punish outlets that fail to heed the PRC line. For example, PRC embassy officials often contact the Press Council of Thailand and Thai Journalists Association to push Thai journalists to cover certain topics in the manner the PRC wants, such as publishing stories that compliment Thailand or criticize the PRC's foes. Since 2018, however, the PRC embassy has shifted tactics, adopting a softer approach in its engagement with the Thai media. While still demanding that Thai journalists follow PRC narratives, the embassy has established a formal public affairs section, similar in name to its U.S. counterpart, and is beginning to award grants with no conditions attached. One such grant, which focuses on Chinese society and culture, is for more than 1 million baht ($31,350 USD) and allows the recipient to choose which topics to cover and select which cities to visit.[22]

Ironically, China Radio International, a PRC state-run radio station, still broadcasts in the Thai language, as it has since it first began propaganda operations against the Royal Thai government and the United States in 1950. However, the station is now dedicated to "introducing China and the world to the Thai" and "promoting understanding and friendship between Chinese and Thai people." Its current news reporting features programs developed in cooperation with Thai broadcasting stations at such education institutions as the prestigious Chulalongkorn University, Naresuan University, and Mahasarakham University.[23]

Regarding media manipulation through funding and advertising, the PRC freely donates funds to organizations such as the Thai Journalists Association. There are also strong indications that PRC-affiliated business interests use advertising funding as a "carrot and stick" technique to ensure that no criticism of the PRC exists in Thai-language and other media. Reported tactics by major Thai business groups with deep relations to PRC business and government organizations include offering to invest in advertising in news media

---

[21] Gershaneck, discussions with Thai and foreign academics.
[22] Gershaneck, discussions with Thai and foreign academics.
[23] Kornphanat Tungkeunkunt, "China's Soft Power in Thailand," Institute of Southeast Asian Studies (Singapore), 3 June 2013.

outlets that propagate PRC narratives and threatening to pull advertising from outlets that do not self-censor on behalf of the PRC.[24]

In 2016, the PRC video game conglomerate Tencent purchased one of Thailand's biggest news and entertainment websites, Sanook.com. While the website's content remains largely Thai-oriented and there appears to be no overt focus on changing Thai perspectives of the PRC, its otherwise sensationalist news coverage carefully avoids any coverage that could be perceived as "anti-China."[25]

Conversely, some Thai media outlets are overtly owned by the PRC. One popular website, Thaizhonghua.com, serves as the media outlet for the Thailand China Information company. The majority of the website's articles are published by Thailand China Network's editorial office and Thaizhonghua's parent agency, *China Daily*, which is the largest Chinese-language newspaper in Thailand. According to Thaizhonghua, the *China Daily* has long-term cooperative relationships with the PRC-run Xinhua News Agency and China News Service, as well as with mainstream Thai news media outlets.[26]

Propaganda and Psychological Warfare as Education and Cultural Programs

The PRC also uses education as an important weapon to exert its influence over Thailand. While Confucius Institutes, Chinese Students and Scholars Associations (CSSA), and Chinese Cultural Centers are chief among these educational tools, it should also be noted that Sino-Thai military education programs have expanded quite significantly since the 2014 coup in Thailand. All have enormous impact on the attitudes and frames of reference of future generations of Thai military leaders, some of whom will inevitably go on to lead the country.[27]

Confucius Institutes, established to promote the spread of Chinese culture and language in foreign nations throughout the world, are ultimately tools of political warfare. Thailand hosts 26 of their number, the most of any country in Asia and more than all ASEAN nations combined. Some reports claim that there are more than 7,000 volunteers in Thailand since the program's inception there in 2006. The funding comes from Hanban, a PRC government entity. According to U.S. intelligence reports, the program limits discussion on topics that the PRC finds sensitive, such as the 1989 Tianan-

[24] Gershaneck, discussions with Thai and foreign academics.
[25] Gershaneck, discussions with Thai and foreign academics.
[26] Gershaneck, discussions with Thai and foreign academics.
[27] Kornphanat Tungkeunkunt, "Culture and Commerce: China's Soft Power in Thailand," *International Journal of China Studies* 7, no. 2 (August 2016): 151–73.

men Square massacre or the current political status of Tibet. The PRC uses Confucius Institutes to instill pro-China viewpoints in the minds both the students as well as the professors molding the thinking of Thailand's future leaders. Further, the program has been characterized as "an avenue to covertly influence public opinion and teach half-truths designed to present Chinese history, government or official policy in the most favorable light."[28]

While Confucius Institute language classes are quite popular in Thailand, scholarships are the program's chief appeal. Each year, many Thai students apply via Thailand's Confucius Institutes to the China Scholarship Council for scholarships that will allow them to study in the PRC. As a result, Thailand ranks highly among foreign countries sending students to China. The PRC also awards annual grants to hundreds of Thai education officials to conduct classroom observations and visits in China. Consequently, the students and officials return to Thailand inculcated with PRC doctrine and perspective, effectively propagandized.[29]

Confucius Institutes also sponsor various events across Thailand, such as the Chinese Cultural Festival held at Chiang Mai University in October 2018. Students from 16 Chiang Mai-area schools participated in the event, which consisted of a question-and-answer session, calligraphy lessons, and group performance competitions related to Chinese language and culture.[30]

According to the *Global Times* and *VOA*, approximately 30,000 Chinese students studied in Thailand in 2016 and 2017; this number is twice the 2012 enrollment.[31] These students are perceived as an "extension of Chinese soft power" and usually belong to CSSAs, which administer Chinese students and scholars studying outside of the PRC at foreign colleges, universities, and other education institutions. Many CSSAs are controversial, since there is a clear line of funding and authority between them and PRC embassies.

Investigations conducted by the *New York Times* and *Foreign Policy* magazine have found that PRC consular officials "communicate regularly with CSSAs, dividing the groups by region and assigning each region to an embassy contact who is responsible for relaying safety information—and the occasional political directive—to chapter presidents." Moreover, several CSSAs "explicitly vet their members along ideological lines, excluding those whose views do not

[28] Natalie Johnson, "CIA Warns of Extensive Chinese Operation to Infiltrate American Institutions," *Washington Free Beacon*, 7 March 2018.

[29] Tungkeunkunt, "Culture and Commerce," 161.

[30] Gershaneck, discussions with Thai and foreign academics.

[31] Zhang Hui, "More Chinese Students Turning to Belt and Road Countries," *Global Times* (Beijing), 20 September 2017; and "Thai Universities Tap into Rising Chinese Demand," *Voice of America News*, 17 January 2019.

align with CCP core interests." CSSAs exert direct political pressure, as well. For example, Chinese students studying in the United States have been told that candidates for upcoming CSSA elections who are CCP members would "receive preferential consideration."[32]

CSSAs have also worked "in tandem with Beijing to promote a pro-Chinese agenda and tamp down anti-Chinese speech on Western campuses."[33] Such organizations have protested a presentation about human rights violations in the PRC, harassed speakers and fellow students regarding positions on such issues as Tibet's sovereignty and the PRC's repression of Uighurs in East Turkestan, and attempted to censor comments at forums about relations between the PRC and Hong Kong.[34] In some instances, members of CSSAs and other PRC student groups have even been accused of spying for Beijing.[35] There is evidence that those groups work very similarly in Thailand.[36]

Finally, there are a growing number of Thai-Chinese cultural centers in Thailand that are supported by the PRC government and Chinese business groups. The Chinese Cultural Center in Bangkok, established by the PRC in 2012, was the first of its kind in Southeast Asia. These centers host cultural activities that are designed to enhance Thai appreciation of the PRC.[37] While there is nothing inherently wrong with celebrating culture, experience shows that such institutions are frequently used on behalf of larger PRC political warfare and influence operations that are detrimental to the interests of their host nations.

High-level Visits, Conferences, and Spies

As noted previously, high-level visits between Chinese and Thai officials are common now, having increased significantly since May 2014. These occasions include trips by Thai prime minister Prayut to Beijing and PRC president Xi Jinping to Bangkok, as well as routine visits made by many senior Thai officials to the PRC. Visits have also extended to other bilateral elements, including cabinet-level officials of nearly all Thai and PRC ministries, heads of businesses and banks, educators, and journalists.

It can be argued that this is simply normal diplomacy and not necessarily political warfare. However, these types of visits are the

[32] Bethany Allen-Ebrahimian, "China's Long Arm Reaches into American Campuses," *Foreign Policy*, 7 March 2018.
[33] Stephanie Saul, "On Campuses Far from China, Still under Beijing's Watchful Eye," *New York Times*, 4 May 2017.
[34] Gerry Shih and Emily Rauhala, "Angry over Campus Speech by Uighur Activist, Students in Canada Contact Chinese Consulate, Film Presentation," *Washington Post*, 14 February 2019.
[35] Saul, "On Campuses Far from China, Still under Beijing's Watchful Eye."
[36] Gershaneck, discussions with Thai and foreign academics.
[37] Tungkeunkunt, "China's Soft Power in Thailand."

heart of united front work, and they are certainly viewed in Beijing as indicators of the success of political warfare operations in Thailand. Visitors routinely appeal to shared economic interests and a common heritage and kinship between the Thai and Chinese people. For example, during a November 2018 visit to Thailand by Zhang Chunxian, vice chairman of the Standing Committee of the National People's Congress, Zhang repeatedly highlighted the "concrete benefits" that Thailand has received from the BRI and "encouraged Overseas Chinese to take the 'proximity advantage' of working with the PRC on it," according to the Thai-language *World Daily* newspaper.[38]

Further, when PRC foreign minister Wang Yi held "strategic consultations" with Thai foreign minister Don Pramudwinai in Chiang Mai in February 2019, Wang stated that "China and Thailand are comprehensive strategic cooperative partners" who can "enhance strategic communication, boost strategic cooperation and work together to make [a] positive contribution to [the] peace, stability and development of the region." He also said the PRC "is willing to join hands with Thailand to push forward the connection between the [BRI] and ASEAN's overall plan on connectivity, promote regional connectivity and sustainable development, successfully hold the China-ASEAN Year of Media Exchanges, lift the level of defense and security cooperation and press forward the development of China-ASEAN relations and the cooperation in East Asia to achieve greater progress." During these strategic consultations, Wang invited Thai prime minister Prayut to attend the second Belt and Road Forum for International Cooperation in Beijing, stating that he hoped Prayut's visit "will serve as an opportunity for the two countries to further boost mutually beneficial and friendly cooperation."[39]

Similarly, conferences and other forums held at major Thai education institutions and universities routinely reflect predominantly PRC participation and perspectives. Often there is a large official PRC contingent, with few or no American or other countervailing voices invited to attend. A think tank called the China Institutes of Contemporary International Relations funds, coordinates, and participates in many of these military and academic conferences as well as other forums and exchanges.[40] That think tank, however, is an arm of the Ministry of State Security, a prime PRC espionage organization that is noted as much for its worldwide disinformation and

---

38 Gershaneck, discussions with Thai and foreign academics.
39 "China, Thailand Hold Strategic Consultations," Xinhua News Agency (Beijing), 16 February 2019.
40 Gershaneck, discussions with Thai and foreign academics.

intelligence operations as for its conduct of legitimate research and analysis.[41]

Cyber Infiltration and Social Media Use

With some exceptions, Thai social media is not typically pro-PRC, so if one reads Thai, it is often easy to spot posts by a PRC-sponsored "online army" of internet trolls. Some bloggers are paid to post articles that will be widely viewed and are designed to change negative perceptions of the PRC. Because PRC tourists are a major irritant in social media complaints about the Chinese, the themes for suggested posts are often akin to "Chinese always look at Thais as friends, so Thais should do the same thing," or "Thais should understand the psychology of Chinese people: Chinese were poor before, so we should understand why they behave the way they do now."[42]

Some websites and bloggers that have garnered popularity in Thailand, such as the New Eastern Outlook, are reportedly sponsored by Russia but contain pro-PRC propaganda themes and messages. There is also some evidence that the PRC-aligned "50-Cent Party" or "50 Cent Army," made up of PRC-paid online commentators who are hired to manipulate public opinion and attack PRC critics and other targets in support of the CCP, does try to influence Thai public opinion. For now, however, those commentators are not perceived as being powerfully influential, as their posts are often poorly written and "childishly worded."[43]

Sometimes the PRC's ultra-nationalist internet trolls, derisively called "Little Pinks," push Thai online audiences in ways that cause the Thais to push back. In April 2020, after a Thai actor "liked" a photograph on Twitter that listed Hong Kong as a country, PRC trolls inundated his social media platforms, and the actor apologized for his "lack of caution [in] talking about Hong Kong." But PRC netizens continued to attack both the actor and his girlfriend, dredging up other alleged transgressions, aided by large propaganda outlets like the *Global Times*. That is when Thais started hitting back online, and the trolling campaign ultimately failed.[44]

[41] Bill Gertz, "Chinese Think Tank Also Serves as Spy Arm," *Washington Times*, 28 September 2011.
[42] Gershaneck, discussions with Thai and foreign academics.
[43] Gershaneck, discussions with Thai and foreign academics.
[44] James Griffiths, "Nnevvy: Chinese Troll Campaign on Twitter Exposes a Potentially Dangerous Disconnect with the Wider World," CNN, 15 April 2020.

CHAPTER SEVEN

PRC Political Warfare against Taiwan: An Overview

We must liberate Taiwan. Although the PRC's planned 1950 invasion of Taiwan was foiled by its intervention in the Korean War, this 1977 propaganda poster supported Beijing's psychological warfare against Taipei and Washington, with Beijing's continuing threat to seize the island by force. Unification with Taiwan remains the primary PRC political warfare objective today.

An overview of Taiwan's relationship with China is necessary to understand the basis of the People's Republic of China's (PRC) sovereignty claims on Taiwan as well as the conduct of its political warfare operations against the island nation. Cross-strait relations between the PRC in mainland China and the Republic of China (ROC) on Taiwan have been much more extensively addressed in academic literature than Sino-Thai relations, so this chapter is structured somewhat differently than chapter five, providing less of a general historical background and focusing more closely on specific aspects of the contentious PRC-Taiwan-ROC relationships and the role of political warfare in those relations.

Mark Stokes and Russell Hsiao at the Project 2049 Institute identify Taiwan as the principal target of PRC political warfare. Political warfare is still the PRC's primary means of destroying the ROC and "reuniting" Taiwan with Communist China. Taiwan's democratic system of government, they say, "presents an existential challenge to [the] political authority" of the Chinese Communist Party (CCP). Moreover, Beijing seeks the "political subordination of the ROC to the PRC under a 'One Country, Two Systems' principle."[1] The CCP's desired final resolution of the Chinese Civil War entails the destruction of the ROC as a political entity and the absorption of Taiwan into the PRC. Beijing prefers to win this last phase of the civil war without resorting to brute military force, though PRC president Xi Jinping has made it clear that he will employ force if he deems it necessary.

Cross-Straits Relations: The Political Status of Taiwan

Chapter three details much of the general history of the PRC's political warfare operations, a great deal of it focused against the ROC and Taiwan, so this overview centers on the question of what political entity currently exercises sovereignty over Taiwan. It is important to examine the evolution of Taiwan's relationship with what eventually became China, its relations with the PRC after its founding in 1949, and the enduring civil war between the CCP and the ROC's Chinese Nationalist Kuomintang (KMT) party.

Reasons for the PRC's relentless political warfare against Taiwan are straightforward. From the 1920s until 1949, Mao Zedong's CCP battled Chiang Kai-shek's KMT for control of China. The CCP eventually prevailed and drove the KMT-led government of the ROC from the mainland to Taiwan. Mao and the CCP then established the PRC, which claimed sovereignty over the entirety of its ever-evolving definition of "China," including Taiwan. However, because the KMT never surrendered, the Chinese Civil War never technically ended, and while the ROC no longer claims to govern all of China, it still asserts its status as a sovereign state on Taiwan.[2]

With American support, the ROC has evolved from an authoritarian government to a vibrant democracy. The PRC, meanwhile, quickly established a tyrannical dictatorship on mainland China that caused the deaths of millions of its own citizens and inflamed insurgencies and civil wars worldwide. Over time, it evolved into an economically and militarily powerful totalitarian state possessing a highly sophisticated political warfare apparatus.

---

[1] Mark Stokes and Russell Hsiao, *The People's Liberation Army General Political Department: Political Warfare with Chinese Characteristics* (Arlington, VA: Project 2049 Institute, 2013), 3.
[2] Steven M. Goldstein, *China and Taiwan* (Malden, MA: Polity Press, 2015), 1–3.

Central to the PRC's legitimacy is its "One China" principle. The simple PRC definition of this principle states that "there is only one China in the world, Taiwan is a part of China, and the government of the PRC is the sole legal government representing the whole of China."[3] The PRC is increasingly capable of forcing the international community to accept its definitions of One China and to acquiesce to, if not wholly support, PRC policies and objectives.

Since most nations now recognize the PRC as the legitimate government of China, the ROC has been increasingly isolated diplomatically.[4] Nevertheless, Taiwan continues to resist the PRC's efforts to persuade or coerce it to abandon its independent status and become a province of the PRC, and it continues to obtain the support needed for its survival. Historical reasons for Taiwan not readily acquiescing to Beijing's coercion include its minimal ties to imperial China's rulers over thousands of years, its close relationship with Japan that was forged by half a century as Tokyo's first colony, and clear recognition of the repressive nature of the CCP. In recent years, reasons also include the trend of "Taiwanization" as the majority of Taiwan's residents now prefer to identify as Taiwanese rather than Chinese.[5]

These factors have strongly shaped Taiwan's political landscape for more than 70 years. Especially significant in historical memory is the bloody repression of Taiwanese citizens by the KMT, including the 28 February 1947 massacre of tens of thousands of civilians by KMT troops. A contemporaneous *New York Times* article cites an eyewitness account that "troops from the mainland arrived [in Taiwan on] March 7 and indulged in three days of indiscriminate killing and looting. For a time everyone seen on the streets was shot at, homes were broken into and occupants killed. In the poorer sections the streets were said to have been littered with dead. There were instances of beheadings and mutilation of bodies, and women were raped."[6] The brutal KMT repression did end there. To this day, that watershed event and its underlying causes create strong Taiwanese antipathy for being absorbed into mainland China.[7]

Following the retreat of the ROC government to Taiwan in 1949, Chiang suspended the nation's constitution and excluded Taiwanese from all but the lowest levels of government. The KMT tried to

[3] "White Paper: The One-China Principle and the Taiwan Issue," Taiwan Affairs Office and Information Office of the State Council, People's Republic of China, 21 February 2000.
[4] Taiwan's overseas presence is extensive, with offices in 73 countries, but most of these missions are unofficial and have no formal status. See Michael Reilly, "Lessons for Taiwan's Diplomacy from Its Handing of the Coronavirus Pandemic," Global Taiwan Institute, Global Taiwan Brief 5, no. 9, 6 May 2020.
[5] Kat Devlin and Christine Huang, "In Taiwan, Views of Mainland China Mostly Negative: Closer Taiwan-U.S. Relations Largely Welcomed, Especially Economically," Pew Research Center, 12 May 2020.
[6] Tillman Durdin, "Formosa Killings Are Put at 10,000: Foreigners Say the Chinese Slaughtered Demonstrators without Provocation," *New York Times*, 29 March 1947.
[7] Goldstein, *China and Taiwan*, 5–6.

"Sinify" the Taiwanese population by imposing mainland Chinese values, history, and language to replace those of Taiwan, which led to resistance. Since democratization in the 1980s, the people of Taiwan strengthened their identity as Taiwanese and viewed the ROC and PRC governments in Taipei and Beijing, respectively, are political equals. Today, many Taiwanese do not believe that Taiwan is a part of China and believe that Taiwan should be independent.[8] Research shows this trend accelerating. In the 30-to-49-year-old age group, those who self-identify as strictly Taiwanese is at 64 percent, while the 50-years-old-and-up group is at 60 percent. Most significantly, in the rising 18- to 29-year-old age group, 83 percent view themselves as strictly Taiwanese.[9]

Taiwan and the United States

The United States has played a central role in allowing Taiwan breathing space to follow its own political path. Accordingly, any discussion of relations between the PRC and ROC, as well as PRC political warfare operations against Taiwan, must include a discussion of U.S. relations with each country. The United States supported the KMT in both the Second Sino-Japanese War and the Chinese Civil War. Although U.S. president Harry S. Truman was inclined to allow the PRC to take control of Taiwan as late as January 1950, he quickly reversed course after the PRC-backed North Korean invasion of South Korea in June of that year.[10]

Since then, the United States has supported the ROC government on Taiwan while remaining ambiguous as to the final sovereignty of the island nation. Since the 1950s, American administrations have employed military forces to defend the ROC against PRC aggression, such as when President William J. "Bill" Clinton deployed two aircraft carrier battle groups to the Taiwan Strait area as a show of force to halt the PRC's threatening missile launches that bracketed Taiwan in 1996. Following the United States' official recognition of the PRC in 1979, Congress ensured the continuation of unofficial diplomatic relations with Taiwan under the guarantees provided by the Taiwan Relations Act (TRA).[11]

While the TRA and U.S. president Ronald W. Reagan's "Six Assurances" afforded Taiwan some confidence the United States would not abandon the island republic, the United States imposed several

---

[8] Goldstein, *China and Taiwan*, 5–6.
[9] Devlin and Huang, "In Taiwan, Views of Mainland China Mostly Negative."
[10] Goldstein, *China and Taiwan*, 19–21.
[11] Taiwan Relations Act, Pub L. No. 96-8, 93 Stat. 14 (1979).

unwritten rules and regulations on the relationship.[12] These self-imposed prohibitions included not allowing the five top officials of Taiwan to come to Washington, not allowing higher level U.S. officials to meet with their Taiwanese counterparts, and not referring to Taiwan as a country.[13]

The triangular relationship between the PRC, the ROC, and the United States has ebbed and flowed since Sino-American rapprochement in the early 1970s. Washington's policy is currently one of "dual deterrence" toward both Beijing and Taipei. U.S. concerns include maintaining the confidence of its allies and friends in the Asia-Pacific region and domestic political constituencies by continuing to support democratic Taiwan against an increasingly assertive China, as well as ensuring that provocative policies resulting from Taiwan's democratic politics do not trigger a violent PRC response. In this dual-deterrence balancing act, the United States has been consistent in its support for a peaceful resolution to the cross-strait impasse.[14]

Since U.S. president Donald J. Trump took office in January 2017, relations between Taiwan and the United States have improved, and they appear set to remain strong as outlined in a recent report from the president to Congress.[15] This support has been consistent: as one example, during an October 2018 speech, Vice President Michael R. "Mike" Pence highlighted the importance of Taiwan-U.S. relations and concluded that "America will always believe that Taiwan's embrace of democracy shows a better path for all the Chinese people."[16]

As continuing indicators of improved relations, in March 2018 President Trump signed the Taiwan Travel Act, which allows high-level diplomatic engagement between Taiwanese and American officials and encourages visits between government officials of the United States and Taiwan at all levels.[17] Further, in March 2020, President Trump signed the Taiwan Allies International Protection and Enhancement Initiative (TAIPEI) Act, designed to increase the scope of U.S. relations with Taiwan and encourage other nations and international organizations to strengthen ties with Taiwan. Of note, the TAIPEI Act intends to "send a strong message to nations

---

[12] Harvey Feldman, "President Reagan's Six Assurances to Taiwan and Their Meaning Today," Heritage Foundation, 2 October 2007.

[13] Gerrit van der Wees, "The Taiwan Travel Act in Context," *Diplomat*, 19 March 2018.

[14] Goldstein, *China and Taiwan*, 3–8.

[15] Donald J. Trump, "United States Strategic Approach to the People's Republic of China," White House, 20 May 2020.

[16] Michael J. Pence, "Remarks by Vice President Pence on the Administration's Policy toward China" (speech, Hudson Institute, Washington, DC, 4 October 2018).

[17] van der Wees, "The Taiwan Travel Act in Context."

that there will be consequences for supporting Chinese actions that undermine Taiwan."[18]

The United States has a One China policy, as Pence noted in his speech, but it is not, of course, the same as the PRC's interpretation. While the PRC's own One China principle offers a useful political warfare narrative, it is largely a myth.

The Myth of "One China"

It is currently the PRC's position that there is only one China, and that Taiwan has always been a part of it. PRC propagandists relentlessly drive home this narrative regarding Taiwan as they do concerning Mongolia, Tibet, Xinjiang, and any other territory that suits its current expansionist aspirations. Historian Edward L. Dreyer explains the insidious effect of this narrative:

> [The "One China" narrative] permits the PRC to deny the legitimacy of any aspirations to independence on the part of the Tibetans, Uighurs, Mongols, or any other minority ethnic group. Since their territories have "always" been part of "China," their histories are, in some sense, part of Chinese history, even if the peoples in question are not native speakers of Chinese and do not identify with the dominant Han nationality. If Taiwan has always been part of China, then surely the PRC government has the right to 'reunify' the island with the mainland, even though the PRC has never exercised any authority over Taiwan.[19]

History neither bears out the claim of One China, nor of China's sovereignty over Taiwan. Throughout recorded history, China was divided for very long periods of time—indeed, for more than 3,000 years, disunity was more common than unity. The "unified China" of PRC mythology consisted primarily of the 18 provinces south of the Mongolian-Manchurian grassland and east of the Himalayas. Taiwan was not part of this empire. Further, Dreyer wrote, "Twice in history China has been part of a multinational empire ruled by non-Chinese people. The Mongol Yuan Dynasty was overthrown by the Ming in 1368, and after the Ming the Manchu Qing Dynasty ruled China from 1644 to 1912."[20]

The Qing initially kept the Chinese and non-Chinese parts of

---

[18] Stacy Hsu et al., "Trump Signs TAIPEI Act into Law," *Focus Taiwan* (Taipei), 27 March 2020.
[19] Edward L. Dreyer, "The Myth of 'One China'," in Peter C. Y. Chow, ed., *The "One China" Dilemma* (New York: Palgrave Macmillan, 2008), 19, https://doi.org/10.1057/9780230611931_2.
[20] Dreyer, "The Myth of 'One China'," 20.

their empire separate, keeping Han Chinese away from Manchuria, Inner and Outer Mongolia, Tibet, and Xinjiang. Toward the end of the dynasty, however, distinctions between Chinese and non-Chinese parts of the Qing empire broke down, and provincial administration became the norm beyond China's traditional boundaries. Major reasons for ending the exclusion of Chinese from the rest of the empire included the mass migration of Chinese into Manchuria and Mongolia and the strengthened ability of the Qing to exercise more consistent control over the region in the face of an "aggressive and expansionist Russian Empire."[21] The extension of Chinese-style administration during the late nineteenth century contributed to the myth of One China existing since ancient times.

Also adding to the false belief of One China was the fact that events were dated "according to the reign of kings or the [names of eras] decreed by emperors." Dreyer argues that this approach to historiography "forced historians to choose a legitimate ruler for every year, even when political authority was actually divided among regimes of comparable strength." For example, of the 1,363 years illustrated in Sima Guang's *Zizhi Tongjian* ("Comprehensive Mirror for Aid in Government"), published in 1084 ACE, China only had a "degree of political unity" for approximately 570 years. The remaining years saw "either independent warlords challenging or ignoring imperil authority, or two or more rival dynasties claiming royal or imperil titles." Even during the seemingly unified periods, massive rebellions occurred.[22]

The Dutch settled on Taiwan in 1624 after abandoning their original outpost in the Pescadores Islands. Following a major survey of the island four years later, they found that it was largely inhabited by aboriginal villagers, with coastal villages harboring at most a few hundred Chinese from Fujian. It was not until 1636, when the Dutch began importing Chinese contract laborers to work their rice and sugar plantations, that a sizable Chinese population began to grow on Taiwan, but initially even these laborers stayed for only a few years, eventually returning to Fujian and taking their earnings with them. Australian historian J. Bruce Jacobs notes that there "were no permanent Chinese communities in Taiwan until the Dutch imported Chinese as laborers," and that "Chinese who came during and after the Dutch period did not think of themselves as 'Chinese'," but rather adopted more local identities based on where they emigrated from.[23]

[21] Dreyer, "The Myth of 'One China'," 20, 26.
[22] Dreyer, "The Myth of 'One China'," 21–22.
[23] Dreyer, "The Myth of 'One China'," 26; and J. Bruce Jacobs, "Paradigm Shift Needed on Taiwan," *Taipei Times* (Taiwan), 16 November 2018.

That is not to say, however, that China and its culture did not impact Taiwan over the centuries. While China and Taiwan were never well-integrated, Taiwan's political, social, cultural, and economic systems all evolved in China's shadow. And although Taiwan was settled initially by peoples from the Malay and Polynesian regions, it was also a major recipient of migrants from mainland China, who brought with them Han Chinese culture, Hokkien and Minnan dialects, and various religious beliefs. The Confucian family system, in particular, eventually dominated Taiwanese society.[24]

Otherwise largely unknown and ignored by China, Taiwan was annexed by the Qing Dynasty in 1684 to prevent its continued use by pirates who were loyal to the Ming.[25] During the seventeenth century, the saga of Koxinga (a.k.a. Zheng Chenggong), a Chinese Ming loyalist who resisted the Qing in mainland China and established a dynasty on Taiwan, unfolded. Koxinga's is a swashbuckling, colorful story involving betrayal, murder, and massive land and sea warfare among pirates, the Dutch, and the Qing. Koxinga's victory over the Dutch on Taiwan in 1662 would later play into PRC political warfare narratives regarding the "liberation" of Taiwan by Chinese from the mainland and victory over foreign colonialism and imperialism.

As Taiwan often served as Koxinga's base of operations, Chinese interest in the nearby island grew.[26] The Qing finally perceived the need to annex Taiwan to control the pirate fleets in the Pescadores Islands, which they did in 1684. Qing-appointed officials on Taiwan reported to the provincial governor of Fujian, but the Qing did not establish normal governance systems on the island, indicating a reluctance to assume permanent annexation. This hesitancy appeared validated during a major rebellion on Taiwan against the Qing in 1786–88.[27] In fact, revolt and rebellion against the Qing on Taiwan were quite common, according to historian George H. Kerr: "Two centuries of ineffective and abusive rule thereafter generated a local Formosan tradition of resentment and underlying hostility toward representatives of mainland authority. Riots and abortive independence movements took place so often that it became common in China to say of Formosa, 'Every three years an uprising; every five years a rebellion'." Kerr notes that there were more than 30 "violent outbursts" in the nineteenth century alone.[28]

In another complex series of events, the issue of Qing sovereign-

---

[24] Steve Yui-Sang Tsang, ed., *In the Shadow of China: Political Development in Taiwan since 1949* (Honolulu, HI: University of Hawai'i Press, 1993), 169–71.

[25] Dreyer, "The Myth of 'One China'," 20.

[26] George H. Kerr, *Formosa Betrayed*, 2d ed. (Upland, CA: Taiwan Publishing, 1992), 26.

[27] Dreyer, "The Myth of 'One China'," 28.

[28] Kerr, *Formosa Betrayed*, 26.

ty over Taiwan became a thorn in the Chinese dynasty's side regarding relations with a modernizing Japan. After the Meiji Restoration of 1868, Japan annexed the Ryukyu kingdom, which then comprised the Ryukyu Islands between Kyushu and Taiwan. When Taiwanese aborigines murdered 54 shipwrecked Ryukyuan sailors in 1871, an inept Qing "foreign ministry" did not recognize Japan's rule of the Ryukyus and disclaimed responsibility for the actions of the aborigines, thereby effectively renouncing sovereignty over Taiwan. Japan eventually sent a naval expedition to exact retribution. The outcome was the eventual Qing recognition of Japan's claim to the Ryukyus and Japan's recognition of the Qing's claim to Taiwan.

During the subsequent Sino-French War (1884–85) and several internal rebellions, the Qing extended greater control over Taiwan and began modernizing the island in ways that were more European than Chinese. Paved streets, electric lights, a modern postal service, and the beginnings of railway and telegraph systems, all of which did not yet exist on the mainland, signified an evolving Taiwanese society that was different than that in mainland China.[29]

Japan's expansionist vision would accelerate Taiwan's modernization in ways that were unforeseen by the island's Qing-appointed governor. The First Sino-Japanese War (1894–95) proved disastrous to the Qing, as Japan won quick victories on land and sea. Consequently, the Qing ceded to Japan, "in perpetuity and full sovereignty," Taiwan and the Pescadores Islands, as dictated by the Treaty of Shimonoseki of 17 April 1895. "Perpetuity," however, lasted just 50 years, for Japan would exercise sovereignty over Taiwan only until 1945.[30]

The 1895 Treaty of Shimonoseki remains significant to this day, for it represents the last occasion in history that Taiwan's territorial sovereignty has been subject to an international accord. Also notable is the fact that Britain's minister to China, Sir Thomas F. Wade, and a former U.S. secretary of state, John W. Foster, were in effect "godfathers" to the treaty, since both England and the United States helped craft the agreement.[31]

The Taiwanese, displeased with their inept Qing rulers and unhappy with the treaty, proclaimed independence as the Republic of Formosa in May 1895 and attempted to fight back against the Japanese occupation of their country. By the end of October, however, Japanese forces had defeated all organized Taiwanese resistance, and Asia's first independent republic was crushed.[32]

[29] Dreyer, "The Myth of 'One China'," 28–29.
[30] Dreyer, "The Myth of 'One China'," 20, 29.
[31] Kerr, *Formosa Betrayed*, 27.
[32] Dreyer, "The Myth of 'One China'," 29–30.

The Japanese proceeded to do more than simply occupy Taiwan—they incorporated Taiwan into Japan's national territory, much like the Ryukyu Islands had been in 1879. Japan's rule was, by Imperial Japanese standards, relatively humane, unlike the brutal treatment it imposed on later colonial conquests such as Korea, the Philippines, and China. This immersion of the Taiwanese into Japanese culture resulted in a people who "seemed more Japanese than Chinese . . . they spoke Japanese, dressed like Japanese, ate Japanese food, and, in some cases, had Japanese names."[33] Ultimately, the people of Taiwan would pay a terrible price under Chinese rule for their Japanese assimilation.

Taiwan, the Republic of China, and Mao Zedong

After Sun Yat-sen's successful revolution in mainland China and the establishment of the ROC on 12 February 1912, the new republic accepted all the Qing Dynasty's treaty obligations and debts. Foreign nations recognized the ROC's sovereignty over all Qing territory as of 1911—which did not include Taiwan, then still a part of Japan.[34] This was the perspective of both the Nationalist KMT and CCP camps for more than 30 years.

During the Second Sino-Japanese War (1937–45) and World War II (1939–45), CCP leader Mao Zedong initially considered Taiwan a separate, occupied nation and supported the idea that Taiwan should be made independent after the war. Several CCP documents and polices from this era reinforce the idea that Mao viewed Taiwan as distinctly separate from China."[35] The most notable evidence of Mao's position can be found in his statement to Edgar P. Snow, an American journalist and CCP sympathizer, made in July 1936. Snow asked, "Is it the immediate task of the Chinese people to regain all the territories lost to Japanese imperialism, or only to drive Japan from North China, and all Chinese territory above the Great Wall?" According to Snow's account, Mao answered:

> It is the immediate task of China to regain all our lost territories, not merely to defend our sovereignty below the Great Wall. This means that Manchuria must be regained. We do not, however, include Korea, formerly a Chinese colony, but when we have re-established the independence of the lost territories of China, and if the Koreans wish to break away from the chains of Japanese

[33] Goldstein, *China and Taiwan*, 14.
[34] Dreyer, "The Myth of 'One China'," 30.
[35] Frank S. T. Hsiao and Lawrence R. Sullivan, "The Chinese Communist Party and the Status of Taiwan, 1928–1943," *Pacific Affairs* 52, no. 3 (Autumn 1979): 446–67, https://doi.org/10.2307/2757657.

imperialism, we will extend them our enthusiastic help in their struggle for independence. The same thing applies for Formosa.[36]

Key CCP documents dated before 1943 routinely addressed Taiwan, but never in the context that Taiwan was part of China. It was often referred to as an ally, much like Korea, in the fight against its Japanese occupiers. Between 1928 and 1943, the CCP consistently recognized Taiwan as a distinct "nation" or "nationality" and acknowledged the "national liberation movement" on Taiwan as a struggle of a "weak and small nationality" that was separate from the Chinese revolution and potentially sovereign. The CCP frequently called for forming a united front with the Taiwanese—specifically the small Taiwanese Communist Party (TCP)—"not because Taiwanese were derivatives of the same Han stock, nor because Taiwanese were also Chinese," but because Taiwan was a small, weak nation oppressed by Japanese imperialism.[37]

The nature of the CCP's early support for the TCP is significant. Established on 15 April 1928 in Shanghai, the TCP was founded as a Nationality Branch of the Japanese Communist Party by order of the Communist International (Comintern). Though the five Taiwanese who attended the convention were CCP members, they supported Taiwan's independence with such slogans as "Long Live the Independence of the Taiwan Nationality," "Overthrow Japanese Imperialism," and "Establish a Republic of Taiwan." In its "Resolution on the Outline of Organization," the TCP cited the 1895 establishment of the Republic of Taiwan as justification for national independence.[38]

After 1943, however, the CCP reversed these positions to be consistent with ROC leader Chiang Kai-shek's views, disavowing Taiwanese ethnic "separateness" and rejecting the independence of political movements on the island. The Allies' Cairo Declaration of 27 November 1943 called for the "unconditional surrender of Japan" and stated that "all the territories Japan has stolen from the Chinese, such as Manchuria, Formosa, and the Pescadores, shall be restored to the Republic of China."[39] The Cairo Declaration was neither a treaty nor a legally binding document, but it is often referred to by both the CCP and KMT as justification for China's claim to Taiwan. Of equal concern, the declaration was historically inaccurate: Taiwan was not "stolen" from China, unless U.S. president Franklin D.

[36] Edgar Snow, *Red Star Over China: The Rise of the Red Army* (London: V. Gollancz, 1937), 88–89. Taiwan was also known as Formosa while under Japanese rule from 1895 to 1945.
[37] Hsiao and Sullivan, "The Chinese Communist Party and the Status of Taiwan," 451.
[38] Hsiao and Sullivan, "The Chinese Communist Party and the Status of Taiwan," 455.
[39] Dreyer, "The Myth of 'One China'," 31–32.

Roosevelt and British prime minister Sir Winston L. S. Churchill believed the United States and England were coconspirators in the theft while helping broker the 1895 Treaty of Shimonoseki. But both wanted to keep China in the war against Imperial Japan at a time when Chiang Kai-shek appeared to be considering a separate agreement with Tokyo to end the fighting in China.[40]

Consistent with the Cairo Declaration, ROC forces accepted the Japanese surrender of Taiwan on 25 October 1945, signifying that the declaration's provisions had been carried out in good faith and were supported by the United States and the larger international community.[41] Although Taiwan's population initially greeted the Chinese mainlanders as liberators, they did not fare will under Chiang's forces, who were "a rag-tag army of often ignorant, undisciplined recruits."[42] The KMT troops treated the Taiwanese with disdain, viewing the islanders as more Japanese than Chinese. The occupying Chinese also resented the fact that Taiwan was prosperous and technologically advanced by mainland Chinese standards and had been spared most of the ravages of the war that mainland China had seen. This disdain took the form of political repression on many levels, most significantly by Taiwanese being excluded from the ROC constitution that was to go into effect in late 1947.

The ROC government, meanwhile, ruled in a corrupt and ineffective way that was far different than how the Japanese authorities had ruled. George H. Kerr, a U.S. naval officer and later a diplomat who was on assignment in Taiwan at the time, described the rapacious nature of the Nationalist rule:

> Looting was carried forward on three levels . . . the military scavengers were at work at the lowest level. Anything movable . . . was fair prey for ragged and undisciplined soldiers. It was a first wave of petty theft, taking place in every city street and suburban village. . . . The second stage of looting was entered when the senior military men . . . organized depots with forwarding agents at the ports through which they began to ship out military and civilian supplies. Next [KMT governor Chen Yi's] own men developed a firm control of all industrial raw materials, agricultural stockpiles and confiscated real properties turned over to them by the vanquished Japanese.[43]

---

[40] Kerr, *Formosa Betrayed*, 25–27.
[41] Goldstein, *China and Taiwan*, 18.
[42] Goldstein, *China and Taiwan*, 14.
[43] Kerr, *Formosa Betrayed*, 114–15.

Chen Yi established monopolies over every economic sector to squeeze Formosans out of business and industry, which caused the cost of living to skyrocket. For example, the cost of foodstuffs shot up 700 percent between November 1945 and January 1947. The Formosan middle class "began to vanish . . . and unemployment became a grave problem." These factors, wrote Kerr, were "the ultimate cause of the 1947 rebellion."[44]

A minor street incident involving official corruption and police brutality sparked the 28 February 1947 massacre of thousands of civilians by mainland KMT troops, during which Taiwan's political, business, and intellectual elites were methodically hunted down, arrested, tortured, and killed and the general populace faced random killings and other sadistic atrocities. Estimates of deaths range from 10,000 to more than 20,000.[45] The protests led to 38 years of authoritarian suppression by the ROC, a period now known as the "White Terror."[46] The ROC denied subsequent pleas from Taiwanese that "Formosans" be entitled to the same rights and treatment as Chinese.[47]

The Chinese Civil War had reignited on the mainland shortly after the end of World War II, and by 1949, KMT armies had fallen back before the increasing victorious CCP forces. Roughly 1.2 million—though some estimates extend up to more than 2 million—mainland Chinese escaped to Taiwan, many of them military personnel and civilian administrators. In May, the ROC expanded its authoritarian rule over Taiwan by imposing martial law and by suspending articles of the constitution. That December, ROC president Chiang Kai-shek and his government evacuated to Taiwan, designating the island as a province under the ROC, which still claimed to rule all of China, and establishing the new national capital at Taipei.[48]

Although comprising only about 15 percent of Taiwan's population, mainland Chinese dominated major government, military, and political positions. Discussion of Taiwanese nationalism or opposition to the KMT was equated with "communist sympathies" and was suppressed as part of the ROC's "de-Japanization and Sinicization" campaign. Consequently, Taiwanese were regularly subjected to systematic harsh treatment.[49] In addition to Communist sympathizers and those merely alleged to be so, the secret police also brutally suppressed the cadre of Taiwan elites who advocated for U.S. trusteeship

[44] Kerr, *Formosa Betrayed*, 114–15.
[45] Goldstein, *China and Taiwan*, 14–15; and Kerr, *Formosa Betrayed*, 310.
[46] Russell Hsiao, "Political Warfare Alert: CCP-TDSGL Appropriates Taiwan's 2-28 Incident," Global Taiwan Institute, Global Taiwan Brief 2, no. 9, 1 March 2017.
[47] Goldstein, *China and Taiwan*, 15.
[48] Goldstein, *China and Taiwan*, 15.
[49] Goldstein, *China and Taiwan*, 15–16.

over Taiwan.[50] Some analysts estimate that as many as 90,000 people were arrested during the White Terror, with about 10,000 actually tried in military courts and some 45,000 summarily executed. Many of those detained were tortured, and many who were not executed were sent "indefinitely" to an infamous Green Island prison camp on off Taiwan's southeast coast.[51]

Historian J. Bruce Jacobs summarizes the KMT regime under the Chiang Kai-shek and his son Chiang Ching-kuo as "rule by outsiders in the interests of the outsiders. It was a dictatorship in which Taiwanese had no power and in which Taiwanese suffered massive and systematic discrimination."[52] Although the ROC suppressed the study of Taiwan's complex history and stressed Taiwan's ties with China, the distinction between the *waisheng ren*, mainlanders from outside the province, and the *bensheng ren*, people from the province, became the focal point for political and cultural division.

Political Warfare in the Continuing Chinese Civil War

Russell Hsiao writes that during the Chinese Civil War, both CCP and KMT forces "spread false information to sow discord in enemy-controlled areas, spreading rumors about defections, falsifying enemy attack plans, and stirring up unrest in an effort to misdirect enemy planning."[53] The onset of the Second Sino-Japanese War and World War II had, however, led to a united front between the two factions and a truce of sorts.

According to Mark Stokes and Hsiao, CCP underground political warfare during that period was divided into several organizations. The Urban Work Department, precursor to the United Front Work Department (UFWD), "focused on ordinary citizens, minorities, students, factory workers, and urban residents." The Social Work Department "concentrated on the upper social elite of enemy civilian authorities, security of senior CCP leaders, and Comintern liaison." Finally, the Enemy Work Department was "responsible for political warfare against opposing military forces."[54]

These departments sought to fulfill three main missions: to "build and sustain a united front with friendly, sympathetic military figures," to "undermine the cohesion and morale of the senior en-

---

[50] Kerr, *Formosa Betrayed*, 369.
[51] Jonathan Manthorpe, *Forbidden Nation: A History of Taiwan* (New York: Palgrave Macmillan, 2005), 204–7.
[52] Jacobs, "Paradigm Shift Needed on Taiwan."
[53] Russell Hsiao, "CCP Propaganda against Taiwan Enters the Social Age," Jamestown Foundation, China Brief 18, no. 7, 24 April 2018.
[54] Stokes and Hsiao, *The People's Liberation Army General Political Department*, 6–7.

emy leaders and create tensions between officer and enlisted ranks," and to "win over and incite defection among those in the middle." Emphasis was placed on "psychological and ideological conditioning of senior enemy defense authorities in order to weaken national will, generate sympathy for CCP strategic goals, and develop clandestine sources of military intelligence." Strategies used included "financial incentives, shame, and promises of leniency."[55]

The surrender of Imperial Japan in September 1945 marked a new chapter in the Chinese Civil War. Having conserved the strength of its Enemy Work Department during the war, the CCP quickly shifted its political warfare efforts from resisting Japan to defeating the KMT and ROC government. Despite the recognition of both parties' legitimacy in October 1945, the civil war recommenced shortly thereafter.[56]

Targeting Taiwan

In 1946, the CCP established the Taiwan Provincial Work Committee, which was "responsible for integrated political-military operations to subvert ROC forces on Taiwan."[57] Cai Xiaoqian, a Taiwanese native, was made secretary general of the committee. Cai had left Taiwan in 1924 to study at Shanghai University, and he was an original standing committee member of the Taiwanese branch of the Japanese Communist Party when it formed four years later. In 1938, he was made director of the CCP's Enemy Work Department, and he deployed to Taiwan in 1946 to conduct united front work in preparation for Chinese occupation of the island. Another Taiwanese native, Cai Xiao, was tasked with training enemy work operatives in Taiwan.

There was also a large pool of Formosans in China from which the CCP could recruit. Many individuals from old, well-established Formosan communities in coastal cities were unable to escape back to Taiwan or elsewhere in the face of the Red Army onslaught. In addition, there was a "very large number of young men who were labor-conscripts in the Japanese Army, stranded in China in 1945 wherever Japanese forces had surrendered." Thousands had no jobs and no place to go, and they were treated roughly by Nationalist forces as "Japanized traitors." Moreover, in 1947, many young men and women from Taiwan sought refuge in China following the 28 February massacre, embittered at the KMT for its brutal abuse and at the United States for not stopping those cruelties. Many "recruits" sim-

---

[55] Stokes and Hsiao, *The People's Liberation Army General Political Department*, 7–8.
[56] Stokes and Hsiao, *The People's Liberation Army General Political Department*, 8.
[57] Stokes and Hsiao, *The People's Liberation Army General Political Department*, 8.

ply had no choice, for refusal to assist the CCP meant being branded a "reactionary" and doomed to an inevitable execution. Many of these Formosans were sent for "re-education" and subversion and sabotage training at the Taiwan Recovery Training Corps camp near Shanghai.[58]

According to Stokes and Hsiao, "Intensified [People's Liberation Army (PLA)] political warfare operations on Taiwan began after the fall of Shanghai in May 1949, when the CCP began deliberate planning for an amphibious invasion that was anticipated in April 1950."[59] Hsiao explains that after the ROC government moved to Taiwan in 1949, "the two sides flooded propaganda and disinformation into enemy-controlled territories to affect public opinion and troop morale."[60] As Communist pamphlets and books were smuggled into Taiwan, Beijing's initial efforts focused on recruiting mainland Chinese officers of the Nationalist army to sabotage Chiang's defense of Taiwan, and to "come home" by defecting to the CCP. While that ploy had worked well with many Nationalist officers during the war on the mainland, it was less successful among those who escaped to Taiwan. Accordingly, subsequent PRC propaganda focused on subverting the mainland civilian refugees there. Meanwhile, the CCP used Hong Kong to facilitate networking between Formosan Communists in Japan, China, and Taiwan.[61]

The following year, ROC counterintelligence operatives revealed the covert CCP operation on Taiwan, resulting in the arrest of Cai Xiaoqian. Cai was recruited by the KMT, and more than 400 CCP agents on the island were subsequently exposed. Other CCP agents escaped to Hong Kong and joined the newly formed Taiwan Democratic Self-Government League, a CCP-backed pro-unification organization that remains in existence today.[62]

In June 1950, North Korea invaded South Korea, igniting the Korean War. United Nations (UN) forces deployed to the peninsula to aid South Korea, and U.S. president Harry S. Truman ordered the U.S. Navy's Seventh Fleet to thwart any foreign attack on Taiwan. Although Chiang Kai-shek volunteered ROC troops to fight alongside the UN forces in Korea, they were not deployed due to U.S. fears of widening the war and involving the PRC. Nonetheless, the PRC attacked UN forces in Korea in October 1950.[63] The Political Department of the Chinese People's Volunteer Army was responsible for all

[58] Kerr, *Formosa Betrayed*, 437–38.
[59] Stokes and Hsiao, *The People's Liberation Army General Political Department*, 8.
[60] Hsiao, "CCP Propaganda against Taiwan Enters the Social Age."
[61] Kerr, *Formosa Betrayed*, 438–41.
[62] Stokes and Hsiao, *The People's Liberation Army General Political Department*, 8.
[63] Goldstein, *China and Taiwan*, 19–20.

political warfare actions against UN forces, while its Enemy Work Department was tasked with handling propaganda and misinformation operations as well as prisoners of war.[64]

After the Korean War ended in an armistice in July 1953, two key events in cross-strait relations occurred. Beginning in September 1954, the First Taiwan Strait Crisis saw the PRC shell and seize several ROC offshore islands in the Taiwan Strait, employing intense propaganda and psychological operations against the ROC that lasted into the following year. In March 1955, the Sino-American Mutual Defense Treaty between the ROC and United States was signed, initiated in large part to deter PRC plans to invade Taiwan.

In 1956, the CCP founded the Taiwan Affairs Leading Small Group (TALSG), a powerful organization responsible for overseeing political warfare operations against Taiwan. Stokes and Hsiao write that the CCP's primary goal during the next two decades was to "undermine the legitimacy of the governing ROC authorities on Taiwan, manage territorial disputes, and counter 'U.S. imperialism'" through propaganda and misinformation operations. For instance, several letters sent to Chiang Kai-shek during that period proposed "direct peace talks" and "a negotiated solution that would grant the authorities on Taiwan a high degree of autonomy."[65] In another example, a 1962 English-language media report out of Singapore claimed that Chiang's "inner circle had reached a secret agreement with the CPP after more than five years of negotiations" and that Chiang "had agreed to accept Taiwan's status as a self-governed autonomous region, but only after [his] passing." Such CCP efforts were intended to undermine resolve on Taiwan and create mistrust between Taiwan and the United States.[66]

In August 1958, the PRC initiated the Second Taiwan Strait Crisis with the same intense artillery shelling and propaganda and psychological operations that had characterized the previous cross-strait conflict. The most severe shelling stopped by the end of the year, but the PRC's political warfare actions continued for nearly three decades. It is notable that the administration of U.S. president Dwight D. Eisenhower was concerned enough about the impact of the crisis on ROC morale that it directly provided supplies and Seventh Fleet support to Taiwan and deliberated use of nuclear weapons in defense of the island nation.

The cross-strait psychological war that began in the 1950s continued through the 1990s. After the Second Taiwan Strait Crisis, both

---

[64] Stokes and Hsiao, *The People's Liberation Army General Political Department*, 8.
[65] Stokes and Hsiao, *The People's Liberation Army General Political Department*, 9.
[66] Stokes and Hsiao, *The People's Liberation Army General Political Department*, 9–10.

the PRC and ROC remained engaged in an "intense international diplomatic contest" characterized by political warfare actions that included "covert operations, subterfuge, and other efforts to encourage defections by enemy officers through psychological warfare." According to Hsiao, "the two sides used megaphones and radio stations to spread propaganda and disinformation into enemy territory" and "utilized balloons and floating carriers to send leaflets and other objects seeking defectors, promising rewards and small gifts including underwear, toys, and cooking oil, among other messages meant to exert a psychological effect on the targeted population." The political warfare contest was perhaps most colorfully symbolized by artillery shelling with warheads full of propaganda leaflets rather than explosives.[67]

While Taiwan remained the PRC's central focus, the CCP turned to other contentious areas, resulting in the occupation of Tibet in 1951 and subsequent Tibetan uprising in 1959, as well as the Sino-Indian border war in 1962. Mao Zedong's Great Leap Forward (1958–62), with its resultant widespread famine and millions of civilian deaths, impacted PRC political warfare activities against Taiwan, as did the Sino-Soviet split (1956–66), which led to bloody border skirmishes in 1969.

During China's Cultural Revolution (1966–76), many of the PRC's political warfare operations were significantly curtailed as Mao threw the PRC into turmoil. However, the PRC achieved a major diplomatic and implicit political warfare victory when the General Assembly of the United Nations voted in 1971 for the PRC to replace the ROC as the UN representative of China. As a result, Taiwan's international standing suffered. In 1970, 68 nations recognized the ROC as "China" while 53 nations recognized the PRC, but by 1977 only 23 nations recognized the ROC while 111 recognized the PRC.[68] The nations that continue to recognize the ROC today remain vital political warfare battlegrounds.

U.S. president Richard M. Nixon's 1972 visit to the PRC attenuated some of Beijing's propaganda and other political warfare activities aimed at Taiwan and its relationship with the United States. Between 1949 and 1972, the PRC framed the Taiwan "problem" in ideological terms by accusing American "imperialists" of "occupying Taiwan," employing the theory of "class struggle" to judge Taiwan's society and routinely interpreting Taiwan's political, economic, and educational systems using Communist ideological jargon.[69]

---

[67] Hsiao, "CCP Propaganda against Taiwan Enters the Social Age."
[68] Goldstein, China and Taiwan, 41.
[69] Hungdah Chiu, ed., China and the Taiwan Issue (New York: Praeger, 1979), 129.

Beginning in 1973, however, focus shifted. The PRC systematically exploited the 28 February 1947 massacre in Taiwan by holding anniversary ceremonies and study sessions to "win over the hearts" of the Taiwanese people. The first meeting hosted approximately 138 participants, nearly one-half of whom were Taiwanese, including KMT party officials, former military officers, government diplomats and administrators, academics, women, and young people. Propaganda themes for the annual meetings included routine calls for Taiwan's "liberation" and its unification with "the motherland," as well as both coercive threats and offers for "peace talks." Oddly enough, the hosts also asserted that Mao inspired the 28 February massacre. By taking credit for the incident, the CCP contrived "to establish the legitimacy and continuity of its leadership between the incident and any future political change on Taiwan."[70]

The Cultural Revolution brought a decade of civil war, chaos, and ruin to mainland China. After its end, the PRC's political warfare infrastructure was reconstituted in the late 1970s, with resultant renewed operations against Taiwan. Up to that point, Beijing's Taiwan policy staff work had been dominated by the PRC's Central Investigation Department, which was focused on intelligence and political warfare operations and which was eventually incorporated into the Ministry of State Security (MSS). This was not necessarily a new PRC model, since during the height of the Chinese Civil War the united front, state security, and liaison work systems worked closely together as underground work entities.

The end of the Cultural Revolution also allowed the CCP to vastly expand its united front mission. United front work was originally focused internally on domestic objectives regarding the various factions and ethnicities in China, especially during the disastrous Great Leap Forward and the bloody Cultural Revolution. But beginning in 1979, Deng Xiaoping broadened the focus of united front work to include Chinese living outside of the PRC. Overseas Chinese were enticed to invest in the PRC to support Deng's "Four Modernizations" of agriculture, industry, national defense, and science and technology in mainland China. The diaspora was also encouraged to support PRC policies and actions within the countries where they resided. This led to a vast increase in funding for the UFWD as well as the PRC's economic revival.[71]

While the deaths of Chiang Kai-shek in April 1975 and Mao Zedong in September 1976 did little to change the nature of the politi-

[70] Chiu, *China and the Taiwan Issue*, 134.
[71] Kerry K. Gershaneck, discussions with senior ROC political warfare officers, Fu Hsing Kang College, National Defense University, Taipei, Taiwan, 2018.

cal warfare competition between the PRC and ROC, the beginning of the Democracy Wall Movement in mainland China in 1978 and economic reforms in the country gave small hope that perhaps the PRC would become less totalitarian. "Cross-strait relations began to liberalize in the 1980s, and the CCP officially shuttered its overt propaganda program in 1991," reports Hsiao. "On the surface, the war without gunfire that had lasted for over 40 years appeared to be over—[but] this could not be farther from the truth. Rather, propaganda and disinformation found new outlets in the mass media and new media."[72]

The China Model, "One Country, Two Systems," and the United Front

On 1 January 1979, the United States formally recognized the PRC and severed official relations with the ROC, which included terminating the 1955 Sino-American Mutual Defense Treaty. In April, the U.S. Congress, expressing little confidence in the stated security assurances toward Taiwan that were coming from President James E. "Jimmy" Carter Jr.'s administration, passed the Taiwan Relations Act, which provided "substantive continuity in the vital security sphere" on "unofficial terms," along with continuity in "commercial, cultural, and other relations."[73]

Meanwhile, Deng Xiaoping announced plans for a Third United Front between the CCP and KMT in December 1979, offering the UFWD a significant role in cross-strait policy. Deng also "outlined a preliminary concept for promoting a 'China model' in place of the international communist movement."[74] That same year, the PRC invaded Vietnam.

One example of a PRC political warfare initiative during this period was the proposal to lure Taiwan into the PRC with the "One Country, Two Systems" idea. Stokes and Hsiao write that in September 1981, PRC officials "outlined a nine-point proposal that called for unification talks between the CCP and KMT on an equal footing, initiation of cross-Strait trade and other functional exchanges, and consultative positions for representatives from Taiwan." In addition to "subordinating Taiwan as a local area under central CCP authority," the proposal also targeted U.S. support for Taiwan. The ROC ultimately rejected the "One Country, Two Systems" concept,

---

[72] Hsiao, "CCP Propaganda against Taiwan Enters the Social Age."
[73] Goldstein, *China and Taiwan*, 56–58.
[74] Stokes and Hsiao, *The People's Liberation Army General Political Department*, 10.

calling instead for unification "under a democratic, free, and non-communist system."[75]

In the end, Hong Kong became the proving ground for the "One Country, Two Systems" idea and remained a key sphere for PRC political warfare. While CCP united front work and intelligence operations had been conducted in Hong Kong for decades, political warfare activities increased dramatically after the signing of the Sino-British Declaration on Hong Kong in December 1984.[76] In time, Hong Kong's experience would make it quite clear that the ROC was wise to reject the PRC's "One Country, Two Systems" formula in 1981. According to Hong Kong independence activist Yau Wai-ching, "China has eroded and nearly destroyed democracy in Hong Kong since taking control of the city from Britain in 1997. Beijing has cunningly manipulated a well-developed political and constitutional framework to undo, step by step, Hong Kong's autonomy. Concepts such as civil liberties and the separation of powers . . . are being abandoned. Fairness and justice, the heart of democracy, are withering."[77]

Hong Kong also played a central role in political warfare competition and in establishing political dialogue during that era. It was in Hong Kong that the CCP established a new tool for "expanding military liaison work out to elites within the broader international community" via the China Association for International Friendly Contact (CAIFC).[78] Using the CAIFC and its various united front organizations, the CCP has co-opted many ROC military officers through programs in the PRC, such as the "Linking Fates" Cultural Festival of Cross-Strait Generals, that bring together ROC retired military officers and senior PRC officials and retired PLA officers.[79] While in the PRC, many ROC attendees are approached with business and financial offers in exchange for their cooperation in support of PRC political warfare objectives.

In 1984, the CCP formed the Carrier Enterprise Corporation in Hong Kong. Initially established as a trading company, the corporation soon expanded into real estate, construction, manufacturing, mining, investment—and political warfare operations. According to Stokes and Hsiao, as many as 20 Carrier subsidiaries in Hong Kong have directed political warfare activities against Taiwan. Next, the CCP established the Alumni Association of the Huangpu (Wham-

[75] Stokes and Hsiao, *The People's Liberation Army General Political Department*, 10–11.
[76] Stokes and Hsiao, *The People's Liberation Army General Political Department*, 11.
[77] Yau Wai-ching, "Democracy's Demise in Hong Kong," *New York Times*, 16 September 2018.
[78] Stokes and Hsiao, *The People's Liberation Army General Political Department*, 11.
[79] Russell Hsiao, "Political Warfare Alert: Fifth 'Linking Fates' Cultural Festival of Cross-Strait Generals," Global Taiwan Institute, Global Taiwan Brief 2, no. 2, 11 January 2017.

poa) Military Academy, a UFWD group tasked with promoting cross-strait unification under the "One Country, Two Systems" concept.[80]

During this time, the PRC also made it a priority to establish a special cross-strait channel of communication to engage ROC leaders in political dialogue. The defection of a China Airlines (Taiwan) pilot who flew to Guangzhou in 1986 made this possible. For the first time since the Chinese Civil War, CCP and KMT authorities carried out direct talks to negotiate the pilot's return to Taiwan. By November 1987, the ROC under President Chiang Ching-kuo lifted its ban on Taiwanese visits to mainland China, marking a significant PRC political warfare success.[81]

Within the ROC political warfare establishment, Chiang Ching-kuo is viewed with great respect, since he founded the ROC military's Fu Hsing Kang College, also known as the Political Warfare Cadres Academy and now a part of Taiwan's National Defense University. As Chiang steered Taiwan from authoritarian rule to democracy, he maintained his strong belief in the necessity of fighting the political war against Beijing. His ideological defense of the ROC was invaluable, but one unfortunate offshoot of his support is that the title and function of the ROC's political warfare profession did not evolve as Taiwan assumed the other trappings of a full democracy. This failure, as well as recognition of abuses during KMT rule and the White Terror, would ultimately undermine Taiwan's ability to counter PRC political warfare as a democracy. Over time, Taiwan's political warfare experts, viewed increasingly as anachronistic holdovers of Leninist ideology and authoritarian rule, gradually lost the respect and trust of Taiwan's elected leadership and people.[82]

Following Chiang's death in January 1988, the CCP worked to establish communications with his successor, Lee Teng-hui. This was accomplished by a neo-Confucian scholar who worked closely with the UFWD's KMT Revolutionary Committee and the Chinese People's Political Consultative Conference. With the founding of the ROC's National Unification Council in 1990, Lee allowed ROC officials to meet with a former PLA General Political Department director and other PRC representatives in Hong Kong in December of that year, and talks regarding confidence-building measures had begun by 1993. As a testament to the scope of this kind of liaison work, Stokes and Hsiao state that "twenty-six meetings between the secret emissaries took place between 1990 and 1995."[83]

The transition of CCP leadership from Deng Xiaoping to Jiang

---

[80] Stokes and Hsiao, *The People's Liberation Army General Political Department*, 11–12.
[81] Stokes and Hsiao, *The People's Liberation Army General Political Department*, 12.
[82] Gershaneck, discussions with senior ROC political warfare officers.
[83] Stokes and Hsiao, *The People's Liberation Army General Political Department*, 12–13.

Zemin resulted in power shifts within the party's official "Taiwan policy community," including a purge of senior PLA military officers and the advent of scandals involving political warfare officials working with the PRC's Ministry of Public Security, the PLA's Intelligence Department, and state-owned enterprises.[84] Reforms and retribution followed. It also coincided with the bloody CCP response to the Democracy Wall Movement in the PRC, which ultimately ended with the literal crushing with tanks and machine-gunning of protestors in Tiananmen Square in June 1989. PRC political warfare operations to cover up or distract from the Tiananmen Square massacre continue in Taiwan through this day and, up to the 2019 PRC crackdown on Hong Kong, proved effective on many university campuses.

In 1991, the ROC officially ended its National Mobilization for the Suppression of Communist Rebellion that was initiated in 1949, and by 1995 President Lee had instituted other democratic reforms that empowered the people of Taiwan, including ending the decades-long cover-up of the 28 February 1947 massacre.[85] All would impact PRC political warfare strategies and operations. As recently as 2017, for example, the CCP tried to co-opt the 70th anniversary of the 28 February incident, as well as the 30th anniversary of the lifting of martial law in Taiwan, by hosting a commemorative event organized by its front organization, the Taiwan Democratic Self-Government League.[86]

Lee's policies and reforms during that time were "cautious but also provocative." He countered PRC propaganda that Taiwan was a province of China by characterizing the claim as a "weird fantasy" and insisting that the ROC and PRC "should coexist as two legal entities in the international arena."[87] Further, increasing transparency about the White Terror in Taiwan and the country's continued movement toward democracy and freedom were also useful in countering PRC influence.

In 1992, representatives of the PRC and ROC met in Hong Kong to determine the nature of future talks, especially whether they "were of a domestic or an international nature." The outcome of these talks, now referred to as the 1992 Consensus, is disputed by both sides to this day, as it essentially reflected very different perspectives on what One China means. Nevertheless, the PRC continues to use the 1992 Consensus today to pressure Taiwan's Tsai Ing-wen administration, and all other nations and international institutions, to accept its interpretation of One China. In recent years,

---

[84] Stokes and Hsiao, *The People's Liberation Army General Political Department*, 13.
[85] Goldstein, *China and Taiwan*, 73–74.
[86] Hsiao, "Political Warfare Alert: CCP-TDSGL Appropriates Taiwan's 2-28 Incident."
[87] Goldstein, *China and Taiwan*, 82–83.

President Tsai's unwillingness to accede to the PRC's version of the 1992 Consensus and One China has led to the PRC's enhanced use of diplomacy, economic warfare, military threats, and political warfare as primary attack vehicles.

During a 1995 speech at Cornell University, where he had earned his doctorate, President Lee highlighted Taiwan's successful democratization and focused on "Taiwanization," which emphasized the history, literature, and culture of Taiwan rather than China. Beijing was very displeased. As the PRC's attitude toward Lee hardened in the run-up to Taiwan's 1996 election, its propaganda organs accused him of advocating for Taiwan's independence and "acting at the United States' direction" to disrupt cross-strait relations.[88]

In July 1995, the PRC demonstrated its hard power in an attempt to influence Taiwanese public opinion by conducting a series of missile tests in the waters surrounding Taiwan and military maneuvers off the coast of Fujian. The following year, to deter the Taiwanese people from voting for Lee in Taiwan's 1996 presidential election, the PRC conducted another show of force just days before the 26 March voting date by launching missiles over the island, conducting massive live-fire and amphibious assault exercises, and disrupting trade and shipping lines around Taiwan. The U.S. response was to dispatch two aircraft carrier battle groups to the area, prompting the PRC to announce the suspension of its missile "tests."[89]

The PRC political warfare effort in 1996 backfired miserably. Lee became the first democratically elected president of the ROC by a wide margin, and 75 percent of the total vote went to candidates opposing Taiwan's unification with the PRC.[90] However, the PRC's political warfare operations did boost the popularity of a new political party called the New Party, which would later be tainted by allegations of conducting espionage operations against Taiwan for the PRC.[91]

Cross-strait relations stalemated during the late 1990s, and "unofficial" talks between Taipei and Beijing stalled as well. Accordingly, the PRC sought to influence Taiwan "by cultivating people-to-people contacts with business figures, local official, and more unification-oriented politicians." Lee's 1998 interview with the German radio station *Deutsche Welle*, in which he denied the PRC's sovereignty over Taiwan, sparked a furious propaganda assault from Beijing and the cancellation of a high-level visit by the head of the Association for

[88] Goldstein, *China and Taiwan*, 86, 93.
[89] Goldstein, *China and Taiwan*, 88–89.
[90] Goldstein, *China and Taiwan*, 88–89.
[91] Jason Pan, "New Party's Wang, Others Charged with Espionage," *Taipei Times* (Taiwan), 14 June 2018.

Relations Across the Taiwan Straits. The PRC cancelled further un-official talks until Taipei accepted Beijing's version of One China.[92]

By the time of Taiwan's second direct presidential election in 2000, the PRC was engaged in ever-increasing and more subtle united front operations. In 2001, it directed the establishment of the China Association for Promotion of Chinese Culture as a principle PLA platform for cross-straits political warfare operations.

The Ascent of the DPP: The Chen Shui-bian Administration

On 18 March 2000, Chen Shui-bian was elected as president of the ROC, leading his Democratic Progressive Party (DPP) to victory over two strong KMT contenders. For the PRC, the DPP was a nightmare, since it supported Taiwan's independence from China and held griev-ances against the mainland KMT government that had repressed the people of Taiwan for so long. Consequently, before the election, the PRC employed a wide range of political warfare and other influence operations to intimidate Taiwan's voters from supporting Chen, as well as to influence Chen's behavior if elected. The PRC State Coun-cil, for example, issued a white paper in February 2000 saying that force might be used against Taiwan if its leaders refuse "the peaceful settlement of cross-strait reunification through negotiations."[93]

Although a supporter of Taiwanese independence, Chen stated publicly that as long as the PRC had no intention of using military force against Taiwan, he would not declare independence or change the ROC's national symbols. Chen faced immense challenges, such as intense political conflicts with the KMT-dominated legislature, the DPP's lack of governing experience, and scandals that plagued his presidency as he sought to reestablish U.S. trust and reassure Beijing that he would approach cross-straits issues constructively. Ultimately, the PRC rebuffed Chen's early efforts at reassurance, relations between the PRC and ROC moved from stalemate to con-frontation, and Chen ultimately overplayed his hand with the Unit-ed States in a way that greatly diminished American confidence and support.

The PRC changed its political warfare strategy from issuing threats to influence Taiwan's public opinion to employing classic united front tactics designed to splinter Taiwan's unity. Specifically, PRC vice premier Qian Qichen suggested that the PRC should "work together with Taiwan compatriots ... that agree on one China ... and

[92] Goldstein, *China and Taiwan*, 92, 95–96.
[93] Goldstein, *China and Taiwan*, 95–96.

unite with all the forces that can be united ... to struggle against separatism." The PRC's primary target was Taiwan's business community, which sought more direct routes and methods for doing business
with mainland China, and it attempted to influence Taiwan's business organizations to accept and promote PRC political positions.[94]

By 2003, Chen's relations with U.S. president George W. Bush
had soured for several reasons. Bush had been highly supportive of
Taiwan upon taking office in 2001, vowing to "do whatever it took" to
help Taiwan defend itself in the event of a PRC attack and providing it with its largest arms sale in a decade. But the 11 September
2001 terrorist attacks against the United States focused American
attention on the Middle East, and Chen's increasing public statements hinting at Taiwan independence, which would likely cause
a cross-strait conflict, caused that period of warmth to "melt away."
Ultimately, Chen played directly into the hands of the PRC by alien-
ating his strongest international ally, the United States, as well as the
people of Taiwan.[95]

At the same time, Chen made great efforts to emphasize Taiwanese identity through a "de-Sinicization" campaign, which disas-
sociated Taiwan from China. For example, Chen ensured that the
subjects of Taiwanese history and culture became central to the
country's secondary education curriculum, while Chinese history
became part of general world history. He also deleted China from
the names of state-run corporations and postage stamps. Chen's efforts seemed aimed at developing a new constitution that would lead
to an independent Taiwan and securing membership in the UN under the name of Taiwan rather than the ROC.

Consequently, the PRC vastly enhanced its political warfare operations against Taiwan. By 2005, Beijing had accelerated its united
front and "people to people" diplomacy, establishing regular contacts with the KMT and Taiwan's People First Party. These high-level
party connections later paved the way for vastly improved relations
between Taiwan and the PRC, as well as between the CCP and KMT,
after the KMT crushed the DPP in Taiwan's 2008 presidential and
legislative elections.[96]

Leading to that devastating defeat, Beijing worked closely with
Washington to "contain Taiwan" and Chen's efforts to change the status quo, which the Bush administration feared meant independence
and, consequently, war. In 2005, the PRC passed the "Anti-Secession
Law," which called for a broad range of exchanges with Taiwan and

---

[94] Goldstein, *China and Taiwan*, 105–6.
[95] Goldstein, *China and Taiwan*, 107–9.
[96] Goldstein, *China and Taiwan*, 110–13.

"peaceful reunification through consultations and negotiations on an equal footing" and set broad conditions under which the use of force against Taiwan would be justified. The PRC also increased a pattern of military intimidation to influence Taiwan's elections and the independence referendum that year, which led many in the U.S. government to believe that the PRC was ready to go to war against Taiwan.[97]

The Ma Era: Rapprochement and Infiltration

Between 2008 and 2016, interactions between Taiwan and the PRC increased quickly and extensively as ROC president Ma Ying-jeou pursued a policy of rapprochement with Beijing. "With rapidly expanding cross-strait travel, academic exchanges and investment," writes J. Michael Cole at the Global Taiwan Institute, "the opportunities for China to engage in political warfare increased exponentially."[98]

The PRC viewed Ma's election as a "historic opportunity" in its efforts to absorb Taiwan into the PRC. Ma endorsed the so-called 1992 Consensus and publicly announced that the PRC and ROC agreed to "separate interpretations" of the One China policy, with Taipei affirming that "China" was the ROC. There is, however, no record that any such agreement between the PRC and ROC was ever made. Ma also sought "meaningful participation" in international organizations, but not membership in the UN. Consequently, Ma was able to reduce tensions and restart stalled cross-strait communications.[99]

Regarding Taiwan's engagement in international organizations and diplomatic access, Ma achieved some success. He claimed credit for Taiwan's participation in the World Health Assembly under the designation of "Chinese Taipei," its assent to the World Trade Organization's Agreement on Government Procurement, and its involvement with the UN's International Civil Aviation Organization. He also obtained for Taiwan "visa-free or visa-on-arrival access to 158 countries and regions, compared with 54 before he took office." In pursuing a policy of "flexible diplomacy," Ma is perceived as having done well.[100]

However, as a result of Ma's attempts at cross-strait rapprochement, the PRC was able to increase its political influence in Taiwan,

---

[97] Goldstein, *China and Taiwan*, 113–17.

[98] J. Michael Cole, "Unstoppable: China's Secret Plan to Subvert Taiwan," *National Interest*, 23 March 2015.

[99] Goldstein, *China and Taiwan*, 120; and Kerry K. Gershaneck, interviews with a senior U.S. Department of State official, various locations, 2018–20.

[100] H. H. Lu and Evelyn Kao, "President Ma Counters Criticism of His Flexible Diplomacy," Central News Agency (Taipei), 29 December 2015.

inflicting serious damage to the ROC's security and national unity and garnering increasing resentment and criticism throughout the country. As PRC media outlets praised Ma and his cross-strait initiatives, Beijing continued to conduct a wide range of political warfare operations and cyberattacks against Taiwan, and PRC intelligence actions expanded significantly.[101]

Academic exchanges between Taiwan and the PRC sent large number of highly educated but underemployed and unemployed Taiwanese, including many with PhDs, to mainland China in search of jobs. With little knowledge of how to identify or resist PRC intelligence enticements, they became easy prey to Confucius Institutes, the MSS, PLA agencies, and other organizations that offered funding for "research" and "consultant" services. These academics were often tasked with reporting on Taiwan's economy, politics, societal problems, security, and other issues of great interest to the PRC political warfare community, which vastly increased Beijing's ability to divide and demoralize the people of Taiwan.[102]

Ma's reign has been characterized as a "dark decade" during Taiwan's intelligence war with the PRC by Jamestown Foundation fellow Peter Mattis, who reports that Taiwan's "intelligence and counterintelligence failures" during the Ma administration damaged its "reputation and sowed doubt about its integrity."[103] In addition to inroads to Taiwanese academics and students, the PRC's political warfare and intelligence operatives also obtained far greater access to retired government officials, particularly military officers and ministerial-level administrators in charge of national defense, economic stability, foreign affairs, and other vital state functions. Many were co-opted with offers of free trips to the mainland and high-paying positions as advisors or directors on the boards of PRC state-owned enterprises.[104]

"Ma opened the door to China's infiltration [in Taiwan], and this led to a large backlash against him yielding too much," said one ROC official, who asked for anonymity. Indeed, Ma's administration faced increasing criticism and protests for its pro-PRC policies, and it soon became mired in bitter domestic policy divisions in the same manner in which Chen Shui-bian's administration faltered.[105]

A high-level cross-strait visit to Taiwan in 2008 was perceived by many Taiwanese as a push for unification with the PRC and led to violent protests. Molotov cocktails were thrown in the streets, and

---

[101] Gershaneck, discussions with senior ROC political warfare officers.
[102] Gershaneck, discussions with senior ROC political warfare officers.
[103] Nadia Tsao et al., "Ma Years 'Dark Decade' in Intelligence War: Analyst," *Taipei Times* (Taiwan), 2 October 2018.
[104] Gershaneck, discussions with senior ROC political warfare officers.
[105] Gershaneck, discussions with senior ROC political warfare officers.

more than 140 police officers were reportedly injured. College students and professors launched a peaceful sit-in, known as the Wild Strawberry Movement, demanding a more reasonable assembly law and a stop to police violence.[106] In 2014, the Sunflower Student Movement, initiated by a coalition of students and civic groups, widely protested Ma's cross-straits trade policies, in part by occupying the legislature.[107]

In November 2015, Ma met with Xi Jinping in Singapore, the first such meeting between the presidents of the PRC and ROC in 66 years. The meeting was perceived as "unequal," and Ma was accused of sacrificing Taiwan's democratic values and attempting to "re-Sinify" the nation.[108] By the end of his administration, many people in Taiwan believed that Ma had gone too far in the direction of PRC-ROC unification at the expense of Taiwan's sovereignty and interests.[109] The DPP, dedicated to establishing a more "Taiwanese" national identity, won the 2016 presidential election by a landslide. Two years later, Ma was found guilty of leaking classified information and thereby violating the ROC's Communications Protection and Surveillance Act, further tarnishing his legacy.[110]

President Tsai and the "Cold Peace"

Following DPP candidate Tsai Ing-wen's election as president of the ROC on 16 January 2016 and her inauguration on 20 May, a "Cold Peace" has defined cross-strait relations. The DPP platform ultimately seeks a sovereign and independent Taiwan, and it accepts neither the PRC's One China principle nor the so-called 1992 Consensus.

As explained by Dr. David D. F. Huang, then at Academia Sinica, the "essential parameters of 'cold peace' are a set of policies carried out by both China and Taiwan." Beijing has indicated that "unless [Tsai] accepted the [PRC's] precondition of the '1992 Consensus,' there would be no official or semi-official communications between China and Taiwan, no international space for Taiwan, and no more 'economic handouts' to Taiwan." Tsai, meanwhile, is reluctant to consent to the 1992 Consensus, since she "was elected president with an ambiguous pledge to maintain the status quo across the Taiwan Strait."[111]

---

[106] Associated Press, "Thousands in Taiwan Protest Talks with China," *New York Times*, 25 October 2008.

[107] Austin Ramzy, "As Numbers Swell, Students Pledge to Continue Occupying Taiwan's Legislature," *New York Times*, 22 March 2014.

[108] Bill Ide, "Taiwan China Historic Talks Fuel Criticism at Home," *Voice of America News*, 8 November 2015.

[109] Goldstein, *China and Taiwan*, 125–28.

[110] Lawrence Chung, "Former Taiwan President Ma Ying-Jeou Sentenced to 4 Months in Prison for Leaking Information," *South China Morning Post* (Hong Kong), 15 May 2018.

[111] David W. F. Huang, " 'Cold Peace' and the Nash Equilibrium in Cross-Straits Relations (Part 1)," Global Taiwan Institute, Global Taiwan Brief 1, no. 12, 7 December 2016.

To counter PRC propaganda, Huang continues, Tsai stated that her government would "respect the 'historical fact' of the 1992 meetings and all developments thus following; would abide by the ROC constitution, and implement existing cross-Strait law and agreements as the previous administration had; and would construct a 'consistent, predictable, and non-provocative' framework of interactions with mainland China." She also stated that there will be "no change of good will toward China, no change of her previous promises, no succumbing to China's pressure, and no return to old ways of cross-Strait confrontation."[112] The CCP is not satisfied with these assurances.

As a result, cross-strait relations between the PRC and Taiwan have developed into deadlock. Public-sector communication channels are cut off and private-sector exchanges reduced, while official channels between the PRC State Council's Taiwan Affairs Office and Taiwan's Mainland Affairs Council and between Taiwan's Straits Exchange Foundation and the PRC's Association for Relations Across the Taiwan Straits have also been disconnected. The PRC's ensuing strategy has been to increase diplomatic, economic, and military pressures on Tsai's government through a wide range of united front and other political warfare activities. The CCP's objectives is to effect regime change in Taiwan or prompt Tsai to mistakenly provoke China.[113]

2018 Midterm Election Interference

Taiwan's midterm elections in November 2018 resulted in resounding defeat at the local level for the DPP and unexpected victory for the KMT, which won mayoralties in Taiwan's three most populous cities. Tsai resigned as leader of the DPP, though she remained Taiwan's president.

While the political issues that drove the election were varied and complex, the PRC's "massive and successful interference in Taiwan's elections" certainly helped impact the outcome, writes Josh Rogin at *The Washington Post*. Beijing "carried out a massive propaganda and social media campaign that spread false news designed to undermine Tsai's government," in which "the island's 23 million citizens were bombarded with anti-Tsai and anti-DPP content through

---

[112] Huang, " 'Cold Peace' and the Nash Equilibrium in Cross-Straits Relations (Part 1)."
[113] David W. F. Huang, " 'Cold Peace' and the Nash Equilibrium in Cross-Straits Relations (Part 2)," Global Taiwan Institute, Global Taiwan Brief 2, no. 2, 11 January 2017.

Facebook, Twitter and online chat groups, promoted by China's '50-cent army' of paid social media trolls."[114]

There are ongoing investigations, under the direction of the ROC National Security Bureau and military intelligence, into allegations of PRC social media engineering and illegal funding of Taiwanese candidates opposing Tsai and the DPP. However, ROC officials acknowledged during several discussions after the election that money laundering and social media engineering are difficult to prove and the investigations themselves are very time consuming.[115]

Another problem acknowledged by DPP officials is that the Tsai government failed to educate the people of Taiwan about PRC political warfare early enough in the administration. "It was only in September [2018] that the DPP began to buy ads regarding 'fake news' and China's influence operations," said one knowledgeable official. By then, the allegations looked to some like an election ploy, and many Taiwanese were skeptical. Others who were buying ads and protesting against the administration's policies took the "fake news" ads to be attacks on their loyalty and integrity.[116]

Rogin notes that after the elections, PRC propaganda organs and Beijing's sympathizers "pointed to Tsai's losses as evidence that her tough stance vis-à-vis China was unpopular and wrongheaded."[117] Those propaganda platforms also depicted the election results as justification for Xi Jinping's strategy of isolating Taiwan and undercutting its international standing since the DPP election victory in 2016.[118]

More ominously, on 1 January 2019, in Xi's first speech ever devoted exclusively to the topic of Taiwan, his tone was threatening. One day after Tsai urged the PRC to settle the Taiwan issue peacefully, Xi declared, "The country is growing strong, the nation is rejuvenating and unification between the two sides of the strait is the great trend of history. . . . We make no promise to abandon the use of force, and retain the option of taking all necessary measures."[119]

2020 Election Interference

Leading up Taiwan's 11 January 2020 national elections, the PRC was emboldened by what it perceived as its midterm election success.

---

[114] Josh Rogin, "China's Interference in the 2018 Elections Succeeded—in Taiwan," *Washington Post*, 18 December 2018.

[115] Gershaneck, discussions with senior ROC political warfare officers.

[116] Gershaneck, discussions with senior ROC political warfare officers.

[117] Rogin, "China's Interference in the 2018 Elections Succeeded—in Taiwan."

[118] Chris Buckley and Chris Horton, "Xi Jinping Warns Taiwan that Unification Is the Goal and Force Is an Option," *New York Times*, 1 January 2019.

[119] Buckley and Horton, "Xi Jinping Warns Taiwan that Unification Is the Goal and Force Is an Option."

Beijing had high hopes for the election of its favored candidate, the KMT's Han Kuo-yu, mayor of Kaohsiung. It was a false hope.

According to a report by the Global Taiwan Institute in October 2019, the PRC used standard military intimidation, along with other tools for election interference in Taiwan that "are more insidious and less understood here in the United States" in the run-up to the 2020 elections. These tools included the employment of criminal gangs, the exploitation of new and traditional media, and United Front-like penetration networks in "grassroots wards, schools, farmers associations, religious organizations, family clans, and even indigenous tribes."[120]

Nevertheless, in Taiwan's 15th presidential and 10th legislative elections, President Tsai and her running mate William Lai won the presidential race by a landslide. They secured a record-breaking 8,170,186 votes, or 57.13 percent, while the KMT, led by Han and Simon Chang, received 38.61 percent of the vote with almost 3 million fewer votes.[121] The people of Taiwan, the only liberal democracy in the Chinese-speaking world, endorsed Tsai's presidency for another four years after her humiliating 2018 local election defeat. Almost as important, Tsai's party retained majority control of the Legislative Yuan.

Han's ascent to the campaign for the presidency was a story of seeming PRC political warfare success. He was "a backbench lawmaker, an unemployed husband and the general manager of an agricultural marketing company" with a "shady private life." Yet, in 2018, he benefitted from an "overwhelming media campaign apparently orchestrated by Chinese agencies and paid for by Taiwan's China-friendly tycoons" to be elected mayor of Taiwan's second largest city, Kaohsiung, which has historically been a DPP stronghold. To support his mayoral campaign, radio and social media were extensively employed. For months, two local media stations controlled by pro-PRC business factions "bombarded the public with a ceaseless stream of flattering news about Han." The stations, TVBS and CtiTV, "allegedly paid local eateries and hotels and other such popular sites . . . to have their broadcasts running 24/7, with algorithms doing a similar job in terms of social media coverage."[122] As part of a broader PRC campaign of disinformation and coercion, similar radio and so-

[120] Gary Schmitt and Michael Mazza, *Blinding the Enemy: CCP Interference in Taiwan's Democracy* (Washington, DC: Global Taiwan Institute, 2019), 12–13.
[121] "60 Countries Have Congratulated Taiwan's President Tsai on Re-election: MOFA," *Taiwan News* (Taipei), 13 January 2020.
[122] Jens Kastner, "Beijing's Man in Taiwan Crashes and Burns," *Asia Sentinel* (Hong Kong), 12 May 2020.

cial media support catapulted Han into the 2020 presidential race as the KMT candidate.[123]

On 31 December 2019, 11 days before the election, the Legislative Yuan passed the Anti-Infiltration Act to help counter election disinformation.[124] Similar to the U.S. Foreign Agents Registration Act, the law penalizes organizations and individuals for secretly acting on behalf of the PRC.[125] Nevertheless, PRC election interference methods identified in the lead-up to the election ranged from "online content farms," to exploiting YouTube, to offline rumor mongering at the all-important village levels in rural Taiwan. According to Puma Shen, an assistant professor at the National Taipei University's Graduate School of Criminology and who specializes in investigating this type of election interference, the social media-based news outlets that have direct affiliations with the CCP are mostly based in China. Other locations include Hong Kong and Malaysia.[126]

Additional steps that the PRC took as part of its political warfare campaign included making Taiwan's media scene more Beijing-friendly. PRC agents "quietly paid five Taiwanese news outlets to publish articles casting China as a land of opportunity that would bring prosperity to Taiwanese." Another line of attack to influence the election involved diplomatic coercion. During Tsai's first presidential term, the PRC "poached more than half a dozen of Taiwan's few remaining diplomatic partners. Two of these countries, Kiribati and the Solomon Islands, switched diplomatic recognition from Taipei to Beijing as recently as September 2019." One PRC propaganda organ threatened that if Tsai was reelected, Beijing would flip all of Taiwan's remaining allies.[127]

The COVID-19 Pandemic Battleground

As COVID-19 began to engulf first the PRC and then the world, Beijing used the virus to intensify military and diplomatic pressure against Taiwan. Taiwan responded to the COVID-19 threat extraordinarily well, ignoring inaccurate information from the World Health Organization (WHO) and Beijing's disingenuous assurances that all was under control. The Tsai administration instituted "early and aggressive measures" learned from its experience fighting the 2003

[123] Bethany Allen-Ebrahimian, "China Steps Up Political Interference ahead of Taiwan's Elections," Axios, 10 January 2020; and Kastner, "Beijing's Man in Taiwan Crashes and Burns."
[124] "How 'Fake News' and Disinformation Were Spread in the Run-up to Taiwan's Presidential Elections," Advox Global Voices, 22 January 2020.
[125] Allen-Ebrahimian, "China Steps Up Political Interference ahead of Taiwan's Elections."
[126] "How 'Fake News' and Disinformation Were Spread in the Run-up to Taiwan's Presidential Elections."
[127] Allen-Ebrahimian, "China Steps Up Political Interference ahead of Taiwan's Elections."

severe acute respiratory syndrome (SARS) outbreak that proved largely effective in stemming the virus spread.[128]

From the onset of the COVID-19 pandemic, Beijing's political warfare apparatus, exploiting strong influence over the WHO and global propaganda networks, was in play. The PRC's influence within the WHO, which excludes Taiwan's membership at Beijing's behest, "undermined global health as the novel coronavirus COVID-19 swept the world in the early months of 2020," according to Anastasya Lloyd-Damnjanovic at the U.S.-China Economic and Security Review Commission. Lloyd-Damnjanovic claims that the "WHO officials consistently ignored Taiwan's attempts to exchange information about the virus and share best practices for containing it."[129] Subsequent efforts by the United States and countries friendly to Taiwan to have the WHO invite Taiwan to the 2020 World Health Assembly were met with a relentless CCP propaganda counterattack. The *Global Times*, among other propaganda organs, slammed the United States and Taiwan for "politicizing a health problem to serve a secessionist agenda that will never succeed."[130] *China Daily* blamed Taiwan for its exclusion from the World Health Assembly, as Taiwan refused to accept the One China policy.[131]

Meanwhile, Beijing increased its coercion and intimidation efforts with a series of military exercises, conducted while the world was distracted by COVID-19, as part of a multifaceted pressure campaign against Taiwan.[132] Chinese military aircraft crossed the median line of the Taiwan Strait three times in the early months of 2020, after only one such incursion in 2019. These line crossings illustrated a "sharp escalation" in military pressure.[133] PLA forces also participated in a two-day joint air and maritime drill in February that involved back-to-back circumnavigating flights around the island, while a Chinese aircraft carrier and attached group of warships sailed near Taiwan in April.[134]

Meanwhile, on 11 May 2020, the CCP employed foreign publications to generate uncertainty and fear that Beijing may be pushed by "nationalist fever" to invade Taiwan during this opportune time. A *South China Morning Post* headline read: "Loud calls on social media urge Beijing to strike while world is busy with coronavirus crisis, but

[128] Anastasya Lloyd-Damnjanovic, *Beijing's Deadly Game: Consequences of Excluding Taiwan from the World Health Organization during the COVID-19 Pandemic* (Washington, DC: U.S.-China Economic and Security Review Commission, 2020).
[129] Lloyd-Damnjanovic, *Beijing's Deadly Game*.
[130] "Chinese FM Slams Taiwan DPP for Colluding with U.S. to Seek WHA Attendance," *Global Times* (Beijing), 15 May 2020.
[131] Li Zhenguang, "Evil Design behind U.S.' Taiwan Rant," *China Daily* (Beijing), 15 May 2020.
[132] Didi Tang, "China's Island War Games 'Simulating Seizure' Rattle Taiwan," *Times* (London), 15 May 2020.
[133] Lloyd-Damnjanovic, *Beijing's Deadly Game*.
[134] Tang, "China's Island War Games 'Simulating Seizure' Rattle Taiwan."

observers say the authorities do not want to be rushed."[135] Beijing reinforced this political warfare gambit with a prominently highlighted *Global Times* report on 23 May stating that, after three decades of Beijing espousing "peaceful re-unification," CCP policy no longer called for that reunification to be "peaceful," and that military force remains "a final solution for the worst case scenario."[136]

The next chapter describes selected contemporary political warfare activities designed to achieve the CCP's goal of taking physical and political control of Taiwan.

[135] Minnie Chan, "China Tries to Calm 'Nationalist Fever' as Call for Invasion of Taiwan Grow," *South China Morning Post* (Hong Kong), 10 May 2020.
[136] Yang Sheng, "Taiwan Separatists Panic as Mainland Drops 'Peaceful' in Reunificiation Narrative," *Global Times* (Beijing), 23 May 2020.

CHAPTER EIGHT

PRC Political Warfare against Taiwan: A Contemporary Analysis

Taiwanese compatriots are our brothers. In addition to continued military threats, Beijing periodically embarked on a more conciliatory approach to peaceful reunification with Taiwan since the mid-1950s. This 1976 poster reflects a United Front Work Department strategy that emphasizes that Chinese and Taiwanese peoples are one, united by blood ties.

A s in chapter six on Thailand, the following analysis will examine selected People's Republic of China's (PRC) political warfare operations against the Republic of China (ROC) on Taiwan.

PRC Goals and Strategies for Conducting Political Warfare against Taiwan

The PRC's primary goal is to "unify China" by bringing Taiwan under Beijing's control as either a province or special administrative region. Intermediate objectives include effecting regime change and ensuring that Taiwan's economic and diplomatic efforts fail. The PRC employs several strategies to achieve its goals, such as employing united front operations and liaison work, violence, economic pressure, military intimidation, and diplomacy to divide Taiwan's society.

While the PRC tried in recent years to "win the hearts and minds" of the Taiwan populace to engineer its hoped-for "unification of China," it has failed to do so. J. Michael Cole at the Global Taiwan Institute writes that the Chinese Communist Party (CCP) has now "abandoned that strategy" and is instead "intensifying efforts to corrode and undermine Taiwan's democratic institutions, create social instability, further isolate Taiwan internationally, and hollow out Taiwan's economy by attracting its talent."[1]

Desired Outcomes of PRC Political Warfare in Taiwan

Ultimately, Beijing seeks to destabilize Taiwan's leadership, demoralize its populace, and destroy its sovereign status to the point that Taiwan either willingly joins the PRC or becomes so internally weak that it cannot defend itself against military assault. Specifically, the PRC hopes to achieve the following outcomes:

- Taiwan is absorbed into the PRC and comes fully under CCP control, thus fulfilling PRC president Xi Jinping's "China Dream" of national reunification.
- The CCP finally resolves the Chinese Civil War on its own terms with the destruction of the ROC as a political entity.
- The People's Liberation Army (PLA) exploits Taiwan's natural resources and strategic location as well as the ROC's national defense technologies, expertise, and manpower to enhance PRC control of the South China Sea and support the defense of the Chinese mainland. Of equal importance, Taiwan provides the PRC the regional power projection platform necessary to break through the chokehold of the first island chain into the Pacific.

---

[1] Dan Southerland, "Unable to Charm Taiwan into Reunification, China Moves to Subvert Island's Democracy," Radio Free Asia, 25 May 2018.

- The influence of the United States in the region becomes seriously, if not fatally, compromised.
- Taiwan's democratic system of government, which presents an existential challenge to CCP political authority, is discredited and effectively destroyed.
- The PRC achieves unchallenged political, military, economic, diplomatic, and cultural dominance, initially throughout the region and ultimately globally.

Themes and Audiences of PRC Political Warfare in Taiwan

The PRC's primary political warfare themes, highlighting the many economic and cultural ties shared between the people of the PRC and Taiwan, include the following:

- There is only One China, and both sides of the Taiwan straits belong to the PRC.
- The peoples of China and Taiwan are kin and must be reunited.
- Taiwan's secessionist position is doomed to fail.
- It is best to join the PRC now since it is at its strongest, while Taiwan is economically stagnant, politically divided, and diplomatically isolated.
- The PRC is strong, while the United States is weak and unreliable.
- Taiwan and the United States' scheme to get Taiwan invited back in the World Health Organization and World Health Assembly is doomed to fail.

Primary Taiwanese audiences of the PRC's political warfare include the news media, business communities, political officials, military leaders, academics, retirees from civil service and education posts, principals of senior high schools, and other elites across all sectors. Secondary audiences include influential social media users, criminal gang leaders and members, and owners of talk radio stations, while tertiary audiences comprise average Taiwanese citizens and students.

Tools, Tactics, Techniques, and Procedures for PRC Political Warfare in Taiwan

Many of the PRC's historical and present-day political warfare operations employed against Taiwan have been discussed in the first four chapters of this book. These include united front operations, the Three Warfares (public opinion/media warfare, psychological warfare, and legal warfare), propaganda, diplomatic coercion, disinformation and misinformation, academic infiltration, business partnering, and the establishment of political parties.

The PRC's current political warfare strategy against Taiwan involves a combination of united front tactics, economic and political pressure, military threats, art and culture, and active measures applied to squeeze the island into submission.

Beijing wages political warfare against Taiwan to undermine the ROC government and suppress political parties and organizations seeking independence for Taiwan. Further, it recruits Taiwan and foreign politicians to advocate for the unification of Taiwan with mainland China.[2] The PRC also employs soft power functions, such as public diplomacy, public affairs, public relations, educational exchanges, and cultural activities.

Active measures include overt violence, cyber warfare, the use of criminal gangs, espionage, subversion, blackmail, deception, coerced censorship and self-censorship, "carrot-and-stick" funding practices, bribery, and coopting once-legitimate news agencies. Finally, the PRC also uses military power short of war, such as PLA live-fire training exercises in the Taiwan Strait, the PLA Navy's transit of Taiwan's waterways, and PLA Air Force overflights of Taiwan's territorial waters.

Below is a detailed examination of some of the most significant PRC political warfare operations and activities, particularly in the realm of united front operations, pan-Red academics and university infiltration, diplomatic strangulation, economic warfare, partnering with criminal gangs, the establishment of new political parties, military intimidation and PLA support, and aggressive cyber operations to exploit Taiwan's new social media environment.

United Front Operations

PRC united front operations against Taiwan are extensive and extraordinarily complex. They support a strategy to divide Taiwanese society by attempting to "sow divisions in Taiwan" and "lure Taiwan-

---

[2] Alexander Bowe, *China's Overseas United Front Work: Background and Implications for the United States* (Washington, DC: U.S.-China Economic and Security Review Commission, 2018), 18–19.

ese people to support pro-China ideas and unification with China."[3] According to Russell Hsiao, executive director of the Global Taiwan Institute, in 2015 the CCP "issued a significant trial regulation on United Front work," which was the "first official regulation issued that comprehensively governs United Front work and more importantly seeks to institutionalize, standardize, and establish procedures regulating this work." The regulation explicitly links "the unification of Taiwan to the goal of the 'great rejuvenation of the Chinese nation' and the 'China dream'."[4]

Senior officers at the ROC's Fu Hsing Kang College, also known as the Political Warfare Cadres Academy, have provided specific insights into PRC political warfare goals against Taiwan. They state that there are different united front strategies pertaining to Taiwan and other overseas countries, which include winning support for PRC policies, increasing PRC influence, and collecting intelligence.[5] Specifically, the PRC's United Front Work Department (UFWD) has a hand in "developing political and business ties with overseas Chinese, bringing investment and research benefits, [and] helping the CCP shape foreign views of China."[6] CCP agencies work to draw overseas Chinese hometown associations, student associations, and other groups into their networks while also attempting to expand their influence over foreign politicians, academics, business leaders, and journalists.

The CCP regulation states that the primary tasks of the united front toward Taiwan are:

- Following the principle of the Central Government's guidance on Taiwan.
- Adhering to the one-China principle.
- Opposing the separatist activities of Taiwan independence.
- Broadly unit[ing] Taiwan compatriots by consolidating the political, economic, cultural and social foundation for deepening peaceful development of cross-strait relations.
- Complet[ing] the great cause of the motherland's unification in the process of realizing the great rejuvenation of the Chinese nation.[7]

[3] Kerry K. Gershaneck, discussions with senior ROC political warfare officers, Fu Hsing Kang College, National Defense University, Taipei, Taiwan, 2018.
[4] Hearing on China's Relations with U.S. Allies and Partners in Europe and the Asia Pacific, before the U.S.-China Economic and Security Review Commission, 115th Cong. (2018) (testimony, Russell Hsiao, Executive Director, Global Taiwan Institute), hereafter Hsiao testimony.
[5] Gershaneck, discussions with senior ROC political warfare officers.
[6] Marcel Angliviel de la Beaumelle, "The United Front Work Department: 'Magic Weapon' at Home and Abroad," Jamestown Foundation, China Brief 17, no. 9, 6 July 2017.
[7] Hsiao testimony.

The ROC government has estimated that the PRC spends more than $337 million annually on UFWD recruiting efforts in Taiwan, and there may be additional "invisible funding" as well.[8] The *Taipei Times* notes that the PRC uses economic incentives to target "local townships, young people and students, Chinese spouses of Taiwanese, Aborigines, pro-China political parties and groups, temples, descendants of Chinese who retain roots in China, labor groups, farmers' and fishermen's associations, and military veterans."[9] As one example of selective targeting, Beijing rewarded eight Kuomintang (KMT) county magistrates in Taiwan who accepted the 1992 Consensus between the PRC and ROC by making swift promises to send Chinese tourists to their jurisdictions and Chinese delegations to purchase their agricultural products. Another approach involves the appointment of prominent Taiwan-born persons to PRC advisory boards such as the Chinese People's Political Consultative Conference, an influential united front political advisory body.

According to University of Miami professor June Teufel Dreyer, the UFWD "sponsors 'exchange' tours to China by Taiwanese students, their teachers, and principals," offers scholarships to some of the PRC's "most prestigious universities," and extends job offers to "the large numbers of PhDs from Taiwan universities who have not been able to find employment there." It has also founded a student baseball league in the PRC, "in which players compete against the backdrop of a large banner reading 'both sides in the Taiwan Strait are one family'." The UFWD especially targets Taiwan's "independence by nature" generation, comprising those "who came of age after the lifting of Taiwan's emergency decrees." These citizens "have no memories of life in China, have grown up under a democratic system, and see no need to declare an independence the country already enjoys."[10]

United front operations impacting the ROC military are multifaceted to an extraordinary degree. Former ROC military officers are often lured to support PRC objectives through business opportunities, appeals to common ethnic heritage, and family ties among those separated when the Chinese Civil War ended in 1949. For example, the Fifth "Linking Fates" Cultural Festival of Cross-Strait Generals, a meeting between retired PRC and ROC military generals in 2017, exposed the many different types of channels used to conduct political warfare operations. The united front operation was supported by

[8] Chung Li-hua and Sherry Hsiao, "China Targets 10 Groups for 'United Front'," *Taipei Times* (Taiwan), 15 January 2018.
[9] Chung and Hsiao, "China Targets 10 Groups for 'United Front'."
[10] June Teufel Dreyer, "A Weapon without War: China's United Front Strategy," Foreign Policy Research Institute, 6 February 2018.

numerous PRC organizations, including the Chinese Foundation for Military Families and Army Support, the China General Network, the Chinese Lien Surname Fraternal Association, the Fujian-Taiwan Exchange Association, two daily newspapers, one Taiwan-based group, and the ROC Association. Russell Hsiao notes that the events sponsors are "usually the State Council's Taiwan Affairs Office or other Taiwan-related [political warfare] organizations."[11]

The myriad of PRC united front organizations connected to the China Association for International Friendly Contact (CAIFC) is daunting enough, but the list of other organizations employed across the PRC's united front is both lengthy and confusing for those not mapping the many interrelationships that exist among them. For example, J. Michael Cole describes the extensive influence web spun by the China Energy Fund Committee (CEFC), a Hong Kong–registered nongovernmental organization that advertises itself as a think tank. The CEFC is run by a former senior official of the PLA Liaison Department-linked CAIFC. The CEFC partners with a wide range of front organizations, foreign governments, and the United Nations (UN). Indirectly, the CEFC runs programs and festivals involving students, academics, entertainers, and religious figures from Taiwan. Cole reports that CEFC engages with the pro-Beijing "Want Want China Times Group" and the pro-unification Fo Guang Shan Foundation for Buddhist Culture and Education to sponsor pro-PRC programs for university students.[12]

The CCP also uses united front proxy organizations to spread "fake news." Hsiao writes that Taiwan's democratic society makes it vulnerable to such attacks: "Observers have noticed a troubling uptick in the infiltration of Taiwan's civil society by proxy organizations associated with [the] CCP's United Front Work Department, with possible financial ties to the PRC government. These united front organizations may then be used to propagate disinformation."[13]

Pan-Red Academics and University Infiltration

PRC united front operations in Taiwan, as elsewhere around the globe, strongly target academia.[14] Based on this author's personal experiences with academic institutions in Taiwan and discussions with security officials and selected Taiwan-based academics, it is clear that Taiwan's key universities have been co-opted to alarming

[11] Russell Hsiao, "Political Warfare Alert: Fifth 'Linking Fates' Cultural Festival of Cross-Strait Generals," Global Taiwan Institute, Global Taiwan Brief 2, no. 2, 11 January 2017.
[12] J. Michael Cole, "Unstoppable: China's Secret Plan to Subvert Taiwan," *National Interest*, 23 March 2015.
[13] Russell Hsiao, "CCP Propaganda against Taiwan Enters the Social Age," Jamestown Foundation, China Brief 18, no. 7, 24 April 2018.
[14] Bowe, *China's Overseas United Front Work*, 3–16.

degrees by academics who have effectively joined the PRC's united front. These pro-PRC academics have incurred the derogatory name "pan-Red professors," for they are no longer seen as KMT-leaning "pan-Blue" or Democratic Progressive Party (DPP)-leaning "pan-Green," but have in effect become agents of influence for the "Red" CCP.[15] These pan-Red academics pose a serious threat to Taiwan's future.[16]

Some pan-Reds openly denigrate Taiwan's democracy and extoll the PRC's totalitarian regime to students who will become tomorrow's teachers, professors, diplomats, judges, attorneys, legislators, military officers, and policy makers. This author has seen pan-Red academics in action and has listened to students describe in detail how these professors propagandize and demoralize their pupils, routinely enforce the prohibition of discussion of topics deemed taboo by the PRC, and use PRC doctrinaire terminology when discussing sensitive subjects. Some co-opted professors exhort students interested in serving as ROC diplomats and military officers "not to serve this regime," but to wait until reunification with the PRC, which, the assert, "will occur in the next few years." The students feel they cannot report this, as no one in a position of authority will hold the offending professors accountable and the students themselves could see their academic careers easily ruined by being accorded bad grades and other forms of retribution.[17]

Numerous students, speaking on the condition of anonymity, have explained that while this talk demoralizes them, they try to ignore it. However, their anecdotal information likely does not reflect the ability of the general student body to inoculate themselves from this near-daily pro-PRC propaganda in their classrooms.

Taiwanese professors and other academic officials are routinely invited to "consult" with PRC officials during all-expense paid trips to the PRC. From discussions with security officials and some professors who accepted invitations to the PRC but were dismayed by attempts to coopt them once there, several trends are apparent. First, academics sometimes leave for the PRC on very short notice to con-

---

[15] Similar to the United States, Taiwan's political party system is color-coded in popular discourse. The DPP leads the pan-Green Coalition, named for the DPP party colors, which normally includes the Taiwan Independence Party, the Taiwan Solidarity Union, and the New Power Party. This coalition favors "Taiwanization" and independence for Taiwan as opposed to "reunification" with the PRC. The KMT leads the pan-Blue Coalition, named for the KMT party colors, which normally includes the People First Party, the New Party and the Non-Partisan Solidarity Union. This coalition favors a Chinese nationalist identity over a separate Taiwanese one as well as close political and economic ties with the PRC. It has historically supported Taiwan's "reunification" with the PRC but now often proclaims that it supports the "political status quo." The author coined the term *pan-Red academic* to describe Taiwanese academics who support Taiwan's absorption into the PRC and who consistently parrot PRC propaganda narratives. Key Taiwan officials and academics with whom the author discussed the term agreed that pan-Red academic is a valid descriptor.

[16] Kerry K. Gershaneck, discussions with Taiwanese academics and government officials, Taiwan, 2018–20.

[17] Kerry K. Gershaneck, discussions with Taiwanese and foreign graduate students, Taiwan, 2018–20.

sult in the PRC for weeks at a time. Second, academics that attend PRC "conferences" and "consultations on reunification" are often offered the promise of academic positions or other rewards in a "re-unified" Chinese academic institution. They are also offered funding for conferences, study, and travel, with the funding being provided under various guises such as think tanks and foundations. Finally, several academics report being offered "entertainment"—generally sexual favors but including other enticements as well—and other perks in the PRC that would, under certain circumstances, lead to entrapment.[18]

Upon return to Taiwan, many of these professors become models of PRC "conditioned behavior." Having succumbed to persuasion, inducement, and/or coercion, as Ambassador Bilahari Kausikan described, they think and act "in such a way that [they] will of [their] own volition do what [the CCP] wants without being told."[19] These co-opted academics will reliably never publicly criticize the PRC for fear of losing future travel, funding, and professional opportunities afforded by the PRC. They are also fearful of being reported to Beijing for even the mildest criticism of the PRC by fellow co-opted Taiwan academics or PRC students.[20]

This author has witnessed this practice repeatedly at academic conferences and forums. The script that plays out is generally as follows: co-opted academics passionately criticize ROC president Tsai Ing-wen's regime and other democratically elected leaders, such as Japanese prime minister Shinzo Abe or U.S. president Donald J. Trump. They will also criticize democracy or, for example, the arbitral court ruling on the South China Sea, in conformance with current PRC propaganda narratives. But when confronted with exposure of their incorrect facts, hypocrisy, or misrepresentations, these academics fall silent. When challenged with sound reason to criticize the totalitarian nature and history of the CCP or questions regarding their lack of intellectual honesty and moral courage by failing to defend democracy and expose totalitarian oppression, these academics avoid eye contact and look at the table. They cannot respond, because to do so would cause them to criticize the PRC, and they know that any criticism of the PRC, however slight, will be reported to Beijing by other pan-Red professors or informants.

Pan-Red professors also refuse to directly and openly confront topics Beijing deems taboo, such as the PRC's illegal occupation of Tibet, its concentration camps in East Turkestan, the brutal suppres-

---

[18] Gershaneck, discussions with Taiwanese academics and government officials.
[19] Bilahari Kausikan, "An Expose of How States Manipulate Other Countries' Citizens," *Straits Times* (Singapore), 1 July 2018.
[20] Gershaneck, discussions with Taiwanese academics and government officials.

sion of civil rights and police-state censorship in the PRC, its illegal occupation of the South China Sea, and the totalitarian and fascist nature of the CCP. Their failure to speak about these subjects enables the PRC's censorship regime to continually expand its reach in Taiwan, swallowing up new topics as forbidden.

Students from the PRC in Taiwan also engage in, and are subject to, PRC political warfare. Beijing cut the number of mainland Chinese students allowed to study in Taiwan by as much as 50 percent beginning in 2017 to punish the Tsai administration, and few Chinese students were allowed back into Taiwan after the advent of the COVID-19 pandemic in January 2020. Nevertheless, these Chinese students have had a dramatic impact on Taiwan's educational institutions.[21] They are a major conduit for transmitting PRC policies and propaganda. Further, these students and their Chinese Students and Scholars Associations at Taiwan universities intimidate and coerce professors and fellow students.

One instance at Chung Yuan Christian University in Taiwan in April 2020 provides a disturbing example of academic harassment and intimidation. It is a textbook case of mainland Chinese student intimidation, pan-Red Academics aiding and abetting that intimidation, and PRC propaganda organs attacking the victim of the intimidation. In April 2020, a professor at Chung Yuan Christian University mentioned the "Wuhan pneumonia caused by the covid-19 virus" in class. A PRC student in the class protested and pressed the charge of "discrimination" against the professor. Rather than defend this professor's academic freedom, the institution made the professor apologize. They apologized in class and said, "As a professor of the Republic of China, I will not discriminate against the students." Four days later, the university asked the professor to issue another apology for the using the phrase "Republic of China." While the Tsai administration then asserted that "institutions of higher education can allow neither self-censorship and interference of teachers' freedom in conducting lectures," PRC propaganda organs such as the *Global Times* initiated sustained attacks on the professor, with lengthy quotes from the aggrieved student and a university threat to prosecute them.[22]

Another vector for PRC political warfare in Taiwan includes the large number of Taiwanese students who study in the PRC. According to the ROC ministry of education, there are approximately 10,000

[21] Study International reports that while 2,136 Chinese students were approved to attend Taiwan universities in 2016, only 1,000 were allowed to do so in 2017. See "China Doesn't Want Its Students to Study in Taiwan," Study International, 7 July 2017.
[22] Fan Lingzhi, "Taiwan Professor Plays Victim in 'Apology' for Discriminatory Remarks against Mainland Student," *Global Times* (Beijing), 12 May 2020.

such students who have studied or are studying in China, whereas prior the pandemic there were 9,300 Chinese students studying in Taiwan. Beijing has recently made it easier for Taiwanese students to attend PRC universities; Taiwanese high school graduates need only show a passing grade to apply, compared to in the past when only those students with top grades or those from Taiwanese international high schools in the PRC could apply.[23] Even more than the Taiwanese academics and others who are lured to the PRC with offers of lucrative jobs and academic status, the students are ill-prepared to fend of the relentless propaganda and other forms of malign influence to which they are routinely subjected.[24]

Diplomatic Strangulation

According to Russell Hsiao, "The PRC is engaged in an intensifying political warfare campaign that is aimed at isolating Taiwan by suppressing the island's international space." Beijing has concentrated great efforts on depriving Taiwan of this international space by coercing or bribing foreign governments to break diplomatic relations with Taiwan.[25] In the spring of 2018, the Dominican Republic and Burkina Faso established ties with the PRC, and that August, El Salvador cut diplomatic ties with Taiwan.[26] Panama, São Tomé and Príncipe, the Solomon Islands, and Kiribati have also severed ties with Taipei, leaving just 15 countries that maintain official diplomatic allegiance with the island nation.[27]

The PRC also pressures countries to evict Taiwan from international organizations, such as the World Health Assembly, the governing body of the World Health Organization, and the International Civil Aviation Organization. Taiwan has seen its title in the World Economic Forum changed from "Chinese Taipei" to "Taiwan, China."[28] In some instances, Beijing threatens foreign companies unless they literally erase Taiwan from their websites. Moreover, in what can only be deemed a bizarre and hypocritical UN policy, Taiwanese citizens who hold ROC passports are forbidden from entering UN facilities in New York City and Geneva, Switzerland. According to Taiwan's representative office in Bern, Switzerland, those Taiwanese

---

[23] "China Doesn't Want Its Students to Study in Taiwan."

[24] Gershaneck, discussions with senior ROC political warfare officers.

[25] Josh Rogin, "China's Interference in the 2018 Elections Succeeded—in Taiwan," *Washington Post*, 18 December 2018.

[26] Chris Buckley and Chris Horton, "Xi Jinping Warns Taiwan that Unification Is the Goal and Force Is an Option," *New York Times*, 1 January 2019.

[27] Chris Massaro, "China Tightens Noose around Taiwan while Challenging U.S. Primacy," Fox News, 3 October 2019.

[28] David W. F. Huang, " 'Cold Peace' and the Nash Equilibrium in Cross-Straits Relations (Part 2)," Global Taiwan Institute, Global Taiwan Brief 2, no. 2, 11 January 2017.

citizens must go through the PRC embassy to get permission to visit the UN, even for issues regarding international human rights.

Finally, Dr. David W. F. Huang writes that alleged Taiwanese lawbreakers who were "accused of crimes in Kenya, Cambodia, Malaysia, and Vietnam were deported (or abducted) to Beijing, rather than to Taiwan," which demonstrates Beijing's supposed "judicial power over Taiwan under the 'One-China' policy." He concludes that such incidents are designed to "punish" the DPP government "for its reluctance to accept the terms of the so-called '1992 Consensus'."[29]

Economic Warfare

Through economic warfare, the PRC seeks to create political problems to ensure that the Tsai administration's economic strategy fails. The PRC has blocked some of Taiwan's trade diversion measures, such as a free trade agreement with Australia, and has greatly reduced the number of tourists it allows to visit Taiwan as well as the number of delegations purchasing Taiwan's products. It has also leveraged internal Taiwan divisions to influence its 2018 elections by offering to work directly with farmers in southern Taiwan to purchase more of their products. Since most of Taiwan's trade is with the PRC, the CCP devotes special attention to Taiwanese business people. Those who endorse policies favorable to China receive special treatment and appointments to PRC organizations, while those who do not find themselves cut off from such opportunities. Further, the Taiwan Affairs Office of the PRC's State Council invites young Taiwanese to start their own businesses in mainland China.[30]

Criminal Gangs

The use of criminal, business, and political organizations is another weapon in the PRC's political warfare arsenal against Taiwan. Former ROC president Lee Teng-hui addressed this challenge, and several ROC political warfare officers that were interviewed by this author state that PRC united front work in Taiwan includes sponsoring organized criminal activities to stir up interethnic conflict and destabilize society.

Paul Huang at *The Epoch Times* writes, "Taiwanese gangs are the cat's paw of the Chinese regime, working for [Taiwan's] unification with the mainland while using violence to subdue those the [PRC] opposes." The Chinese Unification Promotion Party (CUPP) and the Patriot Alliance Association, two criminal-gang-related groups, are useful examples. Both organizations are known for openly advocat-

---

[29] Huang, " 'Cold Peace' and the Nash Equilibrium in Cross-Straits Relations (Part 2)."
[30] Gershaneck, discussions with senior ROC political warfare officers.

ing PRC rule in Taiwan. Chang An-lo, known as the "White Wolf," is founder the Taiwanese branch of the CUPP and leader of Bamboo Union, a large criminal triad in Taiwan. The CUUP, which claims to have 20,000 members, is frequently seen as a recruitment front for the Bamboo Union.[31]

Moreover, Taiwan's news media reports that Bamboo Union and another criminal triad group, the Four Seas Gang, are both "under the influence or even direct control" of China's Ministry of State Security (MSS). The MSS allegedly runs the Fujian-Xiamen bureau of the Taiwan Affairs Office, which was established to control the gangs in Taiwan and recruit Taiwanese gang members to work for the benefit of the CCP.[32]

In addition to providing muscle for political intimidation, organized crime syndicates are "a primary conduit for the Chinese government to funnel an estimated [New Taiwan] NT$35 billion ($1.13 billion USD) in financial support to pro-China parties to run propaganda organizations and political campaigns in an attempt to subvert the (2018) nine-in-one elections." They are also alleged to have "recruited young people to attend political rallies . . . paying each participant NT$1,000 on the condition that they wear CUPP vests and carry Chinese flags."[33]

New Political Parties and a Paramilitary "Youth Association"

In addition to organized crime and political associations, the PRC has also attempted to establish a political party, the New Party, and an associated youth paramilitary organization in Taiwan. June Teufel Dreyer notes that in 2005, more than 20 Taiwanese political figures from both the KMT and DPP who had been sidelined by their parties were invited to "serve as organizing central committee members of a new, pro-Beijing, party." *The Taiwan Crisis*, written by Chinese dissident Yuan Hongbing, confirmed that by 2008, the CCP's politburo "had passed a political strategy for settling the Taiwan issue that listed organizing a political party in Taiwan as its most important united front tactic." The New Party, "which espouses policies that echo those of the CCP, is legitimate under Taiwan law," Teufel Dreyer concludes. It has also been alleged that the party has

---

[31] Paul Huang, "Beating of Students in Taiwan Puts Spotlight on Chinese Regime's Influence," *Epoch Times*, 3 October 2017.

[32] Huang, "Beating of Students in Taiwan Puts Spotlight on Chinese Regime's Influence."

[33] Gary Schmitt and Michael Mazza, *Blinding the Enemy: CCP Interference in Taiwan's Democracy* (Washington, DC: Global Taiwan Institute, 2019), 12–13.

"founded a paramilitary New China Youth Association with the goal of 'wartime control'" of Taiwan.[34]

Military Intimidation and Hybrid Warfare

The strategic focus of the UFWD and PLA is to manipulate international perceptions of One China and undermine Taiwan's international legitimacy, while also "disintegrating" the ROC's will to resist. This combination of military and political warfare capabilities is the foundation of PRC hybrid warfare, according to David R. Ignatius at *The Washington Post*, who asserts that "traditional military combat may be the least of Taiwan's worries." The reason? "Hybrid warfare is cheaper and harder for an open, democratic society such as Taiwan to resist than a conventional military assault," Ignatius argues. "And it's a challenge that Taiwanese experts are struggling to understand and address."[35]

Military intimidation is designed to physically and psychologically wear down an adversary's armed forces and civilian populace. While the PRC's relentless military intimidation against Taiwan, especially since the advent of the Tsai administration in 2016, has been detailed in the previous chapter, recent organizational changes have significantly impacted the PLA's substantial contributions to PRC political warfare against Taiwan.

Beijing's February 2016 establishment of the PLA Eastern Theater Command (ETC), which replaced the Nanjing Military Region (NJMR), was a key milestone for the PRC in the cross-straits security situation. However, even before the establishment of the ETC, the PLA founded a joint command in the NJMR that would have provided improved command and control in a Taiwan-related combat scenario. In December 2015, the CCP's Central Military Commission established a general command unit to control integrated operations of ground, naval, and air forces and established a joint operational command structure for each of the "battle zones" to include the NJMR.[36]

The ETC plays a major role in directing political and military coercion against Taiwan, and its reorganization into the expanded theater command increases it operational capacity. In addition to PLA Ground Force, Navy, and Air Force units, the ETC has operational authority—to include political warfare—over the Anhui, Fu-

---

[34] Teufel Dreyer, "A Weapon without War."

[35] David R. Ignatius, "China's Hybrid Warfare against Taiwan," *Washington Post*, 14 December 2018.

[36] Rachael Burton and Mark Stokes, "The People's Liberation Army Theater Command Leadership: The Eastern Theater Command," Project 2049 Institute, 13 August 2018.

jian, Fuzhou, Jiangsu, Jiangxi, and Zhejiang military districts as well as the Shanghai Garrison.[37]

Much of the PRC's political warfare against Taiwan is directed by the PLA Political Work Department's 311 Base in Fuzhou, which Mark Stokes and Russell Hsiao assert is at "the forefront of applied psychological operations and propaganda directed against Taiwan."[38] Working in concert with the UFWD's complex web of public and ostensibly private entities that constitute Beijing's political warfare apparatus, 311 Base plays a central role within the ETC in the PRC's coercive persuasion campaign against Taiwan. As a deputy corps-level organization, it "carries roughly as much status as . . . [the] six conventional missile brigades that target Taiwan *combined*" and "is actively involved in PLA cyber operations," reports J. Michael Cole.[39]

The Political Warfare Threat in Taiwan's New Social Media Environment

"New information and communication technologies [have] magnified PRC propaganda and disinformation to an unprecedented degree," writes to Russell Hsiao. "The viral aspect of social media has made it an effective tool for propaganda and disinformation."[40]

According to Hsiao, Taiwan boasts one of the highest internet usage and smartphone penetration rates in the world, and it has a vigorous information and communications technology industry with one of the fastest internet speeds in the Asia-Pacific region. The most popular social media platforms in Taiwan are Facebook, LINE, YouTube, and the Professional Technology Temple. The CCP uses this extensive social media network to spread propaganda and disinformation in various ways as a part of its influence operations against Taiwan.[41] Keoni Everington at the *Taiwan News* writes that the PRC "has long regarded Taiwan as a test ground for its cyber warfare techniques, with an average of 100,000 cyber attacks reported per month in 2017 alone." The PRC has also reportedly established its own version of the Russian "troll factory" that takes to social media platforms to influence foreign attitudes and events.[42]

In support of the PRC's troll factory is the PLA Strategic Support Force (SSF), which is responsible for offensive and defensive cyber missions, intelligence operations, and technical reconnaissance. The

[37] Burton and Stokes, "The People's Liberation Army Theater Command Leadership."
[38] Mark Stokes and Russell Hsiao, *The People's Liberation Army General Political Department: Political Warfare with Chinese Characteristics* (Arlington, VA: Project 2049 Institute, 2013), 29.
[39] J. Michael Cole, *Convergence or Conflict in the Taiwan Strait: The Illusion of Peace?* (Abingdon, UK: Routledge, 2017), 68. Emphasis in original.
[40] Hsiao, "CCP Propaganda against Taiwan Enters the Social Age."
[41] Hsiao, "CCP Propaganda against Taiwan Enters the Social Age."
[42] Keoni Everington, "China's 'Troll Factory' Targeting Taiwan with Disinformation Prior to Election," *Taiwan News* (Taipei), 5 November 2018.

PLA reportedly has approximately 300,000 soldiers serving with the SSF, while more than 2 million are alleged to be members of the "50 Cent Army" that manipulates public opinion and attacks PRC critics and other targets in support of the CCP.[43]

According to the ROC's National Security Bureau, the PRC's *modus operandi* is to "spread false news in Taiwan, focusing on cross-strait relations, military defense, and policy implementation by the Tsai administration, among other issues." First, PRC state-run media outlets publish fake news stories about these topics. Next, PLA cyber soldiers and 50 Cent Army members disseminate the disinformation via Facebook, LINE, YouTube, and the Professional Technology Temple.[44] Specific techniques include "circulating fake imagery, in the hopes that it will go viral and be picked up on by traditional media outlets in Taiwan." For example, an image displaying PRC bombers flying near Yu Shan (Jade Mountain) in Taiwan was posted on social media, clearly as a psychological warfare tactic meant to "instill fear in the hearts of the Taiwanese public." The photograph was widely shared on social media before Taiwan's defense ministry could deny the legitimacy of the image.[45]

The PRC also uses disinformation and propaganda on social media platforms to cause social instability in Taiwan by influencing the nation's ongoing pension reform debate. Hsiao writes that users of LINE and other platforms in Taiwan "reported a flood of messages and websites that falsely claimed that the central government was planning to impose draconian restrictions on pensioners," forcing the ROC government to quickly issue a statement denying that charge.[46]

Hsiao also notes that the PRC has reinvigorated another "time-honored tactic" in the new social media era: intentionally concealing or misreporting statements made by Taiwanese officials or ex-officials "to tarnish the person's reputation or mislead the readers into believing that the person supports a particular political position held by the CCP." Both PRC- and Hong Kong-based media outlets employ these tactics against ROC retired generals, national security officials, lawmakers, and even entertainers.[47]

Moreover, the CCP uses computational propaganda, typically in the form of social media, content farms, and bots, to "saturate Taiwan's information space with pro-Beijing political propaganda."

[43] Everington, "China's 'Troll Factory' Targeting Taiwan with Disinformation Prior to Election."
[44] Everington, "China's 'Troll Factory' Targeting Taiwan with Disinformation Prior to Election."
[45] Hsiao, "CCP Propaganda against Taiwan Enters the Social Age."
[46] Russell Hsiao, "China's Intensifying Pressure Campaign against Taiwan," Jamestown Foundation, China Brief 18, no. 11, 19 June 2018.
[47] Hsiao, "CCP Propaganda against Taiwan Enters the Social Age."

J. Michael Cole argues that "computational propaganda has allowed Beijing to insert itself into the battleground of domestic Taiwanese politics, so much so that various (dis)information campaigns can no longer be solely attributed to the KMT and other pan-blue forces." He goes on to explain that Chinese disinformation efforts have recently begun overlapping with "traditional blocking action by opposition legislators and civic groups opposed to reforms," which includes "protests against pension reform, government plans to limit the . . . burning of large quantities of incense and ghost money at Buddhist temples, and limits for the Tsai administration's Forward-looking Infrastructure Development Program."[48]

Finally, it is important to note the use of the Chinese web platform WeChat in Taiwan. Combining many of the features of Facebook, Twitter, WhatsApp, and Skype, WeChat is the single largest web platform for news and communication in the Chinese-speaking world, with half a billion users in the PRC alone. It is owned and operated by the Chinese web company Tencent, which reportedly cooperates very closely with the PRC's state security apparatus. Accordingly, WeChat works alongside the PRC's propaganda apparatuses to track the communications of possible dissidents and to censor content, comments, and links deemed unfavorable to the CCP and its worldview. Since many Taiwanese citizens use WeChat, the long arm of PRC's security arm is able to censor communications within Taiwan's borders.[49] As one example, by March 2020, WeChat had assisted the PRC's global COVID-19 propaganda campaign by blacklisting more than 500 keywords related to the coronavirus, and was found to have the capability to identify "certain users and [create] a portfolio about them, feeding other aspects of the [Chinese Communist Party's] transnational repression apparatus."[50]

Equally disturbing, the CCP uses WeChat and other social media platforms as a united front weapon to mobilize Chinese both within the PRC and abroad to organize street protests, as has been evidenced in major demonstrations in U.S. cities and student protests against campus free speech in Canada.[51] If it has not already been used to coordinate united front and other political warfare operations in Taiwan, WeChat's use in North America for such purposes proves the efficacy of social media platforms in PRC operations against Taiwan.

[48] J. Michael Cole, "Will China's Disinformation War Destabilize Taiwan?," *National Interest*, 30 July 2017.
[49] Gershaneck, discussions with senior ROC political warfare officers.
[50] Alexa Grunow, "WeChat Uses International Accounts to Advance Censorship in China," Organization for World Peace, 11 May 2020.
[51] Julie Makinen, "Chinese Social Media Platform Plays a Role in U.S. Rallies for NYPD Officer," *Los Angeles (CA) Times*, 24 February 2016; and Gerry Shih and Emily Rauhala, "Angry over Campus Speech by Uighur Activist, Students in Canada Contact Chinese Consulate, Film Presentation," *Washington Post*, 14 February 2019.

CHAPTER NINE

Conclusions and Recommendations

Wave of anti-American rage along the Huangpu River, 1961. This poster depicts Chinese demonstrations against American capitalism and the U.S. military along the Bund in Shanghai.

The purpose of this book is to examine the People's Republic of China's (PRC) political warfare in sufficient detail to provide recommendations for the United States to successfully combat this existential threat to America and its partners and allies. As was evidenced during the Cold War, if the United States displays the strength and leadership to fight, friendly and allied nations will follow.

PRC political warfare entails a relentless, multifaceted onslaught of strategies, tactics, techniques, and procedures. However, each government's responses to these attacks are quite different, as reflected in the two country studies herein. Thailand's ruling establishment, for example, seems amenable to PRC influence operations and does not seek to publicly confront or expose them. This approach is based on Thailand's unique history, geography, business ties, and current political situation regarding China. Nevertheless, PRC political warfare has the clear potential to limit Thailand's sovereignty and its historical flexibility to "bend with the wind" to protect its national interests. The government of Taiwan, on the other hand, realizes the existential danger that PRC political warfare poses to its continuance as a self-ruling, vibrant democracy. For many historical, political, and ethnic reasons, Taiwan faces both external and self-imposed constraints on how to deal with the threat. While it attempts to resist PRC political warfare within its limited maneuvering space, Taiwan has failed to develop a comprehensive approach to confronting the threat, and there currently exists no coherent strategic or operational framework for doing so.

Other countries and regions vital to the United States have demonstrated disturbing temerity under the Chinese Communist Party's (CCP) political warfare assault. Notable recent examples related to the COVID-19 pandemic include the European Union, under pressure from Beijing, delaying and then heavily watering down a report documenting the massive PRC disinformation campaign, as well as Southeast Asian nations self-censoring regarding the PRC's egregious actions during the pandemic.[1]

Ideally, this book will help the United States lead its own united front of free, like-minded nations to deter, counter, and defeat PRC political warfare. Further, other countries under assault can benefit from this work as they assess their own vulnerabilities, capabilities, and strategies in the face of Beijing's political warfare campaigns against them. Given strong, visionary, and agile leadership, the following recommendations are achievable. To deter, counter, and ultimately defeat PRC political warfare, the United States should consider the following actions.

Identify the PRC Threat by Its Rightful Name: Political Warfare

The PRC is engaged in war against the United States. It is not mere competition or malign influence, but war by PRC definition. Words matter. Ideally, correct terminology leads to proper national goals, objectives, policies, and operations. That is precisely why American diplomat George F. Kennan outlined both his successful Cold War-era strategies of containment and counterpolitical warfare in straightforward terms. But national leaders must educate internal and external audiences that the PRC is engaging in political warfare

---

[1] Eric Chan and 1stLt Peter Loftus, USAF, "Chinese Communist Party Information Warfare: U.S.-China Competition during the COVID-19 Pandemic," *Air Force Journal of Indo-Pacific Affairs* 3, no. 2 (May 2020); and Sophie Boisseau du Rocher, "What COVID-19 Reveals about China-Southeast Asia Relations," *Diplomat*, 8 April 2020.

against the United States and explain, in general terms, why and how it plans to confront the threat.

Develop a National Strategy to Counter PRC Political Warfare

Through legislation, the United States should mandate a national strategy, appoint a highly respected coordinator for political warfare within the U.S. National Security Council (NSC), establish a strategic operational center of gravity like the Cold War-era U.S. Information Agency (USIA) with broader authority than the existing Global Engagement Center and external to the U.S. Department of State, and develop counterpolitical warfare career paths in diplomatic, military, and intelligence organizations.[2] The Center for Strategic and Budgetary Assessments study by Ross Babbage provides an excellent delineation of steps to be taken to build a strategy. The United States must first state its goals in combating political warfare and then develop a "theory of victory" and an end state. It should also determine if its chief aim is to "force a cessation of authoritarian state political warfare and instill greater caution" in regimes such as the PRC or Russia or to "facilitate the demise of these regimes and their replacement by liberal democratic alternatives."[3]

Rebuild National Institutions to Counter PRC Political Warfare

The U.S. executive and legislative branches of government must revive the nation's ability to engage in information operations and strategic communication similar in scope to the capabilities that were developed during the Cold War. This means establishing a twenty-first-century USIA equivalent, which ideally would be under direct control of the NSC.

Pending legislation and funding authorization that begins the slow process of reestablishing this USIA equivalent, the command and control organization that unifies the national effort could be a standing Joint Interagency Task Force (JIATF) modeled on the JIATF-West counterdrug organization headquartered at Camp Smith, Hawaii. This JIATF could begin operations quickly and

---

[2] The Global Engagement Center has been criticized for being too heavily focused on the threat of Russia, with little focus on sophisticated Chinese disinformation and information warfare operations, and for failing to help educate the American public about the PRC threat. See Bill Gertz, "Inside the Ring: Global Engagement Secrecy," *Washington Times*, 11 March 2020.
[3] Ross Babbage, *Winning Without Fighting: Chinese and Russian Political Warfare Campaigns and How the West Can Prevail*, vol. I (Washington, DC: Center for Strategic and Budgetary Assessments, 2019), 80.

would start the process of building cooperation with the private sector, civil society, the legal community, and the news media.

Rebuilding institutions also includes reestablishing the Ronald W. Reagan administration-era Active Measures Working Group, as well as better coordinating the work of the U.S. State Department, the Global Engagement Center, other cabinet-level strategic communications and public affairs structures, and the Broadcasting Board of Governors, which oversees the Voice of America, Radio Free Europe/Radio Liberty, Radio Free Asia, Radio and Tv Martí, and the Middle East Broadcasting Networks.[4]

Establish Education Programs Regarding PRC Political Warfare

The U.S. Departments of State and Defense, especially, should establish courses of varying lengths for senior-level and intermediate-level professionals. Entry-level courses should also be planned for students within the Foreign Service, military, intelligence, commerce, public affairs, and academic communities. This education program would be voluntary for individuals within private-sector industries and nongovernmental organizations but compulsory for government workers, federal contractors, and students attending U.S. government education institutions. Similarly, the private sector and civic groups should initiate public information programs in coordination with news media organizations.

The focus of these courses will be on building internal defenses within the most highly valued PRC target audiences: elected officials, senior policy makers, thought leaders, national security managers, and other information gatekeepers. Similar governmental, institutional, and public education programs were employed successfully during the Cold War, with threat briefs and public discussion a routine part of each. To help propel this education effort forward, the outline for a notional five-day counterpolitical warfare program of instruction is contained in the Appendix of this book.

As a related important initial step, U.S. officials should conduct a content analysis of what is being taught about PRC political warfare at U.S. government education and training institutions. Based on this author's discussions at the Defense Information School and Foreign Service Institute, there are no courses at these foundational schools designed to address political warfare. Discussions with recent graduates of National Defense University, the Army War Col-

---

[4] Michael Dhunjishah, "Countering Propaganda and Disinformation: Bring Back the Active Measures Working Group?," *War Room*, 7 July 2017.

lege, and the U.S. Naval War College indicate there is no formal education being offered on this threat at those institutions, either.

It is also important to assess prior and planned guest lectures, conferences, and symposiums at these education and training institutions as they pertain to PRC political warfare. As one rationale, it is perplexing that speakers such as a widely recognized CCP member and a relentlessly pro-PRC former Australian prime minister were invited to provide keynote addresses to the U.S. Military Academy (West Point) and Naval Academy, respectively. Education institution leadership must be held accountable regarding what and how they teach future U.S. military and diplomatic leaders about both the PRC military and the political warfare threat, as well as how they defend their institutions against being used as platforms for hostile political warfare operations.

Immediately available mass-education instruments include public affairs and media assets within the Departments of State and Defense. As was done during the Cold War, public affairs can be used today to educate internal and external audiences about PRC political warfare and routinely expose such operations publicly. As a matter of policy, the U.S. government's public affairs assets should be used to counter propaganda generated by such organs as the *People's Liberation Army Daily* newspaper, as well as to expose united front operations such as efforts by the China Association for International Friendly Contact to co-opt retired U.S. military officers. By exposing those political warfare operations on a sustained basis in U.S. government publications, internal and external audiences learn over time the nature of the PRC threat.

Establish an Asian Political Warfare Center of Excellence Think Tank

An Asian Political Warfare Center of Excellence (APWCE) would be similar to the Finland-based European Centre of Excellence for Countering Hybrid Threats, as would its mission: "To develop a common understanding of PRC political warfare threats and promote the development of a comprehensive, whole-of-government response at national levels in countering PRC and other political warfare threats."[5] The APWCE would be a whole-of-government effort, but in practice its primary U.S. government sponsors would be the Department of Defense, Department of State, Department of Commerce, Central Intelligence Agency, Federal Bureau of Investi-

---

[5] Kerry K. Gershaneck, "PRC Threat Obliges Political Defense," *Taipei Times* (Taipei), 10 July 2019.

gation (FBI), and United States Agency for International Development.

The APWCE will provide the intellectual foundation and education needed to develop and synchronize counterpolitical warfare and offensive political warfare capabilities, but it would not have authority to conduct or coordinate those operations.

Notional APWCE functions would be to:

- Encourage strategic-level dialogue and consulting between and among like-minded nations, in Asia and throughout the world.
- Investigate and examine political warfare operations targeted at democracies by the PRC and map the vulnerabilities of participating nations to improve their resilience and response.
- Conduct tailored training and arrange scenario-based exercises for practitioners aimed at enhancing the individual capabilities of and interoperability among participants in countering PRC political warfare threats.
- Conduct research and analysis into PRC political warfare methods to counter such operations.
- Invite and engage in dialogue with government and nongovernmental experts and practitioners from a wide range of professional sectors and disciplines to improve situational awareness of PRC and other political warfare threats. Typical participants would be practitioners, scholars, policymakers, congressional staff, journalists, strategists, campaign planners, legal specialists, and selected civil servants as well as foreign service, military, intelligence, and law enforcement officers.

Ultimately the APWCE's curriculum would comprise a wide range of courses of varying duration. However, because the United States is far behind the PRC in this fight, a short introductory course should be established immediately. The notional five-day program of instruction provided in the following appendix allows for rapid initiation of the APWCE's proposed education and training mission. With strong, agile leadership and competent faculty and staff, an initial APWCE training program could be put in place within 30 days.

Investigate, Disrupt, and Prosecute PRC Political Warfare Activities

The U.S. Department of State, Department of Defense, Department of Justice, FBI, and Intelligence Community each play key roles on countering PRC political warfare. Based on past U.S. failures in countering political warfare operations and prosecuting espionage prosecutions, as described by Peter Mattis in his testimony before Congress in 2018, it is imperative to review existing laws, legislation, and policies that apply to PRC political warfare to ensure the existence of clear mission statements, requirements for action, and assessments of success.[6]

Screen, Track, and Expose PRC Political Warfare Activities

In this author's discussions with FBI, military intelligence, and Department of State officials, it is apparent that combatting PRC political warfare has not received the priority it deserves to compete successfully in resource battles within government bureaucracies. As Mattis highlights, "the Executive Branch has failed to prosecute or botched investigations into Chinese espionage," which are more straightforward to prosecute than political warfare and other influence operations.[7] The Intelligence Community and Department of Justice personnel that perform counterpolitical warfare are likely the same who conduct counterespionage, and for them to succeed there is a need for better analytical, investigative, and legal training.

Routinely Expose Covert and Overt PRC Political Warfare Operations

Through legislation and/or executive order, the United State should mandate an annual, NSC-led, publicly disseminated report on the CCP's political warfare against the United States. The annual report would be similar to the Reagan-era annual report on Soviet active measures, with focus on PRC united front interference and influence operations. It would include practical advice for ordinary citizens about how to recognize and avoid those threats. According to Mattis, an annual report on the CCP's activities would force "government agencies to come together to discuss the problem and make decisions about what information needed to be released for public consump-

---

[6] *Hearing on U.S. Responses to China's Foreign Influence Operations, before the House Committee on Foreign Affairs, Subcommittee on Asia and the Pacific,* 115th Cong. (2018) (testimony by Peter Mattis, Fellow, Jamestown Foundation), hereafter Mattis testimony.

[7] Mattis testimony.

tion." It would also "have the beneficial effect of raising awareness and convening disparate parts of the U.S. Government that may not often speak with each other. A classified annex could be produced for internal government consumption."[8] This annual report should be augmented by periodic publicly disseminated reports on PRC political warfare in geographic regions and against institutions such as the United Nations and the news media.

As the Hudson Institute suggests, one way to operationalize the public's exposure to PRC political warfare is for the U.S. executive branch to work with academic institutions, journalists, think tanks, and other organizations to map out political warfare operations and expose those that can be publicly uncovered without harming national security. One approach is to design a "united front tracker" that can expose PRC political warfare fronts, enablers, and operatives and hold them accountable. This tracker could, for example, reveal the myriad of groups engaged in united front activities, such as taxpayer-funded conferences at universities and academic institutions that parrot PRC propaganda themes. By exposing political warfare operations on a sustained basis, the United States can better inform its citizens of the threat they face and how best to contend with those threats. Such a tracker could also be used to publicly shame united front and other political warfare operations. That kind of shaming can be quite beneficial, as was proven when the U.S. government took forceful action against Republic of South Africa influence operations during the apartheid era with the United States Comprehensive Anti-Apartheid Act of 1986.

Other steps that should be taken include publicly identifying those involved in foreign censorship and influence in the news media. Most Americans are likely unaware that PRC-based news organizations act as organs of the CCP and that their reporting is directed by the CCP Propaganda/Publicity Department, as opposed to the often-independent reporting of commercial news media organizations. It is also important to publicize business organizations and public relations and law firms involved in lobbying on behalf of the PRC, as well as academics and universities that support PRC political warfare.

Raise the Costs for CCP Interference

Too often, the U.S. government has been weak in confronting PRC transgressions, even on American soil, by overriding U.S. law en-

---

[8] Mattis testimony.

forcement officials and thereby accommodating illegal PRC intelligence activities. For example, consider the May 2017 incident in New York City, when the FBI was prevented by the Department of State from arresting several high-ranking Chinese Ministry of State Security officials and other intelligence personnel who were conducting an illegal mission in violation of their U.S. visas. "Beijing faces few if any consequences for its interference inside the United States," Mattis notes. It is long past time to raise the cost of PRC political warfare within the United States. When PRC embassy and consulate officials travel to universities to "threaten students or turn them out for a rally," as they have done to foment counter-Hong Kong protest rallies and disrupt the layover of Taiwan's president in Honolulu, the U.S. government "can revoke their diplomatic status," and "travel restrictions can be placed on such officials."[9]

Take Legal Action against PRC Officials and Affiliates Engaged in Civil Rights Offenses

Although ostensibly a student support association, the real mission of Chinese Students and Scholars Associations (CSSA) is to penetrate academia to subvert democratic institutions and engage in espionage against foreign countries, academics, and Chinese students matriculating abroad. Confucius Institutes, meanwhile, engage in various forms of censorship, coercion, and surveillance of Chinese students and academics. To help counter those actions, Mattis suggests leveraging civil rights legislation such as "Conspiracy Against Rights" (U.S. Code, Title 18, Section 241). Legal action could be taken against CSSAs, Confucius Institutes, and other united front and undercover CCP intelligence and security officials "who threaten, coerce, or intimidate Chinese people (or others) in the United States." Specifically, this provision "makes it unlawful for two or more persons to conspire to "injure, oppress, threaten, or intimidate any person in any State, Territory, Commonwealth, Possession, or District in the free exercise or enjoyment of any right or privilege secured to him by the Constitution or laws of the United States, or because of his having so exercised the same."[10]

[9] Mattis testimony.
[10] Mattis testimony.

Encourage Academic Study that Focuses on Combating PRC Political Warfare

The U.S. government should support research into this existential challenge and how to contain, deter, and/or defeat it; provide funding to students in the field; and offer special high-level recognition and awards.

Pass Legislation to Diminish the Offensive Power of PRC News and Social Media

Freedom of the press must be scrupulously safeguarded in democracies, but allowing totalitarian states such as the PRC to dominate the democracies' news media is the path to national suicide. Legislation, combined with exposure and public shaming, would help diminish the harm that the PRC does through its insidious infiltration of the news media.

Initially, simple steps can be taken, such as passing legislation that requires reciprocity pertaining to news media, social media, and entertainment sectors. Legislation should be passed stating that no PRC-affiliated entity or person should be allowed to buy or engage in any news media, business, education, or entertainment activities in the United States that U.S. citizens cannot do in the PRC. Implicit in this is the requirement that U.S. citizens be allowed to engage in the activity in the PRC without interference, which would allow for free speech, lack of censorship, and no intimidation through direct threats to corporate business interests and physical harassment of individual journalists and their families. Legislation should also be passed that supports and encourages Chinese-language publications, social media, and broadcasts that counter PRC propaganda outlets globally. Finally, U.S. government officials and civic organizations should confront American news media outlets that parrot PRC political warfare narratives.

APPENDIX

Curriculum for a Five-Day Counter-PRC Political Warfare Course

T he purpose of this appendix is to provide a rationale, pedagogy, and curriculum for education and training programs to counter People's Republic of China (PRC) political warfare, with particular focus on a notional five-day counterpolitical warfare course. Although designed for rapid implementation by the proposed Asian Political Warfare Center of Excellence (APWCE), other organizations in the United States and countries under PRC political warfare attack may adopt and tailor this course to meet the urgent need to rapidly build capacity to combat this existential threat.

Background
The PRC is engaged in political warfare against most countries of the world. This is an aggressive brand of total war that integrates all aspects of PRC national power into its political warfare campaigns. Open societies normally lack a whole-of-government understanding and response to the political warfare threat and therefore typically establish weak applicable laws and policies to combat it. Consequently, those nations lack national counterpolitical warfare policies, strategies, organizations, and resources. Worse, as many countries do not realize that they are under attack or are in denial of that fact, they are unwilling and/or unable to effectively respond.

Most countries lost the ability to recognize and combat political warfare nearly three decades ago after the end of the Cold War. The United States, which has historically provided national security focus and resources for its global network of allies and coalition partners, does not teach about PRC political warfare at either the Foreign Service Institute or the Defense Information School, premier institutions where diplomats and military officers prepare to compete on the information battlefield. Further, there are no systematic courses at its National Defense University or various war colleges. Other countries face similar challenges.

Democracies are particularly vulnerable to political warfare because they lack the necessary education about the threat and because the open nature of free societies offers numerous pathways for the PRC to engage in influence and coercion operations. Many authoritarian nations choose to ignore PRC political warfare in their own countries, obtaining validation for their dictatorships from the PRC's totalitarian rule or fearing they may anger the Chinese Communist Party if they confront it. In order to effectively combat the PRC political warfare threat, democracies must refocus their national security cultures and initiate new governmental and public education programs.

Meaningful study of PRC political warfare requires a broad curriculum of extended duration, longer than the five-day course proposed herein. Ultimately, some degree- and certificate-granting institutions, particularly those funded by the U.S government, should incorporate such in-depth curriculum in national security-related programs. In the absence of existing curriculum and programs of study, this notional course provides a relatively easy-to-implement introduction to orient key audiences to critical aspects of PRC political warfare and how to counter it.

Public Education and Training Program Focus

Counter-PRC political warfare education and training should do the following:

- Lay the foundation that political warfare is now a part of the "perpetual rhythm of struggle" on the continuum of conflict.[1]
- Teach how to identify, map, and fight PRC political warfare and assess outcomes.
- Teach how to build enduring legal mechanisms, policies, institutions, and organizations to counter PRC political warfare.
- Develop a network of diplomatic, military, intelligence, law enforcement, legal, and security practitioners and scholars.

In general, the focus of these education and training programs should be on how democratic nations can counter political warfare through a variety of strategies and tactics that range from educating internal audiences about the threat to raising the price of PRC coercion and manipulation. Foundational teachings should illustrate how to identify and track PRC political warfare, engage in strategic

---

[1] George F. Kennan, "The Inauguration of Organized Political Warfare," Office of the Historian of the State Department, 4 May 1948.

communications, develop thought processes to devise useful policies and actions, and build an internal defensive capacity for a long-term political warfare fight.

In addition to teaching defensive actions, courses should educate on skills and tools that can be used to fight back, such as addressing how to introduce asymmetric cost-imposing measures and other offensive strategies and tactics. For example, although the PRC is much more difficult to influence than open democracies, it is more fearful of external ideas and information because of its tenuous legitimacy and massive concentration of wealth and power. Therefore, innovatively introducing alternative perspectives that counter PRC narratives and expose political and economic corruption as well as ineptitude can impose significant costs.

Notional Course Outline

A notional five-day counter-PRC political warfare course should cover the following:

- History of PRC political warfare
- Theory, doctrine, and practice of PRC political warfare
- Terminology
- Political warfare mapping
- National strategic communication planning
- News media and social media
- Intergovernmental coordination
- Civil society engagement
- Legal and law enforcement implications
- Defensive and offensive strategies
- Contemporary political warfare campaigns and case studies

The content of each topic should be tailored specifically for counterpolitical warfare operations. For example, higher-level training courses focusing on national strategic communication planning should teach how to think about strategic communications in countering hostile political warfare. Notional content should include the following:

- Hostile political warfare problem research and analysis
- Friendly political warfare-related strengths, weaknesses, opportunities, and threats

- Counterpolitical warfare campaign objectives, duration, themes, and messages
- Key audiences
- Strategies, tactics, and messages and the tools necessary to convey them
- Scheduling campaign milestones and events
- Budget, personnel, and other resources
- Evaluation criteria and tools
- Coordination with allies, partners, and civic society

Lower-level training courses, meanwhile, should focus on how to execute aspects of this counterpolitical warfare strategic communications framework (table 2).

By the end of the education or training course, students should be able to perform basic mapping of political warfare influence operations (figure 1).

Figure 1. CCP circles of influence

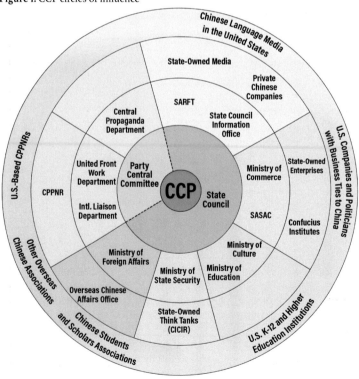

Jonas Parello-Plesner and Belinda Li, The Chinese Communist Party's Foreign
Interference Operations: How the U.S. and Other Democracies Should Respond
(Washington, DC: Hudson Institute, 2018), 15, adapted by MCUP

Table 2. Political warfare course five-day schedule

	Day 1 Understanding PRC Political Warfare	Day 2 Detecting Political Warfare	Day 3 Strategies to Counter Political Warfare	Day 4 Tools and Practical Applications	Day 5 Practical Application and Expert Exchange
Class 1: 0830–1030	Welcome and Course Introduction	Mapping PRC Political Warfare Operations	Combatting PRC Political Warfare	Strategic and Crisis Communications	Participant Case Studies
		Break: 1030–1045			
Class 2: 1045–1230	Overview: The Three Warfares Plus	United Front Operations	Legal and Law Enforcement Implications	Building the Counter-political Warfare Plan	Tabletop Exercise #2
		Lunch: 1230–1330			
Class 3: 1330–1515	PRC Political Warfare Tools	Influence Operations and Special Measures	Whole-of-Government Cooperation	Tabletop Exercise #1	Tabletop Exercise #2 Assessment
		Break: 1515–1530			
Class 4: 1530–1730	Selected Political Warfare Country Case Studies	Assessing PRC Political Warfare Effectiveness	Engaging News Media and Civil Society	Tabletop Exercise #1 Assessment	Course Assessment and Closing Remarks

Compiled by the author, adapted by MCUP

Students will also learn how to map target audiences and influence means (table 3).

Realistically, it will be difficult for all participants to fully absorb the theory and terminology required to become true political warfare specialists in just five days. But it is vital that government officials and key public leaders begin building a foundation to understand these topics. They must also begin learning how to identify, map, and fight PRC political warfare, assess outcomes, and build enduring legal mechanisms, policies, institutions, and organizations to counter the threat.

Extended courses, such as those at the National Defense University or equivalent educational institutions, should focus on national-level political warfare-related objectives, policies, organizing principles, strategies, campaign plans, and legal framework from a U.S. and friendly/allied perspective, as well as from the PRC perspective. The courses should culminate in a student's development of a country-specific counterpolitical warfare campaign plan or comprehensive supporting campaign plans. All courses should provide students the opportunity to discuss unique political warfare challenges they face in their home countries and exchange lessons learned and best practices. All courses should also include practical application tabletop exercises, during which students develop solutions to hostile political warfare campaigns and operations in a "war room" environment.

Faculty and Students

For this course, faculty should be selected from those with firsthand knowledge of the topics on which they are recruited to speak. This field of candidates includes political warfare planners and operatives, intelligence officers, journalists, social media experts, strategic communications and information operations practitioners, and seasoned academics with demonstrated experience and expertise in the field.

In assessing prospective faculty, candidates with a doctorate or a professorship at a prestigious university may not be as important as those candidates with real-world practical knowledge and hard-won experience. In general, there has been little rigor within U.S. academia invested in the research and analysis of PRC political warfare. Most of the useful work on this topic has been completed by organizations and individuals outside prestigious universities. This author recommends avoiding the recruitment of "instant experts" who have recently discovered the topic, regardless of academic pedigree.

Table 3. CCP targets of influence

	Building Relationships	Establishing Joint Ventures	Lobbying	Using Market Access as Leverage	Providing Supplemental Financing	Purchasing Majority Shares of Companies
Independently Owned Chinese Language Media	X	X		X	X	X
U.S. K-12 and Higher Education	X	X			X	
U.S. Academic Institutions	X				X	
U.S. Politicians	X		X	X	X	
U.S. Companies with Ties to China	X	X		X	X	
U.S. Mainstream Media	X	X		X	X	X
Chinese Students and Scholars Associations	X				X	
Overseas Chinese Groups	X					

Jonas Parello-Plesner and Belinda Li, The Chinese Communist Party's Foreign Interference Operations: How the U.S. and Other Democracies Should Respond *(Washington, DC: Hudson Institute, 2018), 45, adapted by MCUP*

Initially, students should represent a cross section of high- to mid-level civil servants and foreign service officers, as well as military, intelligence, and law enforcement officers with career growth potential or who serve in particularly sensitive planning, operations, and public information/public diplomacy billets. Expertise must be built across the whole of government, so officials from all departments, ministries, and agencies should be required to participate. After the program has matured during the course of a year, non-government leaders and other influential persons should then be invited to participate in the course. These include trusted business and industry leaders, news media executives, journalists and editors, educators and professors, and elected officials.

Conclusion

The United States and many other democracies are ill-prepared to confront and defeat PRC political warfare, as are certain authoritarian states that do not desire to become vassals or tributary states of Beijing. Within the United States and other nations that oppose PRC hegemony, it is essential to begin a systematic education program to teach government officials across the board—not just national security specialists—about the threat and how to counter it.

This proposed rationale, philosophy, methodology, and notional curriculum for a five-day counter-PRC political warfare education course provides a solid basis for establishing a systematic governmental and public education program. It should be adapted as needed and implemented immediately, while efforts continue to develop longer-duration education and training programs at governmental and civilian institutions of higher learning.

SELECTED BIBLIOGRAPHY

"60 Countries Have Congratulated Taiwan's President Tsai on Re-election: MOFA." *Taiwan News* (Taipei), 13 January 2020.

Akbar, Arifa. "Mao's Great Leap Forward 'Killed 45 Million in Four Years'." *Independent* (London), 17 September 2010.

Albert, Eleanor, and Beina Xu. "The Chinese Communist Party." Council on Foreign Relations, 27 September 2019.

Allen-Ebrahimian, Bethany. "China's Long Arm Reaches into American Campuses." *Foreign Policy*, 7 March 2018.

———. "China Steps Up Political Interference ahead of Taiwan's Election." Axios, 10 January 2020.

Anderson, Benedict. "Riddles of Yellow and Red." *New Left Review* 97 (January/February 2016): 6–20.

Associated Press. "Thousands in Taiwan Protest Talks with China." *New York Times*, 25 October 2008.

Audjarint, Wasamon. "Submarine Deal Shows Thailand's Growing Reliance on China." *Nation* (Thailand), 1 June 2017.

Babbage, Ross. *Winning without Fighting: Chinese and Russian Political Warfare Campaigns and How the West Can Prevail*, vols. I and II. Washington, DC: Center for Strategic and Budgetary Assessments, 2019.

Birtles, Bill. "China's President Xi Jinping Is Pushing a Marxist Revival—but How Communist Is It Really?" Australian Broadcasting Corporation, 3 May 2018.

Blackwell, Tom. "How China Uses Shadowy United Front as 'Magic Weapon' to Try to Extend Its Influence in Canada." *National Post* (Toronto), 28 January 2019.

Blanchard, Ben. "China's Top Paper Says Australian Media Reports Are Racist." Reuters (London), 10 December 2017.

———. "U.S. Plays down Tension with China, Upbeat on Military Exchanges." Reuters (London), 22 February 2014.

Blaxland, John, and Greg Raymond. *Tipping the Balance in Southeast Asia?: Thailand, the United States and China*. Washington, DC: Center for Strategic & International Studies; Canberra, Australia: Strategic & Defence Studies Centre, Australian National University, 2017.

Boisseau du Rocher, Sophie. "What COVID-19 Reveals about China-Southeast Asia Relations." *Diplomat*, 8 April 2020.

Boot, Max, and Michael Scott Doran. "Political Warfare." Council on Foreign Relations, 28 June 2013.

Bowe, Alexander. *China's Overseas United Front Work: Background and Implications for the United States.* Washington, DC: U.S.-China Economic and Security Review Commission, 2018.

Brady, Anne-Marie. "Exploit Every Rift: United Front Work Goes Global." In David Gitter et al., *Party Watch Annual Report, 2018.* Washington, DC: Center for Advanced China Research, 2018.

Brahm, Laurence. "Nothing Will Stop China's Progress." *China Daily* (Beijing), 2 October 2019.

Buckley, Chris, and Chris Horton. "Xi Jinping Warns Taiwan that Unification Is the Goal and Force Is an Option." *New York Times*, 1 January 2019.

Burton, Rachael, and Mark Stokes. "The People's Liberation Army Theater Command Leadership: The Eastern Theater Command." Project 2049 Institute, 13 August 2018.

Buruma, Ian. "The Tenacity of Chinese Communism." *New York Times*, 28 September 2019.

Campbell, Charlie. "Thailand PM Prayuth Chan-ocha on Turning to China over the U.S." *Time*, 21 June 2018.

Cardenal, Juan Pablo, Jacek Kucharczyk, Grigorij Mesežnikov, and Gabriela Pleschová. *Sharp Power: Rising Authoritarian Influence.* Washington, DC: National Endowment for Democracy, 2017.

Chan, Eric, and 1stLt Peter Loftus, USAF. "Chinese Communist Party Information Warfare: U.S.-China Competition during the COVID-19 Pandemic." *Air Force Journal of Indo-Pacific Affairs* 3, no. 1 (May 2020).

Chan, Minnie. "China Tries to Calm 'Nationalist Fever' as Calls for Invasion of Taiwan Grow." *South China Morning Post* (Hong Kong), 10 May 2020.

Chen, Liu. "U.S. Should Stop Posing as a 'Savior'." *PLA Daily* (Beijing), 27 September 2019.

Chia, Jasmine. "Thai Media Is Outsourcing Much of Its Coronavirus Coverage to Beijing and That's Just the Start." *Thai Enquirer* (Thailand), 31 January 2020.

Chin, Josh. "Trump's 'Meddling' Claim Plays into China's Trade Narrative." *Wall Street Journal*, 27 September 2018.

"China Doesn't Want Its Students to Study in Taiwan." Study International, 7 July 2017.

"China: Release Abducted Swedish Bookseller." Human Rights Watch, 17 October 2016.

"China, Thailand Hold Strategic Consultations." Xinhua News Agency (Beijing), 16 February 2019.

China's National Defense. Beijing: Information Office of the State Council of the People's Republic of China, 1998.

"China's Repressive Reach Is Growing." *Washington Post*, 27 September 2019.

"Chinese FM Slams Taiwan DPP for Colluding with U.S. to Seek WHA Attendance." *Global Times* (Beijing), 15 May 2020.

Chung, Lawrence. "Former Taiwan President Ma Ying-Jeou Sentenced to 4 Months in Prison for Leaking Information." *South China Morning Post* (Hong Kong), 15 May 2018.

Chung Li-hua, and Sherry Hsiao. "China Targets 10 Groups for 'United Front'." *Taipei Times* (Taiwan), 15 January 2018.

Ciccotta, Tom. "Multiple Universities Refuse to Cooperate with Federal Investigations into Ties to China." Breitbart, 21 May 2020.

Cohen, Michael K. "Greenpeace Working to Close Rare Earth Processing Facility in Malaysia: The World's Only Major REE Processing Facility in Competition with China." *Journal of Political Risk* 7, no. 10 (October 2019).

Cole, J. Michael. *Convergence or Conflict in the Taiwan Strait: The Illusion of Peace?* Abingdon, UK: Routledge, 2017.

———. "Unstoppable: China's Secret Plan to Subvert Taiwan." *National Interest*, 23 March 2015.

———. "Will China's Disinformation War Destabilize Taiwan?" *National Interest*, 30 July 2017.

Conley, Heather A. "The Arctic Spring: Washington Is Sleeping through Changes at the Top of the World." *Foreign Affairs*, 24 September 2019.

Cooper, Cortez A., III. "China's Military Is Ready for War: Everything You Need to Know." *National Interest*, 18 August 2019.

Copp, Tara, and Aaron Mehta. "New Defense Intelligence Assessment Warns China Nears Critical Military Milestone." *Defense News*, 15 January 2019.

Cordesman, Anthony H., and Steven Colley. *Chinese Strategy and Military Modernization in 2015: A Comparative Analysis*. Washington, DC: Center for Strategic and International Studies, 2015.

Costello, John, and Joe McReynolds. *China's Strategic Support Force: A Force for a New Era*. Washington, DC: National Defense University Press, 2018.

Danby, Nick. "China's Navy Looms Larger." *Harvard Political Review*, 5 October 2019.

Davis, Anthony. "China's Loose Arms Still Fuel Myanmar's Civil Wars." *Asia Times* (Hong Kong), 28 January 2020.

De la Beaumelle, Marcel Angliviel. "The United Front Work Department: 'Magic Weapon' at Home and Abroad." Jamestown Foundation, China Brief 17, no. 9, 6 July 2017.

Denyer, Simon. "Command and Control: China's Communist Party Extends Reach into Foreign Companies." *Washington Post*, 28 January 2018.

Department of Defense Dictionary of Military and Associated Terms. Joint Publication 1-02. Washington, DC: Joint Chiefs of Staff, 2004.

Devlin, Kat, and Christine Huang. "In Taiwan, Views of Mainland China Mostly Negative: Closer Taiwan-U.S. Relations Largely Welcomed, Especially Economically." Pew Research Center, 12 May 2020.

Dhunjishah, Michael. "Countering Propaganda and Disinformation: Bring Back the Active Measures Working Group?" *War Room*, 7 July 2017.

"Dictionary: Fascism." *Merriam-Webster*, accessed 7 October 2019.

"Dictionary: Totalitarianism." *Merriam-Webster*, accessed 7 October 2019.

Doehler, Austin. "How China Challenges the EU in the Western Balkans." *Diplomat*, 25 September 2019.

Dreyer, Edward L. "The Myth of 'One China'." In Peter C. Y. Chow, ed. *The "One China" Dilemma.* New York: Palgrave Macmillan, 2008.

Durdin, Tillman. "Formosa Killings Are Put at 10,000: Foreigners Say the Chinese Slaughtered Demonstrators without Provocation." *New York Times*, 29 March 1947.

Eckstein, Megan. "Berger: Marines Focused on China in Developing New Way to Fight in the Pacific." *U.S. Naval Institute News*, 2 October 2019.

Everington, Keoni. "China's 'Troll Factory' Targeting Taiwan with Disinformation Prior to Election." *Taiwan News* (Taipei), 5 November 2018.

Fan Lingzhi. "Taiwan Professor Plays Victim in 'Apology' for Discriminatory Remarks against Mainland Student." *Global Times* (Beijing), 12 May 2020.

Fanell, James E., and Kerry K. Gershaneck. "White Warships and Little Blue Men: The Looming 'Short, Sharp War' in the East China Sea over the Senkakus." *Marine Corps University Journal* 8, no. 2 (Fall 2017): 67–98, https://doi.org/10.21140/mcuj.2017080204.

Feldman, Harvey. "President Reagan's Six Assurances to Taiwan and Their Meaning Today." Heritage Foundation, 2 October 2007.

Garnaut, John. "Australia's China Reset." *Monthly* (Australia), August 2018.

Gershaneck, Kerry K. "China's Plan for Conquest of the South Pacific." *Asia Times* (Hong Kong), 7 September 2018.

———. "China's 'Political Warfare' Aims at South China Sea." *Asia Times* (Hong Kong), 3 July 2018.

———. Discussions with Senior ROC Political Warfare Officers, Fu Hsing Kang College, National Defense University, Taipei, Taiwan, 2018.

———. Discussions with Taiwanese Academics and Government Officials, Taiwan, 2018–20.

———. Discussions with Taiwanese and Foreign Graduate Students, Taiwan, 2018–20.

———. Discussions with Thai and Foreign Academics, Thailand, 2013–18.

———. Discussions with Thai Military Officers, Thailand, 2013–18.

———. " 'Faux Pacifists' Imperil Japan while Empowering China." *Asia Times* (Hong Kong), 10 June 2018.

———. Interview with a Senior U.S. Department of State Official, Bangkok, Thailand, 30 December 2016.

———. Interviews with a Senior U.S. Department of State Official, Various Locations, 2018–20.

———. "PRC Threat Obliges Political Defense." *Taipei Times* (Taiwan), 10 July 2019.

———. "Taiwan's Future Depends on the Japan-America Security Alliance." *National Interest*, 7 June 2018.

———. "Under Attack: Recommendations for Victory in the PRC's Political War to Destroy the ROC." *Fu Hsing Kang College Academic Journal*, 1 June 2019.

———. "WHO Is the Latest Victim in Beijing's War on Taiwan." *Nation* (Thailand), 22 May 2018.

Gertz, Bill. "Chinese Think Tank Also Serves as Spy Arm." *Washington Times*, 28 September 2011.

———. "Controversial State Department Nominee in Trouble." *Washington Free Beacon*, 15 May 2018.

———. "Global Engagement Secrecy." *Washington Times*, 11 March 2020.

———. "Warfare Three Ways: China Waging 'Three Warfares' against United States in Asia, Pentagon Says." *Washington Free Beacon*, 26 March 2014.

"Global Brands Better Stay Away from Politics." *Global Times* (Beijing), 7 October 2019.

"Global Engagement Center: Core Mission & Vision." U.S. Department of State (website), accessed 25 May 2020.

Goldstein, Steven M. *China and Taiwan*. Malden, MA: Polity Press, 2015.

Griffiths, James. "Nnevvy: Chinese Troll Campaign on Twitter Exposes a Potentially Dangerous Disconnect with the Wider World." CNN, 15 April 2020.

Groot, Gerry. "The Rise and Rise of the United Front Work Department under Xi." Jamestown Foundation, China Brief 18, no. 7, 24 April 2018.

Grossman, Derek, et al. *America's Pacific Island Allies: The Freely Associated States and Chinese Influence*. Santa Monica, CA: Rand, 2019, https://doi.org/10.7249/RR2973.

Grunow, Alexa. "WeChat Uses International Accounts to Advance Censorship in China." Organization for World Peace, 11 May 2020.

Gungwu Wang and Chin-Keong Ng, eds. *Maritime China in Transition, 1750–1850*. Wiesbaden, Germany: Harrassowitz Verlag, 2004.

Halper, Stefan A. *China: The Three Warfares*. Washington, DC: Office of the Secretary of Defense, 2013.

Hearing on China's Relations with U.S. Allies and Partners in Europe and the Asia Pacific, before the U.S.-China Economic and Security Review Commission, 115th Cong. (2018). Testimony by Russell Hsiao, Executive Director, Global Taiwan Institute.

Hearing on China's Worldwide Military Expansion, before the House Permanent Select Committee on Intelligence, 115th Cong. (2018). Testimony by Capt James E. Fanell, USN (Ret).

Hearing on Strategic Competition with China, before the House Committee on Armed Services, 115th Cong. (2018). Testimony by Aaron L. Friedberg, Professor of Politics and International Affairs, Woodrow Wilson School, Princeton University.

Hearing on Strategic Competition with China, before the House Committee on Armed Services, 115th Cong. (2018). Testimony by Ely Ratner, Maurice R. Greenburg Senior Fellow for China Studies, Council on Foreign Relations.

Hearing on U.S. Policy in the Indo-Pacific Region: Hong Kong, Alliances and Partnerships, and Other Issues, before the Senate Foreign Relations Committee, Subcommittee on East Asia, the Pacific, and International Cyber Policy, 116th Cong. (2019). Testimony by David R. Stilwell, Assistant Secretary of State for East Asian and Pacific Affairs, U.S. Department of State.

Hearing on U.S. Responses to China's Foreign Influence Operations, before the House Committee on Foreign Affairs, Subcommittee on Asia and the Pacific, 115th Cong. (2018). Testimony by Peter Mattis, Fellow, Jamestown Foundation.

"How 'Fake News' and Disinformation Were Spread in the Run-up to Taiwan's Presidential Elections." Global Voices, 22 January 2020.

Hsiao, Frank S. T., and Lawrence R. Sullivan. "The Chinese Communist Party and the Status of Taiwan, 1928–1943." *Pacific Affairs* 52, no. 3 (Autumn 1979): 446–67, https://doi.org/10.2307/2757657.

Hsiao, Russell. "CCP Propaganda against Taiwan Enters the Social Age." Jamestown Foundation, China Brief 18, no. 7, 24 April 2018.

———. "China's Intensifying Pressure Campaign against Taiwan." Jamestown Foundation, China Brief 18, no. 11, 19 June 2018.

———. "Political Warfare Alert: CCP-TDSGL Appropriates Taiwan's 2-28 Incident." Global Taiwan Institute, Global Taiwan Brief 2, no. 9, 1 March 2017.

———. "Political Warfare Alert: Fifth 'Linking Fates' Cultural Festival of Cross-Strait Generals." Global Taiwan Institute, Global Taiwan Brief 2, no. 2, 11 January 2017.

Hsu, Stacy, et al. "Trump Signs TAIPEI Act into Law." *Focus Taiwan* (Taipei), 27 March 2020.

Huang, David W. F. " 'Cold Peace' and the Nash Equilibrium in Cross-Straits Relations (Part 1)." Global Taiwan Institute, Global Taiwan Brief 1, no. 12, 7 December 2016.

———. " 'Cold Peace' and the Nash Equilibrium in Cross-Straits Relations (Part 2)." Global Taiwan Institute, Global Taiwan Brief 2, no. 2, 11 January 2017.

Huang, Paul. "Beating of Students in Taiwan Puts Spotlight on Chinese Regime's Influence." *Epoch Times*, 3 October 2017.

Hungdah Chiu, ed. *China and the Taiwan Issue*. New York: Praeger, 1979.

Ide, Bill. "Taiwan China Historic Talks Fuel Criticism at Home." *Voice of America News*, 8 November 2015.

Ignatius, David R. "China's Hybrid Warfare against Taiwan." *Washington Post*, 14 December 2018.

Jacobs, J. Bruce. "Paradigm Shift Needed on Taiwan." *Taipei Times* (Taiwan), 16 November 2018.

Jain, R. K., ed. *China and Thailand, 1949–1983*. New Dehli: Radiant, 1984.

Jiang, Joseph P. L. "The Chinese in Thailand: Past and Present." *Journal of Southeast Asian History* 7, no. 1 (March 1966): 39–65; https://doi.org/10.1017/S0217781100003112.

Johnson, Bridget. "DOJ Asked to Probe China's Use of INTERPOL Notices to Persecute Dissidents." PJ Media, 30 April 2018.

Johnson, Ian. "Who Killed More: Hitler, Stalin, or Mao?" *New York Review of Books*, 5 February 2018.

Johnson, Natalie. "CIA Warns of Extensive Chinese Operation to Infiltrate American Institutions." *Washington Free Beacon*, 7 March 2018.

Kania, Elsa B. "The PLA's Latest Strategic Thinking on the Three Warfares." Jamestown Foundation, China Brief 16, no. 13, 22 August 2016.

Kasit Piromya. Interview with the Author, Bangkok, Thailand, 1 May 2018.

Kastner, Jens. "Beijing's Man in Taiwan Crashes and Burns." *Asia Sentinel* (Hong Kong), 12 May 2020.

Kausikan, Bilahari. "An Expose of How States Manipulate Other Countries' Citizens." *Straits Times* (Singapore), 1 July 2018.

Kennan, George F. "The Inauguration of Organized Political Warfare." Office of the Historian of the State Department, 4 May 1948.

Kennedy, Conor M., and Andrew S. Erickson. *China Maritime Report No. 1: China's Third Sea Force, the People's Armed Forces Maritime Militia: Tethered to the PLA*. Newport, RI: U.S. Naval War College, 2017.

Kenney, Kristie. Speech at the Honolulu International Forum, Pacific Forum, Honolulu, HI, 9 August 2013.

Kerr, George H. *Formosa Betrayed*. 2d ed. Upland, CA: Taiwan Publishing, 1992.

King, Amy. "Hurting the Feelings of the Chinese People." *Sources and Methods* (bog), Wilson Center, 15 February 2017.

Kremidas-Courtney, Chris. "Hybrid Warfare: The Comprehensive Approach in the Offense." Strategy International (London), 13 February 2019.

Kurlantzick, Joshua. *Charm Offensive: How China's Soft Power Is Transforming the World.* New Haven, CT: Yale University Press, 2008.

Larter, David B. "Senior Intel Officer Removed after Controversial Comments on China." *Navy Times* 10 November 2014.

Li, Eric X. "The Rise and Fall of Soft Power: Joseph Nye's Concept Lost Relevance, but China Could Bring It Back." *Foreign Policy*, 20 August 2018.

Li Zhenguang. "Evil Design behind U.S.' Taiwan Rant." *China Daily* (Beijing), 15 May 2020.

Lian, Yi-Zheng. "China Has a Vast Influence Machine, and You Don't Even Know It." *New York Times*, 21 May 2018.

Lim, Preston, and Rachel Brown. "SinoTech: Department of Justice Launches Initiative to Address Chinese Economic Espionage." Lawfare, 14 November 2018.

Link, Perry. "China: The Anaconda in the Chandelier." *New York Review of Books*, 11 April 2002.

Lintner, Bertil. "A Chinese War in Myanmar." *Asia Times* (Hong Kong), 5 April 2017.

———. "In a High-Stakes Dance, China Charms Bhutan." *Asia Times* (Hong Kong), 31 July 2018.

Liou, Jenn-Shing. "Seriously Facing the Promulgation of CPC United Front Guidelines." Xinhua News Agency (Beijing), 22 September 2015.

Lloyd-Damnjanovic, Anastasya. "Beijing's Deadly Game: Consequences of Excluding Taiwan from the World Health Organization during the COVID-19 Pandemic." U.S.-China Economic and Security Review Commission, 12 May 2020.

Lopez, C. Todd. "Southcom Commander: Foreign Powers Pose Security Concerns." U.S. Southern Command, 6 October 2019.

Lu, H. H., and Evelyn Kao. "President Ma Counters Criticism of His Flexible Diplomacy." Central News Agency (Taipei), 29 December 2015.

Lum, Thomas, et al. *China and the U.S.: Comparing Global Influence.* Hauppauge, NY: Nova Science Publishers, 2010.

———. *Comparing Global Influence: China's and U.S. Diplomacy, Foreign Aid, Trade, and Investment in the Developing World.* Washington, DC: Congressional Research Service, 2008.

Mahnken, Thomas G. *Secrecy & Stratagem: Understanding Chinese Strategic Culture.* Sydney, Australia: Lowy Institute for International Policy, 2011.

———. "The United States Is Not Doing Enough to Fight Chinese Influence." *Foreign Policy*, 19 October 2018.

Mahnken, Thomas G., Ross Babbage, and Toshi Yoshihara. *Countering Comprehensive Coercion: Competitive Strategies against Authoritarian Political Warfare*. Washington, DC: Center for Strategic and Budgetary Assessments, 2018.

Makinen, Julie. "Chinese Social Media Platform Plays a Role in U.S. Rallies for NYPD Officer." *Los Angeles (CA) Times*, 24 February 2016.

Malik, Mohan. "Historical Fiction: China's South China Sea Claims." *World Affairs* 176, no. 1 (May/June 2013): 83–90.

Manthorpe, Jonathan. *Forbidden Nation: A History of Taiwan*. New York: Palgrave Macmillan, 2005.

Mao Zedong. *Selected Works of Mao Tse-Tung*. Beijing: Foreign Language Press, 1965.

Massaro, Chris. "China Tightens Noose around Taiwan while Challenging U.S. Primacy." Fox News, 3 October 2019.

Mattis, Peter. "A Guide to Chinese Intelligence Operations." *War on the Rocks*, 18 August 2015.

———. "An American Lens on China's Interference and Influence-Building Abroad." *Open Forum*, Asan Forum, 30 April 2018.

———. "Contrasting China's and Russia's Influence Operations." *War on the Rocks*, 16 January 2018.

McCormick, Andrew. " 'Even If You Don't Think You Have a Relationship with China, China Has a Big Relationship with You'." *Columbia Journalism Review*, 20 June 2019.

McMahon, Fred. "China—World Freedom's Greatest Threat." Fraser Institute, 10 May 2019.

Monaco, Nicholas J. *Computational Propaganda in Taiwan: Where Digital Democracy Meets Automated Autocracy*. Oxford, UK: University of Oxford, 2017.

Mosher, Steven W. *Bully of Asia: Why China's Dream Is the New Threat to World Order*. Washington, DC: Regnery, 2017.

———. *Hegemon: China's Plan to Dominate Asia and the World*. San Francisco, CA: Encounter Books, 2000.

Nanuam, Wassana, Patsara Jikkham, and Anucha Charoenpo. "NCPO Boosts China Trade Ties." *Bangkok Post* (Thailand), 7 June 2014.

Newsham, Grant. "China 'Political Warfare' Targets U.S.-Affiliated Pacific Islands." *Asia Times* (Hong Kong), 5 August 2019.

———. "Chinese Psyops against America: One Hell of a Success." *And Magazine*, 1 December 2019.

"Nowhere Feels Safe: Uyghurs Tell of China-led Intimidation Campaign Abroad." Amnesty International, accessed 19 June 2020.

Nye, Joseph S., Jr. "Get Smart: Combining Hard and Soft Power." *Foreign Affairs* 88, no. 4 (July/August 2009): 160–63.

Pan, Jason. "New Party's Wang, Others Charged with Espionage." *Taipei Times* (Taiwan), 14 June 2018.

Parello-Plesner, Jonas, and Belinda Li. *The Chinese Communist Party's Foreign Interference Operations: How the U.S. and Other Democracies Should Respond*. Washington, DC: Hudson Institute, 2018.

Pence, Michael J. "Remarks by Vice President Pence on the Administration's Policy toward China." Speech, Hudson Institute, Washington, DC, 4 October 2018.

"Penetration of Leading Social Networks in Taiwan as of 3rd Quarter 2017." Statista, accessed 19 November 2018.

Percival, Bronson. *The Dragon Looks South: China and Southeast Asia in the New Century*. Westport, CT: Praeger Security International, 2007.

Phaicharoen, Nontarat, and Wilawan Watcharasakwet. "Thai Military Suspends Deals on Foreign Weapons while Nation Battles COVID-19." BenarNews (Bangkok), 22 April 2020.

Pillsbury, Michael P. *The Hundred-Year Marathon: China's Secret Strategy to Replace America as the Global Superpower*. New York: Henry Holt, 2015.

Pongsudhirak, Thitinan. "A Recalibration between Thailand and the Outside World." *Bangkok Post* (Thailand), 2 October 2015.

Psychological Operations, Joint Publication 3-13.2. Washington, DC: Joint Chiefs of Staff, 2010.

Qiao Liang, Col, and Col Wang Xiangsui. *Unrestricted Warfare: Assumptions on War and Tactics in the Age of Globalization*. Beijing: PLA Literature and Arts Publishing House, 1999.

Qin, Amy, and Julie Creswell. "China Is a Minefield, and Foreign Firms Keep Hitting New Tripwires." *New York Times*, 8 October 2019.

Ramzy, Austin. "As Numbers Swell, Students Pledge to Continue Occupying Taiwan's Legislature." *New York Times*, 22 March 2014.

Ratner, Ely. "Learning the Lessons of Scarborough Reef." *National Interest*, 21 November 2013.

———. "The State Department is Tilting Dangerously toward China." *Foreign Policy*, 24 August 2017.

Raymond, Gregory Vincent. *Thai Military Power: A Culture of Strategic Accommodation*. Copenhagen, Denmark: NIAS Press, 2018.

Reilly, Michael. "Lessons for Taiwan's Diplomacy from Its Handling of the Coronavirus Pandemic." Global Taiwan Institute, Global Taiwan Brief 5, no. 9, 6 May 2020.

Reynolds, E. Bruce. " 'International Orphans': The Chinese in Thailand during World War II." *Journal of Southeastern Asian Studies* 28, no. 2 (September 1997): 365–88, https://doi .org/10.1017/S0022463400014508.

Ringen, Stein. "Totalitarianism: A Letter to Fellow China Analysts." *ThatsDemocracy* (blog), 19 September 2018.

Robertson, Matthew P. "Examining China's Organ Transplantation System: The Nexus of Security, Medicine, and Predation, Part 2: Evidence for the Harvesting of Organs from Prisoners of Conscience." Jamestown Foundation, China Brief 20, no. 9, 15 May 2020.

Robinson, Linda, et al. *Modern Political Warfare: Current Practices and Possible Responses.* Santa Monica, CA: Rand, 2018, https:// doi.org/10.7249/RR1772.

Rogers, William P. *United States Foreign Policy, 1969–1970: A Report of the Secretary of State.* General Foreign Policy Series. Washington, DC: U.S. Department of State, 1971.

Rogin, Josh. "China's Interference in the 2018 Elections Succeeded— in Taiwan." *Washington Post*, 18 December 2018.

Rolland, Nadège. "China's Counteroffensive in the War of Ideas." Real Clear Defense, 24 February 2020.

Rushford, Greg. "How China Tamed the Green Watchdogs: Too Many Environmental Organizations Are Betraying Their Ideals for the Love of the Yuan." *Wall Street Journal*, 29 May 2017.

Ryan, Mark A., David Michael Finkelstein, and Michael A. McDevitt, eds. *Chinese Warfighting: The PLA Experience Since 1949.* Armonk, NY: M. E. Sharpe, 2003.

Saul, Stephanie. "On Campuses Far from China, Still under Beijing's Watchful Eye." *New York Times*, 4 May 2017.

Schmitt, Gary, and Michael Mazza. *Blinding the Enemy: CCP Interference in Taiwan's Democracy.* Washington, DC: Global Taiwan Institute, 2019.

Shambaugh, David. "China's Soft-Power Push: The Search for Respect." *Foreign Affairs* 94, no. 4 (July/August 2015): 99–107.

Shao Dan. "Chinese by Definition: Nationality Law, Jus Sanguinis, and State Succession, 1909–1980." *Twentieth-Century China* 35, no. 1 (2009): 4–28, https://doi.org/10.1179/tcc.2009.35.1.4.

Shih, Gerry, and Emily Rauhala. "Angry over Campus Speech by Uighur Activist, Students in Canada Contact Chinese Consulate, Film Presentation." *Washington Post*, 14 February 2019.

Shinkman, Paul D. "Chinese Army No Longer a Threat, Top U.S. General Says." *U.S. News & World Report*, 14 May 2013.

Slavin, Erik. "What Happens When a Navy Officer Gets Real on China?" *Stars and Stripes*, 24 February 2014.

Smith, J. Y. "George F. Kennan, 1904–2005: Outsider Forged Cold War Strategy." *Washington Post*, 18 March 2005.

Snow, Edgar. *Red Star Over China: The Rise of the Red Army*. London: V. Gollancz, 1937.

Sonoda, Koji. "Ex-diplomat: U.S. Must 'Figure out a Way to Work with China." *Asah Shimubn* (Japan), 6 November 2018.

Southerland, Dan. "Unable to Charm Taiwan into Reunification, China Moves to Subvert Island's Democracy." Radio Free Asia, 25 May 2018.

Spalding, BGen Robert, USAF (Ret). *Stealth War: How China Took Over while America's Elite Slept*. New York: Portfolio/Penguin, 2019.

Stokes, Mark, and Russell Hsiao. *The People's Liberation Army General Political Department: Political Warfare with Chinese Characteristics*. Arlington, VA: Project 2049 Institute, 2013.

Sun Tzu. *The Complete Art of War*. Trans. by Ralph D. Sawyer. Boulder, CO: Westview Press, 1996.

Taber, Robert. *The War of the Flea: A Study of Guerrilla Warfare Theory and Practice*. New York: Citadel Press, 1970.

Taiwan Relations Act, Pub L. No. 96-8, 93 Stat. 14 (1979).

Tang, Didi. "China's Island War Games 'Simulating Seizure' Rattle Taiwan." *Times* (London), 15 May 2020.

Tatlow, Didi Kirsten. "Mapping China-in-Germany." *Sinopsis* (Prague), 2 October 2019.

Teng Biao. "Has Xi Jinping Changed China?: Not Really." ChinaFile, 16 April 2018.

Teng Pei-ju. "China Appoints Taiwanese Man to Top Advisory Board." *Taiwan News* (Taipei), 26 January 2018.

Teufel Dreyer, June. "A Weapon without War: China's United Front Strategy." Foreign Policy Research Institute, 6 February 2018.

———. "China's United Front Strategy and Taiwan." *Taiwan Insight* (England), 19 February 2018.

"Thai Universities Tap into Rising Chinese Demand." *Voice of America News*, 17 January 2019.

"The Day the NBA Fluttered before China." *Washington Post*, 7 October 2019.

Tong, Chee Kiong, and Kwok B. Chan. *Alternate Identities: The Chinese of Contemporary Thailand*. Leiden, Netherlands: Brill, 2001.

Trump, Donald J. "United States Strategic Approach to the People's Republic of China." White House, 20 May 2020.

Tsang, Steve Yui-Sang, ed. *In the Shadow of China: Political Development in Taiwan since 1949*. Honolulu: University of Hawai'i Press, 1993.

Tsao, Nadia, et al. "Ma Years 'Dark Decade' in Intelligence War: Analyst." *Taipei Times* (Taiwan), 2 October 2018.

Tungkeunkunt, Kornphanat. "China's Soft Power in Thailand." Institute of Southeast Asian Studies (Singapore), 3 June 2013.

———. "Culture and Commerce: China's Soft Power in Thailand." *International Journal of China Studies* 7, no. 2 (August 2016): 151–73.

"Uni Alumni Blast U.S. 'Meddling' in Coup." *Bangkok Post* (Thailand), 2 June 2014.

"United Front Upgraded by Creation of Special Leading Small Group." *Chinese Communist Party News* (Beijing), 31 July 2015.

"Up to One Million Detained in China's Mass 'Re-Education' Drive." Amnesty International, 24 September 2018.

U.S.-China Military Contacts: Issues for Congress. Washington, DC: Congressional Research Service, 2015.

Van der Wees, Gerrit. "The Taiwan Travel Act in Context." *Diplomat*, 19 March 2018.

Van Slyke, Lyman P. *Enemies and Friends: The United Front in Chinese Communist History*. Stanford, CA: Stanford University Press, 1967.

Wang, Zheng. *Never Forget National Humiliation: Historical Memory in Chinese Politics and Foreign Relations*. New York: Columbia University Press, 2012.

Watson, Burton, trans. *The Analects of Confucius*. New York: Columbia University Press, 2007.

"White Paper: The One-China Principle and the Taiwan Issue." Taiwan Affairs Office and Information Office of the State Council, People's Republic of China, 21 February 2000.

Wong, Alan, and Edward Wong. "Joshua Wong, Hong Kong Democracy Leader, Is Detained at Bangkok Airport." *New York Times*, 4 October 2016.

"World against the CCP: China Became the Target at the World Health Assembly." Chinascope, 21 May 2020.

Xi Jingping. "Full Text of Xi Jinping's Report at 19th CPC National Congress." *China Daily* (Beijing), 4 November 2017.

Xinhua. "China Slams Use of Bringing up Human Rights Issues with Political Motives as 'Immoral'." *Global Times* (Beijing), 12 December 2018.

Yang Han and Wen Zongduo. "Belt and Road Reaches out to the World." *China Daily* (Beijing), 30 September 2019.

Yang Sheng. "Taiwan Separatists Panic as Mainland Drops 'Peaceful' in Reunification Narrative." *Global Times* (Beijing), 23 May 2020.

Yau Wai-Ching. "Democracy's Demise in Hong Kong." *New York Times*, 16 September 2018.

Yeh, Joseph. "Beijing's Routine Exercises Psychological Warfare: Expert." Central News Agency (Taipei), 22 April 2018.

Yuan, Li. "China Masters Political Propaganda for the Instagram Age." *New York Times*, 5 October 2019.

Zawacki, Benjamin. "America's Biggest Southeast Asian Ally Is Drifting toward China." *Foreign Policy*, 29 September 2017.

———. "China's Belt and Road Paves over Rules and Rights." *Asia Times* (Hong Kong), 28 August 2019.

———. Interview with the Author, 4 April 2016.

———. *Thailand: Shifting Ground between the U.S. and a Rising China.* London: Zed Books, 2017.

Zhang Hui. "More Chinese Students Turning to Belt and Road Countries." *Global Times* (Beijing), 20 September 2017.

Zhen, Liu. "China's Latest Display of Military Might Suggests Its 'Nuclear Triad' Is Complete." *South China Morning Post* (Hong Kong), 2 October 2019.

INDEX